Introducing Greek Philosophy

Introducing Greek Philosophy

M. R. Wright

University of California Press
Berkeley   Los Angeles

University of California Press, one of the most distinguished university presses in the United States, enriches lives around the world by advancing scholarship in the humanities, social sciences, and natural sciences. Its activities are supported by the UC Press Foundation and by philanthropic contributions from individuals and institutions. For more information, visit www.ucpress.edu.

University of California Press
Berkeley and Los Angeles, California

Published simultaneously outside North America by
Acumen Publishing Limited.

Cataloging-in-Publication data for this title is on file
with the Library of Congress.

ISBN 978-0-520-26146-4 (cloth : alk. paper)
ISBN 978-0-520-26148-8 (pbk. : alk. paper)

Manufactured in the United Kingdom

17   16   15   14   13   12   11   10
10   9   8   7   6   5   4   3   2   1

The paper used in this publication meets the minimum requirements of
ANSI/NISO Z39.48-1992 (R 1997) (*Permanence of Paper*).

For all my grandchildren, dearly loved

Contents

Preface

In the following pages we shall meet a remarkable group of thinkers who faced many of the main issues that concern humanity, and developed the discipline of philosophy as a way of clarifying and understanding them. Where only fragments and summaries survive, the conclusions are elusive, and discussions of the original views are still open-ended. On the other hand, even where there is a considerable body of original texts available, as is the case with Plato and Aristotle, although they have been subject to centuries of interpretation, analysis and commentary, their core meanings remain debatable. We can therefore join the Greeks in their exploration of perennial issues not in the spirit of reading history but more in the expectation of meeting ideas that are worth further investigation. These philosophers challenged their predecessors and competed with each other in the quest for solutions, and we too can, as it were, sit down with them and discuss the same problems. With Greek plays, successive generations have found ways of interpreting the tragedies that throw new light on their dramatic developments. Watching a modern-dress *Oedipus*, in an English translation, can be a gripping and emotional experience. Similarly with philosophy: despite the unfamiliar background and the language differences there can still be engagement with the issues involved. A serious study of Greek philosophy is in itself a philosophical exercise, demanding but rewarding.

Introducing Greek Philosophy starts with the necessary chronological outline of the main figures involved and their interconnections in the emergence of philosophical thinking in the sixth to third centuries BCE. The material presented here is mainly restricted to this timescale, although there are references to the earlier epic poetry of Homer and Hesiod and the reactions it provoked and to those later Latin writings of Lucretius and Cicero from the last century of the Roman Republic, which are important sources for some of their Greek predecessors. Once this framework is established, there follows an analysis of the variety of linguistic forms the Greek philosophers adopted in their writings, such as dialogue, narrative, myth, poems, letters, essays and hymns, as they made use of different types of media for new ways of thinking. We shall also track influences, borrowings and subversions in the literary forms to illustrate the competitive interchange of ideas.

The topics of the six chapters that follow the introductory material are chosen as especially relevant to philosophy today. The Greeks were the first to wrestle with these issues, and what they had to say is still pertinent and provocative. In cosmology there is ongoing interest concerning the first beginnings of the universe, its basic constituents and its mathematical structures; today, as in the past, there is a search for a "theory of everything". The nature of the divine is continually relevant in the fierce debates for and against the existence of god, the dangers inherent in fanatical religious belief and the idea of purposeful creation set against evolution and natural law. The processes of thought as abstract or material, connections between character and self-identity, and the understanding of mind, perception and language are difficulties for present-day psychologists, neurologists and computer scientists, as well as for philosophers. In the great varieties of opinions and beliefs that surround us, what guarantees are there of certainty and sure knowledge, or should we admit to general doubts, and work only with probabilities? Now, as formerly, there are also endless political debates, concerning, for example, the qualities required in leadership, the advantages of democracy, the suppression of tyranny, coopera-tion and confrontation between the state and its citizens, and espe-cially the tension between power and law. The vast majority of us are uncertain about the quality of life and the pursuit of happiness. The conflicting claims of wealth and possessions, ambition and political power, pleasure, duty, love and friendship are as hard to assess for us as for the ancient Greeks. Should we suffer injustice or retaliate? Can goodness or good citizenship be taught? Is virtuous behaviour due to habit and disposition, home environment, the right schooling, a matter of choice or conditioned by our genes? It is worth exploring what intelligent and articulate philosophers from the past had to say on such perennial problems. A brief appendix to the discussion of these topics has been added, concerned with the secondary sources and fragmentary nature of much of the available evidence. The range of possible interpretations of their testimony adds to the interest in the study of these pioneers.

I am grateful to my daughter Cathy and to my husband for reading an early draft of the manuscript from the point of view of interested amateurs in the subject; their own clear thinking helped to clarify potentially obscure material. Giannis Stamatellos commented on the work as a text for present and intending students, and I drew on his expertise in later Greek philosophy for assistance with the Epilogue. From Acumen I wish to thank Steven Gerrard for his encouragement and sound advice, and Kate Williams for her patience and attention to details throughout, and for designing the map.

M. R. W.
Aberystwyth

Chronology

Single dates are approximate for the mature work of the persons named.

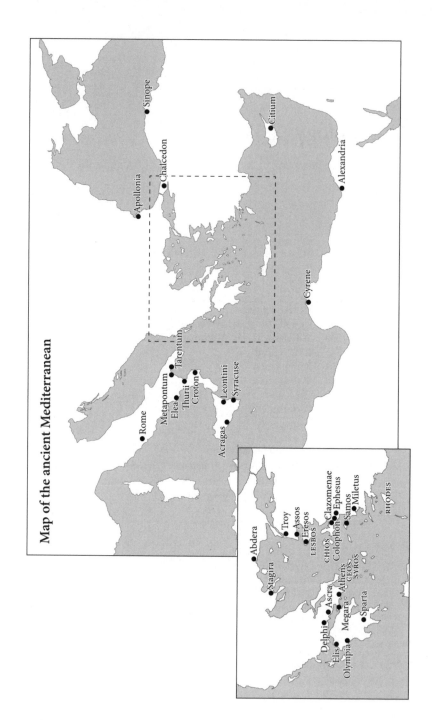

Map of the ancient Mediterranean

1. Mapping the territory

When, at the opening of his *Metaphysics*, Aristotle mused on the origins of philosophy, he characterized the philosopher by his ability to generalize, to abstract universal principles from individual instances, and to cope with problems beyond the comprehension of the average mind. He further contrasted the man of experience who knows facts with the man of wisdom who asks "Why?", and suggested that it was through curiosity that individuals now and in the beginning became philosophers, first asking the obvious questions, and then gradually worrying about more complex issues (*Metaphysics* 982b12). Aristotle goes on to suggest that there is an inborn craving for knowledge – not for practical purposes but for its own sake – and that in its pursuit the most satisfying human life is to be found.

Such a philosophical way of thinking came into the public domain in the early sixth century BCE, and in a specific area, namely the islands and western coast of Asia Minor, known collectively as Ionia. Mutual exchanges between Ionia and the older civilizations of the Babylonians, Hebrews, Phoenicians and Egyptians had increased in the sixth century BCE with trade expansion, the spread of Greek colonies and the inexorable westward encroachment of Persian power. Political movements in the Greek world generally, together with the emergence of city-state democracies, fostered independent argument, reflection and decision-making, as constitutions and laws were hammered out within the *polis*, rather than being externally imposed. The city centre was no longer a palace from which a ruler issued edicts, but an open public space, the

1

agora, in which social and political issues were continually discussed, and then given formal expression as the result of individual voting in the assembly. Instead of submissive acceptance of a single authority on the part of the populace there were speeches for and against difficult decisions to be made, dialogue between the parties involved and personal choices concerning the decision on which side to cast one's vote. The new politics therefore contributed to the spread of public speaking and independent judgement. The emerging science of medicine was also important in the development of intellectual skills. It involved a method of abstraction from individual case studies to the establishment of general principles, and these could then be applied to new instances; in this way the necessary combination of theoretical reasoning and practical expertise was acquired. This method was also being extended to abstract mathematical calculations and to principles of law, both of these disciplines becoming important as land was divided and constitutions drawn up in the recently founded colonies.

In all these activities verbal expression was crucial, and the Greek language was proving a tool of precision, especially with the practice (unknown to the Semitic languages) of introducing vowels and their signs between the consonants. The language developed into a lucid, elegant and concise means of communication, inherently balanced, and capable of fine nuances of meaning. With the adaptation of the Phoenician alphabet and the spread of literacy through the population (where previously knowledge of letters had been the preserve of an elite class), what was said in this language could then be written down and published extensively, then read at leisure, studied and criticized. In an amazingly swift movement of people and ideas, Presocratic philosophy[1] swung over from Ionia and the east to the opposite side of the Greek world, to the colonized towns of southern Italy and Sicily. It moved with Xenophanes as he travelled throughout Greece from his native city of Ionian Colophon; Pythagoras migrated from the eastern island of Samos to the Italian Croton; Parmenides settled in neighbouring Elea; and Empedocles rose to prominence in Sicily. It was not until the time of Pericles in the fifth century that Athens emerged as the third and most enduring centre of philosophy, attracting intellectuals from all over the Greek world. Anaxagoras and Democritus were drawn to Athens from the east, sophists came there from western and northern colonies to captivate the new generation of aspiring politicians, and then, in the fourth century, Aristotle moved down to Athens from Thrace, followed soon after by Epicurus from Pythagoras' island of Samos and the Stoic Zeno from Cyprus. Only Socrates and Plato were native Athenians.

Antecedent to the emergence of philosophical thinking was the legacy of the Homeric epics: the *Iliad*, the war poem of the last year of the siege of Troy, and the *Odyssey*, which tells of the return home of the Greek hero Odysseus from Troy to Ithaca. Throughout the Greek world these were a unifying factor, known, quoted and used authoritatively in a variety of contexts. In the history of philosophy the poems are most relevant for their ethics and theology.[2] Moral principles were adapted to the changing political climate, and success at "being best" moved from prowess in the battlefield to wielding power and influence in the city-state. A greater challenge, however, was to the Homeric divinities. These had been portrayed as gods and goddesses, in form and dress like human beings, tall and powerful, jealous, spiteful, quarrelling among themselves, interfering in mortal affairs, intent on revenge for any slight to their prestige and, most notably, untouched by age or death. The philosophical attack on this Homeric theology, along with its replacement by other views on what it means to be divine, was started by some of the Presocratics and was continued most notably by Plato and then, on different grounds, by the Epicureans. Theological disagreements began the long-standing quarrel between poetry and philosophy.

The traditional version of the gods and their origins found in the Homeric poems was then supplemented by Hesiod, who came from Ascra in Boeotia, the region that contained Mount Helicon. This was thought to be the home of the Muses, whom Hesiod claimed as the inspiration of his works, which were also composed in the Homeric epic metre. One of the two poems attributed to Hesiod is the *Theogony*, roughly contemporary with the Book of Genesis in the eighth to seventh century BCE, and relating a comparable theme of the initial division of dark and light, and the emergence of the cosmic masses of earth and sky. Hesiod uses a genealogical model of mating and begetting rather than a creator god to explain the arrangement of the world-system, the articulation of the earth's surface into its natural features and the appearance of meteorological phenomena. The succession myths of the gods and their great battle with the Titans were woven into this material as well as an aetiology for the discovery of fire (in the myth of Prometheus), an interpretation of the sufferings that are integral to human history and an explanation for advances in law and culture. Hesiod did not invent his material (except perhaps for some of

3

the names to complete various lists) but collected it from a number of sources, and then wove it all into a story that involved a comprehensive account of theological myth, contemporary cult practices, phenomena of the physical world and events in human life. The poem is important as a bridge connecting ideas from the ancient Near East with the new lands of Hellas,[3] and as mediating between the myth-making of the past and the search for non-mythical explanations of the world as we know it.

Between Hesiod and the first philosophers lurk the shadowy figures of Orpheus, Musaeus and Epimenides. They are credited with cosmogonies that begin with such vague Hesiodic entities as Chaos, Night, Aither and Erebus, and relate the subsequent production of an egg, and the emergence of a significant personage or personification from it. Another early mythographer, Pherecydes of Syros, narrated a different genealogy starting from Zas (i.e. Zeus) and Chronos (Time), which involved the biological model of a tree rather than an egg to explain the first beginnings, and also, spread upon the tree, an embroidered cloth that portrayed the natural features of earth and sea.

The three Milesians

It was from the main city of the Ionian coast, the busy port of Miletus, with its close links to the hinterland, that the first named philosophers – Thales, Anaximander and Anaximenes – came. Their interests and methods, which involved in particular a search for a unifying account of the origins and present diversity of the physical world, became known as Milesian or Ionian. Thales was on the list of the Seven Sages, and sayings attributed to him formed part of the repository of received wisdom. He wrote nothing himself, but, as far as we can judge from the comments of Aristotle (*Metaphysics* 983b20), he explained the source of life, which continues to nourish and maintain an animate world, by the abiding presence of one stuff – "water". He was said to base his theory on observations that both semen, the source of life, and nourishment, which supports it, are moist, that heat is generated and fuelled by moisture, and the buoyancy of water keeps the earth that floats on it stable. Aristotle admits that he is filling in gaps, and there is no way of knowing how far Thales' own arguments went, but three features are incontrovertible: the expectation that the complexities of the world can be readily explained in physical rather than theological terms, a new confidence in the explanation offered and the stimulus provided for others to criticize, adapt and develop the first attempts at such an explanation.

Anaximander, Thales' successor, wrote down his thoughts in the first recorded prose work in European literature. Only one sentence survives, probably dealing with opposites such as hot and cold, wet and dry: "From the source from which they arise, to that they return of necessity when they are destroyed, for they suffer punishment and make reparation to one another for their injustice according to the assessment of time" (DK 12B1).[4]

Here the opposites are viewed as "things", acting and reacting on each other like quarrelsome neighbours. At some time or place one encroaches on its counterpart, and that in turn, at another time or place, makes good the loss and itself becomes the aggressor. Gains and losses balance out overall in a cosmic equilibrium (known as *isonomia*), which is exemplified in the succession of bright days and dark nights, hot, dry summers and cold, wet winters.

In Anaximander's cosmology, according to the ancient sources, the whole system of balanced opposition began when something capable of producing hot and cold was separated off from the "limitless" (*apeiron*), the vast and characterless origin of all things. As a result of a violent rotation this developed into a fiery sphere surrounding a mist-shrouded earth, and then the various features of the world emerged. Explanations were given for the appearance of sun, moon and stars at proportionate distances, and for eclipses, storms, earthquakes and the like. The earth was thought to be drum-shaped, with living things on the under-surface (literally the "antipodes", feet opposite feet), and to stay where it is in the centre because there is no reason for it to move in one direction rather than another. Anaximander is credited with drawing the first map, centred on Greece, and for introducing the *gnōmon* (a form of sun-dial to mark hours, solstices and equinoxes) from Babylon. He also suggested that the human race originated, not from earth, but from creatures in the more protected environment of the sea.

These first moves in the study of nature, which were to develop into the different sciences of meteorology, geography and anthropology, were firm strides rather than faltering steps. It was thought that the world could be made intelligible in its own terms and the results justified by reason, argument and observation; these results were then made public and available for scrutiny and criticism.

Anaximander's views were indeed immediately challenged by his fellow townsman Anaximenes, who, like Anaximander, wrote in prose, of which one sentence is extant: "As our soul (*psyche*), which is air, maintains us, so breath (*pneuma*) and air (*aer*) surround the whole world" (13B2). In this fragment there is a new use for the word *psyche* (soul), which is no longer viewed as a shadow of the former self flitting endlessly in the realm of the dead, but as the ever-present principle of life, which holds together, strengthens and controls the individual. In addition a connection is established between the relationship of soul/air to us and breath/air to the whole world order, so that it too is alive and controlled. Anaximander's indeterminate "limitless" now has a character, that of the air we breathe, essential for life and an obvious candidate for the boundless source of that life. Anaximenes then argued that all things could be derived from this one intermediate and indeterminate substance according to differences in quantity: when thinner, air would have the appearance of fire; when thicker of mist; then it could condense further to become water; and further still to produce earth and rocks. We have the understanding here of the functioning of a "first principle" that explains and is responsible for the original emergence and subsequent maintenance of life.

Pythagoras of Samos

The island of Samos is close to Miletus and the Ionian coast. Pythagoras was one of its most famous citizens, but he was compelled, most likely for political reasons, to emigrate, and he, and his philosophy, moved westwards, over to Croton, the Achaean colony in southern Italy. His influence increased in the Italian towns, and he again became involved in local politics, "honoured by the men of Italy", according to one of the few direct references to him by Aristotle (*Rhetoric* 1398b14). Pythagoras himself retired to the neighbouring city of Metapontum, but there were various attacks on his followers in subsequent years, and it is reported that their houses and meeting places were burnt down, until Achaeans from the Peloponnese finally restored order. The most famous of these early followers were Philolaus of Croton (470–390 CE) and his younger contemporary, the mathematician Archytas of Tarentum, who was said to have been a close friend of Plato.

Pythagoras was an oral teacher and left no writings. He is named only once by Plato as "teaching a way of life still called Pythagorean", and it is said that his followers were interested in music and astronomy (*Republic* 530d, 600b). Aristotle is similarly noncommittal, and speaks indirectly of "the Italians called Pythagoreans", "some of the Pythagoreans" or "the so-called Pythagoreans" when quoting views attributed to them. By his time many strange stories concerning Pythagoras himself were circulating, and Aristotle collected some of them into an essay *On the Pythagoreans*, from which only a few quotations survive. Much later there came the emergence of the "Neo-Pythagorean" movement with the revival of Plato's philosophy in Neoplatonism, and many versions of a "Life of Pythagoras" were written, most notably by Porphyry and Iamblichus in the third century CE, but for the most part based on dubious authority.

Three interests however can with some confidence be attributed to Pythagoras himself, and these were important in early philosophy. The first is in the development of mathematics. The details of the famous "Pythagorean proof" – that the square on the hypotenuse of a right-angled triangle is equal to the sum of the squares on the adjacent sides – is probably later, from the mathematician Euclid, but the principle was known, and led to the discovery of irrational numbers.[5] This created difficulties for arithmetic, and resulted in more attention being given to geometry (the study of plane figures), stereometry (the study of solid figures) and astronomy (the study of bodies in movement). The second interest was in music and harmonic theory. When it was discovered that something as beautiful and abstract as a melody depended on the exact mathematical ratios of the lengths of vibrating strings on the lyre, it was suggested that the planets, moving at proportionate speeds, might also produce different notes of the octave as they circled the heavens, resulting in the "harmony of the spheres". And, if mathematical ratios were essential in these different contexts, perhaps the principle should be extended, and everything might have a numerical basis. The examples we have are very simple – justice as four (still remaining in the expression "four-square"), marriage as five, which is the sum of the first odd and even numbers (3 + 2, the unit being discounted) – but the underlying principle of a formal mathematical structure for apparently random phenomena was of crucial importance. The third interest was in the soul in two particular contexts: it was thought that music could be used as therapy to calm souls in an emotional state and so bring individuals into harmony with their surroundings, and the idea of transmigration of the soul on the death of one body to another of the same or a different species was adopted. The evidence for this is from Pythagoras' near contemporary, Xenophanes of Colophon, who quotes an anecdote about Pythagoras recognizing the voice of a friend in the yelp of a puppy. It is a joke from a group of satires, but its point is confirmation that transmigration was a well-known Pythagorean belief.

Xenophanes of Colophon

Xenophanes, like Pythagoras, came from the eastern Mediterranean, and was forced to emigrate, in his case when the Persians defeated the Lydians in 546 BCE and took control of the Ionian cities. He tells us in his own words that he spent sixty-seven years of a long life "wandering up and down the land of Hellas" (21B8.2), including a considerable time among the western Greeks of Sicily. Xenophanes is known mainly for his attack on the anthropomorphic attributes and immoral behaviour of the Olympian gods as portrayed by Homer and Hesiod. In his own account he put forward the idea of one god, motionless, intelligent, seeing and hearing "as a whole", and activating everything by the power of thought. But he did regard sure knowledge – of gods and the other subjects of which he spoke – to be unattainable by human beings; they can only assent to what is probable, and act according to opinion and belief. This distinction between the mental states of *epistēmē* (having knowledge) and *doxa* (holding opinions) opened up the subject of a "theory of knowledge" as an important branch of philosophy.

Heraclitus of Ephesus

Both Pythagoras and Xenophanes were treated with disdain by their immediate successor their Ionian neighbour Heraclitus, from the famous city of Ephesus. He accused them (22B40) of a quantity of learning (*polymathia*) that was devoid of understanding (*nous*). He himself spoke of *logos*, the true analysis and description of the way things are, but which is unnoticed by humanity, as the waking world eludes the sleeper. Individual effort and motivation are needed to interpret the *logos*. There is a hidden meaning to be discovered in the unseen but powerful "harmony" maintained between opposed forces that characterizes the underlying nature of things, and results in their overall unity. Anaximander's idea of opposites as warring factions restrained and controlled by a cosmic equilibrium is adapted by Heraclitus to show their mutual interdependence. There are even some cases in which opposites become "the same": when opposite predicates can be truly applied to the one subject. In a further development Heraclitus explains the unseen harmony in divine terms, where "god" is identified with concurrent or successive opposite states, and, conversely, the opposite states are unified in the "one wise".

This divine principle is also identified with the physical structure of the world, in terms of ever-living, intelligent and all-controlling fire. Fire takes its place in the cycle of changes of the world masses yet is also the standard by which the transitions are regulated, just as gold is exchanged in barter at the same time as the *amount* of gold involved sets the standard for the measure of the exchange. The "formula" sense of *logos* is also relevant here, in the proportions that are measured out at different times and places to ensure the permanence of the cosmos. The fire is never still, since its preservation depends on the intake of fuel followed by the exhalation as heat. Fire therefore, like a river, instantiates the tag attributed to Heraclitus: "everything is on the move" (*panta rhei*) – all things are constantly changing and yet are ever the same. There are within the individual soul the same "turnings" of fire through water to earth and back through water to fire, but best and wisest is the soul in a "fiery" state, a state achieved through the repression of indulgence, which literally was thought to make the soul "wet". Heraclitus encourages us to follow him in awaking to a realization of the true nature of the external world and also to engage in self-searching, drawing on the soul's limitless resources for increasing enlightenment.

Parmenides of Elea

Xenophanes, Heraclitus' predecessor, was reported by Aristotle to have been the teacher of Parmenides, being the first to "one-ify" (*henizein*, a word made up for this context), and Plato says that Parmenides' type of philosophy started with Xenophanes or even earlier. There was a tendency to link philosophers in terms of master–pupil relationships between well-known individuals, which made for a tidy, if not always accurate, chronology. Nevertheless it is clear that philosophic ideas that had started in Ionia were now circulating in southern Italy and Sicily and provoking strong reactions of support and criticism from opposite ends of the Greek world. Xenophanes had joined the migration from east to west after the Persian conquests in Ionia, and one result of this migration was the founding of the Ionian colony of Elea in southern Italy. Parmenides was in the second generation of the new citizens, and made the little town so famous that his philosophy could be known simply as "Eleatic". Zeno, his younger contemporary and fellow citizen, confirmed the tradition.

Parmenides presented his material in the restrictive form of Homeric epic verse. His one poem divides into three sections: a long prologue (preserved entire); some preliminaries and the main extended argument of the *Alētheia* (Road of truth); and the *Doxa* (Road of opinion), of which only a little remains. The prologue describes a journey taken by a young man in a chariot driven by the daughters of the Sun, crossing the vault of the sky, descending into the west through gates unbarred by the personification of Justice, and then travelling along a broad highway to a meeting with an unnamed goddess. She assures him that his journey is in due order, and gives him instructions to master two programmes: the unshaken heart of truth and the opinions of mortals. The rest of the poem consists of her exposition of them.

The *Alētheia*, which follows this prologue, is the first sustained stretch of argument in European literature, and many would claim that philosophy as such only starts here with Parmenides. The section opens with the most basic assumption: that reasoning and intelligent speech require an object, expressed simply by *esti* (is). Its opposite (is not) has to be rejected as literally a non-starter, for to say or think something that is not there to be spoken or thought of is peculiarly self-refuting. Once this is established a series of deductions can be made. There can be no generation or destruction, since generation would involve "is" coming from "is not" and destruction a move from "is" to "is not"; "is not" has to be rejected in both cases. Furthermore, if there can be no single generation or destruction, there obviously cannot be a series of starts and stops, but just a continuation of "is". An additional argument is that if there is no reason to start at one time rather than another then there will be no initial generation.[6] Next the goddess denies movement and change since, from the previous argument that "is not" cannot become "is", what is not the case cannot come to be so, and, since "is not" cannot become "is", what is true at one time cannot not be true at another. This brings the further implication that there is no way of distinguishing past from future, so *esti* is to be understood in terms of a tenseless present. Finally, it is deduced that with the denial of movement comes the denial of room for movement. Since a gap is a spatial "is not" (and "is not" is rejected spatially as well as temporally), there can be no gaps. This means that there is no alteration of consistency, but what there is is "equal to itself" in every direction; it is compared to a sphere, both in the perfect balance around the centre and in being "the same all over".

The road of human opinion is now described in the third part of Parmenides' poem, the *Doxa*. This is the road that is travelled by most people, described as "dazed, uncritical crowds", who are misled by what they see and hear, and do not understand the basic contradictions involved in their everyday assumptions. What there is is all that there is, so that it is truly unique, but, once the first wrong move is allowed, of having two entities rather than one, a plausible cosmos can be generated. Here the two entities are called "fire" (understood as bright and hot) and "night" (which is dark and cold). It is clear from the few surviving lines that this cosmos was explained in detail, presented by the goddess as a *dialectical* device, to win an argument "so that no one else's thinking shall outstrip you" (28B8.61). After the earlier onslaught on illogical thinking, in this context Parmenides is happy to adapt some features from Heraclitus: a central, controlling deity, the earliest concept of an "element" as an unchanging unit in composition and the development of a physical correlation between the thinking subject and the object thought.

Zeno of Elea

At the beginning of the dialogue named after Parmenides, Plato describes a (probably fictitious) visit to Athens by "father Parmenides" along with his younger colleague Zeno, also from Elea. The dialogue features a reading by Zeno of some of his own arguments, which are discussed by Socrates, the third character in the dialogue. Zeno explains that the purpose of his book was to support Parmenides against those who mocked him for the apparently ridiculous consequences of accepting the existence of only one entity. Zeno pays the mockers back with interest by showing that even more absurd conclusions follow from the seemingly obvious assumption that there is more than one thing in existence. Zeno's method, in the arguments preserved by the later Aristotelian commentator Simplicius, was to take the hypothesis that "there are many things in existence" and draw contradictory conclusions from it. "Many things", for example, can be shown to have no size at all, and to be infinitely big. If one asks how many the "many things" are, they will be found to be both a definite number and an unlimited plurality. And if one asks "Where are they?" the two possible answers are both unacceptable, for either they are nowhere, or they are in a place, which is in a place in a place, and so on indefinitely. Such arguments introduced difficulties concerned with spatial extension, numerical series and infinite regress that were to exercise logical minds over the centuries.

Further puzzles, of which there are only indirect reports, also deal with these topics. "Millet seed" is a puzzle about what can be heard. One seed makes no sound when dropped, a bushel of seeds makes a loud sound, but it is impossible to mark a division in the series from one seed to a bushel such that less than that number of seeds makes no sound when falling, and more than that does produce an audible sound. The most famous of Zeno's puzzles are the four dealing with moving objects: "Dichotomy", "Arrow", "Achilles and the tortoise" and "Stadium". These illustrate how confused thinking about temporal as well as spatial finite and infinite divisibility in the assumption of plurality generates the following paradoxes: it is impossible to traverse a set distance; a flying arrow is at rest; Achilles cannot overtake the tortoise; and a given time is equal to twice that time.

Zeno's aim in his puzzles and dilemmas is avowedly polemical. He subjects the obvious and generally accepted assumptions – (i) that there are many things in existence and (ii) that they move – to a devastating analysis; the resulting contradictory or absurd conclusions require a rejection or at least a re-examination of these assumptions. This is as far as his support of Parmenides goes. There is no evidence to suggest that Zeno positively advocated monism (that what there is is a single entity), but some to suggest that he was aware that there might be logical difficulties about hypothesizing and characterizing even one thing.

Melissus of Samos

The philosophy that started in the Italian town of Elea now went eastwards, to Pythagoras' island of Samos, and found an advocate in Melissus, a general who is said to have sunk the Athenian fleet in 441 BCE. He adopted the main arguments of Parmenides' *Alētheia*, but introduced some modifications of his own. He agreed with Parmenides' elimination of generation and destruction (since these involve prior and posterior temporal states of nothingness), and with the conclusion that what there is exists eternally. But if nothingness is applied to space there can be no spatial boundary (for outside the boundary would be emptiness, and this is not allowable as a spatial "is not"); therefore, Melissus argues, what there is must extend without limit. It is, however, without body (*sōma*), having no bulk or parts or means of apprehension or awareness, and, since it extends without limit, it would have no shape, to make it recognizable as a distinct entity. The language here is coming close to that used by Anaximander earlier of his *apeiron*, limitless in space and time.

Melissus also follows Parmenides in eradicating movement and change, including the slightest alteration in arrangement or structure, since the minimum possible change, by as much as a single hair, would involve ultimate destruction "in the whole of time" (30B7, 10). Furthermore, if there could be many things, as the experience of our senses suggests, then each would be as immutable as the one. But Melissus is ready (in B8) with a lively refutation of the assumption that we can trust our senses: if we see or hear anything correctly, then that would stay as it was first seen and heard, but the senses also record constant change; we cannot be perceiving things both statically as they are and as constantly changing, so the evidence recorded by eyes and ears is unreliable.

Empedocles of Acragas

The first reactions to the Eleatic thesis, which had started in the west with Parmenides and Zeno, and was supported in the east by Melissus, came from Empedocles back in Sicily, and from Anaxagoras in Clazomenae, an eastern Ionian city. The movement of arguments and counter-arguments to and fro across the Mediterranean that characterizes Presocratic thought only settled in Athens at the end of the fifth century, with the arrival of Anaxagoras, Democritus and the sophists there. Empedocles was roughly contemporary with Zeno and Melissus, and like them he supported Parmenides in some respects, retaining Eleatic wording and Parmenides' medium of the Homeric hexameter, but other arguments were adapted or modified, to take into account the observed plurality and change of the physical world. Empedocles agreed that continuity in time and extension in space could not be broken up by nothingness, and that there was no absolute generation or destruction. He effected a compromise between Eleatic logic and the perceived cosmos by admitting the existence of more than one thing, but not more than a limited plurality of four, which could not be increased or diminished in any way. Apparent generation and destruction are to be explained in terms of the arrangement and rearrangement of these four "roots" – named as earth, air, fire and water – in movements initiated by opposed universal principles of attraction and repulsion, which he called *Philia* (Love) and *Neikos* (Strife or Hate). Empedocles admitted change in so far as these elements come together and disperse, but denied it to each of the elements, which he saw as four independent equals, eternal and homogenous, never losing or altering their individual characteristics. In their eternity and changelessness the elements could be viewed as divine, and, in addition, the complete union of the four into one at periodic intervals was also called "god" by Empedocles, for it met the Eleatic criteria of self-sufficiency, steadfastness and uniformity, and had the spherical shape to which Parmenides had compared the balance and "sameness all over" of what there is. This divine state of perfection, however, comes to an end when, at the regularly appointed time, Strife invades, the whole begins to break up into its component parts and the conflict between the attraction and repulsion of elements starts anew.

Empedocles also included in his poem *On Nature* a detailed account of the structure and functioning of organic life. He was a pioneer in morphology and embryology, and his physiological interests centred in particular on respiration, the movement of blood in the body and the mechanics of perceiving and thinking. In a version of the "ladder of life" (*scala naturae*), he suggested that simple elements were alive in that they could be aware of and respond to their like; plants and animals have a composite structure and so can respond to more complex external phenomena. Human beings are still more sophisticated and aware, for their heart-blood, which Empedocles claimed controls intellectual functioning, contains all the elements in more or less exact proportions, so that human beings are capable of more advanced thought. Most superior is the divine state, apparent in the cosmos when the elements are completely intermingled in perfect harmony, and also in the individual who, in the highest ranks of human life, and as a result of right intention and intellectual endeavour, attains to an apprehension of the divine and eventual assimilation to it. In what is probably a separate poem, known as *Katharmoi* (Purifications), and addressed not to a privileged student but to the general citizen body of Acragas, there is an exhortation to a particular lifestyle. This means fostering harmony between ourselves and respect for others because of the kinship of human beings and animals. We all have a similar physical structure, and are involved in the struggle for domination between the cosmic forces of Love and Hate.

Anaxagoras of Clazomenae

The Milesian Anaximenes, as we have seen, first related the physical constituent of the soul to the like character of air that encircles the cosmos. Heraclitus exploited the relationship between internal human and external divine intelligence in the form of fire, Parmenides (in the *Doxa*) put forward a theory of thinking that was dependent on the proportion of the mixture of light and dark in the individual at any one time, and Empedocles connected his own thinking with the divine in the physical relationship of elements. This trend of relating internal to external intelligence in terms of composite structure reaches a climax with the next Presocratic, Anaxagoras of Clazomenae, in his theory of *Nous* (Mind) as a substance that is both a source of knowledge and power directing and controlling the external world and the distinguishing feature of human reason.

Anaxagoras came to Athens from Ionia, and stayed for many years. He associated with the statesman Pericles in his youth and had a considerable influence on him, in particular fostering an interest in science.[7] But early in Pericles' career some of his associates were targeted by his political opponents. Anaxagoras was consequently tried and sentenced to exile on a charge of impiety, specifically for saying that the sun was merely a hot stone, and the moon a lump of earth. In exile Anaxagoras chose to return to Ionia, to the town of Lampsacus.[8] His one book was already written and on sale in Athens. Socrates read it but was disappointed that the theory of mind given in it was purely mechanical, with no concern for working towards "what was best" (*Apology* 26d).

Starting at the beginning, Anaxagoras claimed that once "all things were together" (59B1). This would seem to mean that there was a complete and uniform fusion of all the elementary components of the cosmos, in contrast to Empedocles' mixtures of particles of earth, air, fire and water, which retain their individual characteristics. Furthermore, in denying the existence of a minimum smallest or a maximum largest, Anaxagoras showed in effect the irrelevance of size to the complexity of material, for "in everything there is a portion of everything". Following

15

the Eleatic denial of ultimate generation or destruction, Anaxagoras explained growth, change and the variety of visible transformations not by a repositioning of parts of a limited number of elements, but by the emergence in a new arrangement of ingredients that had always been present and now become prominent.[9] And he suggested that what had always been present was a total mingling of portions of earth, "seeds" of plants, animal tissues and such traditional opposites as wet and dry, hot and cold, and bright and dark.

An original process of separation and articulation in a vortex, initiated by the universal Mind, first brought heavier parts of this basic mixture towards the centre and parts that were mainly air and *aithēr* moved out to encircle it, so that a recognizable cosmos emerged. Unlike the traditional world picture, however, no spatial or temporal limits were set to the process, so that Anaxagoras had the strikingly modern thesis of an infinitely expanding universe. In the movements of division and accretion on the earth itself there is further articulation, but all the separating parts still keep the complexity of the original fusion, and so are able to develop in unlimited ways. In insisting that there is no way of cutting off or isolating a bit of pure hot or cold or the like, Anaxagoras is moving towards a realization that these opposites are not substances, as previously assumed, but *qualities* characterizing substances and inseparable from them. This again is a significant advance.

Diogenes of Apollonia

Diogenes of Apollonia (a Milesian colony on the Black Sea, perhaps founded by Anaximander) was younger than Anaxagoras, and like him came to Athens and settled there. Diogenes was affected by his birthplace in that he stayed firmly in the tradition of the early philosophers from Miletus, explaining all that there is as arising from the same substance. This principle may take on different forms at different times, but eventually everything returns to the same origins. He revived the view of Anaximenes that it is air that is the basic substance, and, through the process of thinning and thickening, Diogenes posited an innumerable number of opposites, with rare and dense, hot and cold, as primary. The character of (warm) air as necessary for life was again revived, and a clear emphasis placed on it as being intelligent and the stuff of soul. In this Diogenes also comes close to Anaxagoras' theory of universal and individual Mind (*Nous*), but more clearly aligns its infinity and eternity to divinity. He even goes so far as to suggest a universal purpose at work, arranging everything in the best possible manner (64B3). Diogenes' main interest, however, may well have been in medicine rather than cosmology. A long fragment (B6), concerned with the network of veins in the body and the circulation of air through them, probably comes from a medical treatise *On the Nature of Man*, comparable to the one in the Hippocratic corpus, and another quotation (B5) explains the working of the different senses (sight, hearing, smell and taste) in terms of the movement of air in the organs.

The atomists Leucippus and Democritus

Although roughly contemporary with Socrates, the atomists belong here with the "Presocratic" group because they produced a physical theory that brought to a natural end the investigation of the composition and structure of the cosmos initiated by the Milesians. Probably Leucippus initiated the theory, using a rather exotic vocabulary, and further details and supporting arguments were provided by Democritus, but the two are usually taken together and referred to as the (early) atomists. They were both from Abdera, on the north-east coast of Greece; Democritus later visited Athens and perhaps settled there, where he was disappointed to find that no one had heard of him.

Like Empedocles and Anaxagoras, the atomists accepted the Eleatic denial of absolute generation and destruction. Pluralism has to be understood in the strict sense that, since many cannot come from one, the many things always exist, and these were called atoms (*atoma*, literally "uncuttables"). Such atoms were described as solid, eternal, immutable minimal units, too small to be seen, of different shapes and sizes but having no qualitative differences, and being physically if not theoretically indivisible. To be able to move and initiate change they require room for movement, and here "is-not" – denied by Parmenides, and by Empedocles and Melissus in its spatial application as *kenon* (empty space) – is given a blatantly paradoxical existence: nothing (*mēden*, "void") is as real as thing (*den*, "atom"). Atoms moving in void account for all that there is.

Leucippus and Democritus supposed that the present world order arose as a result of a rotation of a group of atoms in the void, and there was a consequent "sifting" of the heavier atom clusters to the centre of the grouping and the lighter outwards, with the whole held together in an envelope of enclosing atoms. Eventually, however, as a result of pressure from within and external bombardment, they concluded this structure would fall apart. Given limitless material and unlimited space it is obvious that world orders other than ours are forming and disintegrating elsewhere. Such movements and groupings of atoms in space are the result of "necessity" following physical laws, but the atomists are at odds with all previous thinkers in attributing no morality, intelligence or divinity to the workings of nature. Empedocles had compared the mingling of elements to that of a limited number of colours in a two-dimensional painting, but here the variety of phenomena is to be explained rather as arrangements of basic units and empty spaces, much as the vivid scenes and characters in the *Iliad* arise from a limited number of letters in different groupings interspersed with spaces. Qualities such as colours and tastes are the result of conventional ways of talking, for in reality there are only atoms and void. Because of these conventions, and given the small size of the atoms and the intangibility of void, the senses are no reliable guide to what there really is. They can only record the apparent results of the interaction of the elemental units in space, and so provide a "bastard" kind of knowledge, expressed in arbitrary and conventional language. In this contrast of what is generally accepted and what is actually the case, the atomists bring to a conclusion Ionian and Eleatic ways of thinking and open up the ensuing sophistic debate on the conflicting claims of *nomos* (human law and tradition) and *physis* (natural law).

The sophists come to Athens

The radical shift in philosophy in the fifth century BCE is linked to political events in Athens at the time. The Presocratics came mainly from the fringes of the Greek world, from Ionia in the east and the western colonized towns of southern Italy and Sicily, but Athens was eventually acknowledged as the centre and leader of the Greek world. At the beginning of the century, after the victories over the Persians at Marathon and Salamis, Athens under Themistocles freed the Ionian Greeks from Persian rule and began to develop a maritime empire, which depended on a strong democracy to provide the citizen manpower for its ships. With the founding of the Delian league, the allies and islanders contributed funds rather than men to the Athenian navy, which further bolstered Athenian supremacy. Under Pericles in the mid-fifth century Athens became the political and cultural centre of Greece, but unrest among the allies and Sparta's growing suspicions of Athenian successes led to the Peloponnesian War, the shocking loss of life in the Sicilian Expedition and the eventual defeat of Athens by the Spartans at Aegospotami in 405 BCE; the democratic leaders were then exiled and the Spartans imposed the rule of the Thirty Tyrants on the Athenian people. But the democrats returned soon after, the tyrants were overthrown and there was uneasy peace until the rise of Thebes and eventually the threat from Macedon.

All these events affected the direction and development of philosophy. The excitement and opportunities of Periclean Athens attracted the brightest minds from across the Greek world, including the Presocratics Anaxagoras and Democritus, and also the itinerant professors known as "sophists". Among these were Protagoras from Abdera, Democritus' home town, Prodicus from the island of Ceos, Hippias from Elis on the southern mainland, and Thrasymachus from Chalcedon on the Bosphorus. Gorgias came from Leontini in Sicily, and Euthydemus and his brother from the island of Chios; they moved from there to Thurii in southern Italy and thence to Athens. The extensive travels of these sophists inclined them to relativism, in the sense that they found that traditions and beliefs vary from one place to another according to local custom (*nomos*). When they discussed ethics, however, in relative terms, the exposure to conflicting judgements was seen by the more conservative Athenians to have unwelcome and even dangerous consequences.

The sophists had wide interests, covering language, grammar and literary criticism, law, rhetoric and public speaking, history, politics and anthropology. Some were interested in science and mathematics, but generally these topics were seen as irrelevant to the main purpose of public achievements. The ambitious, talented and privileged youth of Athens could no longer be satisfied with the traditional education, which focused on the Homeric poems and physical training, but required a form of higher education for a successful political career, and this the sophists were able to supply. They fostered the ability to argue one's case in public, to win over the assemblies and councils to one's point of view and to help one's friends and discomfit one's opponents on the political scene, and in particular they taught and practised the skills of arguing for and against a given topic. Historians and dramatists had long used this device, when opposed arguments relating to a course of action were presented as contrasting persuasive appeals by

19

individual advisers or protagonists. In the hands of the sophists this expertise was readily passed on to their students, who became adept at making the weaker argument appear the stronger, and, in unscrupulous hands, the unjust argument was powerful enough to defeat the just. Most sophists aimed to improve the young in their care, to make them better citizens, but it seemed that some did encourage their students to challenge received wisdom, and, with their verbal dexterity, to confuse and disturb their seniors. In particular the sophists were open to the charge, relentlessly pressed by Socrates and Plato, that they did not have understanding of the topics they spoke on, and relied on fostering persuasive techniques rather than working out the truth in the given context.

Socrates

Socrates was the first philosopher from Athens itself. He so loved the city that he left it only once, on compulsory military service, and, when he did take a walk outside the walls, as described in the rural setting of Plato's *Phaedrus*, he was gently mocked for being so overcome by the charm of the countryside. Although at the heart of fifth-century thinking, Socrates wrote nothing, and what we know of him comes mainly from four sources. For his contemporary, the comedy writer Aristophanes, he was hardly distinguishable from the sophists or some of the earlier Presocratics. In his play *Clouds*, Aristophanes portrays Socrates as engaged in running a school, charging fees, busy with meteorological studies and teaching unscrupulous arguments, making the worse, the more unjust cause, defeat the better; all this the Socrates in Plato's *Apology* vehemently denies. In some of the biographical works of Xenophon, however, who was also a near contemporary, Socrates appears unexceptional, giving advice on common practical problems, and ready to die not for great principles, but because his faculties were becoming weak in old age. Xenophon was basically a military man, and it may well be that, while admiring Socrates as "the best and happiest of men", the subtleties of Socratic arguments eluded him. Aristotle, writing later, rarely mentions Socrates, but the few remarks relating to him are most valuable. He attributes two innovations in philosophy to Socrates: inductive argument and universal definition (i.e. in searching for "what a thing is" he would take what is common to a number of instances and make deductions accordingly). Aristotle also links Socrates to two ethical "paradoxes", namely that "no one does wrong willingly" and "virtue is knowledge" (*Metaphysics* 1078b28; *Eudemian Ethics* 1216b3).

The main evidence for Socrates' character and philosophical originality, however, is to be found in the writings of Plato, but there is an immediate difficulty in separating the historical Socrates from the Platonic character. In the so-called "early" works of Plato, Socrates is shown engaged in direct dialogue with one or more respondents, attempting to clarify their thoughts regarding various ethical traditions and beliefs. The exception is the *Apology*, Plato's version of Socrates' defence at his trial on charges of impiety and corrupting the young. In the course of this speech the main characteristics attributed to him by Aristophanes are repudiated, and, unlike the Socrates of Xenophon, his readiness to die relates to his refusal to abandon the life of philosophy. In Plato's central dialogues, Socrates is more clearly a spokesman for Plato's own views, especially relating to the metaphysical theory of forms and the immortality of the soul; in the later works of Plato, Socrates is often not the main speaker, or not even present. It is possible therefore to trace with some caution a number of stages in Plato's portrayal of Socrates. First there is a defence of Socrates' life and work, and a presentation of him engaged in arguments that tend to negative conclusions, followed by the introduction of positive Platonic material intermingled with Socratic biography. Then there are writings that are almost wholly Platonic, generally to the exclusion of Socrates. Finally there are the *Laws*: a long exposition delivered by a visitor to Athens from Crete, which contains much dogmatic material on political issues, and in some ways is even anti-Socratic in its repression of free speech as a threat to ordered government.[10]

Despite the differences between these four sources there is general agreement on some aspects of Socrates' life and work. He was Athenian-born, the son of a stonemason and a midwife. He was indifferent to material well-being and ignored physical discomfort, usually going barefoot and dressed in the same tunic whatever the weather. In appearance he was short, stout and snub-nosed, which would put him at a disadvantage in a society where physical beauty was especially prized, but there was the compensation of his charisma, a magnetic personality that was both attractive and unsettling. He was distinguished for his resolution and courage during his military service, and for his independent spirit, shown once as a member of the Council when he was the only one to vote against an illegal trial, and again when he refused to obey an order sent out by the Thirty Tyrants. He was eventually tried on charges of impiety and corrupting the young in 399 BCE by a duly assembled jury of 501 judges and condemned to death; he refused to attempt to escape and was executed according to the law by being given a draught of hemlock.

Socrates was well known for his anti-democratic views, based on a belief that government was a skill that required a certain expertise, and consequently he had a tendency to criticize present and past statesmen for having no true understanding of the art of politics. When the Athenian democracy was strong, under Pericles, it could take such criticism, and it was only when it was in a more fragile state, as its supporters were trying to restore democratic rule after the Thirty Tyrants had been established and then overthrown, that it seemed appropriate to silence Socrates for a time. He was probably brought to trial on the expectation that conviction would lead to his temporary departure from the city, but Socrates deliberately provoked the members of the jury, refused to flatter or entreat them, and chose death and philosophy rather than exile and the abandonment of his life's work.

In Plato's "Socratic" dialogues, Socrates himself claims to know nothing, but to act like a midwife in encouraging the birth of other people's ideas and then testing them. This claim was reinforced by a statement from Apollo's Oracle at Delphi that "no one was wiser than Socrates". Socrates interpreted this as meaning that in saying that he knew nothing (which gave him the reputation for being "ironic") Socrates was deemed by the god superior to those who thought they were wise when they were not; it was only when false knowledge was removed and ignorance admitted that one was ready to search for the truth. This goal of understanding was, Socrates believed, the highest human endeavour, and should be pursued at all costs with a constant testing of one's own beliefs and those of other people, summed up in the conclusion that "an unexamined life is not worth living" (*Apology* 38a).

Socrates' method of practising philosophy was known as *elenchos*:[11] a cooperative dialogue between questioner and respondent to reach an agreed conclusion on the subject under discussion. Such a dialogue was preferable to listening to a lecture or reading a book in a one-sided exposition, where little progress could be made. The search for agreement usually involved the definition of a moral term, such as courage or piety or virtue itself, which would cover the various instances of the related action. The respondent would make two or three suggestions and amendments, which were all shown by Socrates to involve ambi-guities, contradictions or absurdities, and the end result was a bewil-derment known as *aporia* (literally "no way out"). Although no definite conclusion to the discussion was reached, some advances would have been made, and the exercise was of mutual benefit in that error was removed, ignorance admitted and the stimulus provided to think more positively about what the answer might be. Generally the advances that were made in the *elenchos* exercise were towards a realization that a definition of a virtue involved a certain understanding of the nature of the virtue and of the benefits gained from acting accord-ingly. When this line of argument was pursued it could result in the paradoxes that "virtue is knowledge" and "no one does wrong will-ingly". The overall result was a tendency towards a search for an "art of living" in the underlying assumption that living rightly involves a skill (*technē*) comparable to that of medicine or pottery, in that a knowledge of principles applied in given situations would result in a successful end product. If, therefore, one *knows* that one's true good lies in acting rightly, then one would act accordingly, and conversely if one does not understand that it is worse (and not in one's interest) *to do* rather than *to suffer* wrong, then this ignorance is to be remedied not by punish-ment but by education.

Plato and Socrates

This linking of virtue to knowledge, along with the quest for defini-tions of underlying realities and the requirement of wisdom in polit-ical leaders, had a lasting influence on Socrates' most famous follower, Plato of Athens. This influence was compounded by Socrates' own unflinching adherence to moral principles and his condemnation by his fellow citizens. On Socrates' execution in 399 BCE, a disillusioned Plato, now twenty-eight years old, abandoned the political career expected of someone with his aristocratic family connections, and went travelling to Italy and Sicily. On a second visit to Syracuse in Sicily it is said that he attempted, without success, to groom the heir to the throne, the young Dionysius II, for the role of "philosopher-king". Plato eventually settled back in Athens and continued his with-drawal from personal involvement in the politics of the city. Instead he established the Academy, an informal society of the brightest young minds, where there were programmes of research into philosophical and mathematical problems, as well as training and advice for those who were interested in social and political issues. In the daily life of the Academy, dialogues may well have been composed and enacted, and there may have been public readings and the performance of rhetorical set pieces. We hear of one reading, by Plato himself, of his *Phaedo*, and a lecture with the title "On the Good".[12] One puzzle is that Aristotle, who was a member of the Academy for twenty years, never seems to have approached Plato directly, or raised questions on difficulties he had with some aspects of Platonic metaphysics.

Twenty-six works are contained in the Platonic corpus, as well as a further nine of more doubtful authenticity;[13] thirteen *Letters* and some mysterious "unwritten doctrines" are also attributed to Plato. Taking just the accepted works we find that they vary in length from a few pages of *Ion* to longer dialogues such as *Gorgias*, with ten books of *Republic* and twelve of *Laws*. They are usually all known as "dialogues", although some, such as *Apology*, *Timaeus* and *Laws*, are in the form of almost continuous exposition, and four contain a substantial one-person narrative of the fate of the soul after death. No chronological ordering of the works so far attempted has won general approval, but it is possible to suggest various groupings.

The "early works" are closely connected with Socrates and have him as the main speaker, engaged, as we have seen, in dialogue with one or more respondents. Most are in the form of "definition dialogues", concerned with the search for a general definition of a moral term, which Socrates requires as the necessary basis for any discussion of it; they end in failure, although considerable progress is made in eluci-dating the term. These dialogues are: *Laches* on courage, *Euthyphro* on piety, *Charmides* on *sōphrosynē* (self-restraint, or temperance), the first book of *Republic* on justice, *Hippias Major* on beauty, *Lysis* on friendship and *Meno* on virtue itself. *Hippias Minor* and *Ion* are concerned with a critique of the Homeric poems and some moral consequences, and *Cratylus* deals more with language, discussing the origins of words and their relation to reality. Literary criticism and linguistics were topics on which many sophists claimed expertise, and Socrates is shown engaged with some sophists more directly on these and related topics. He banters with Euthydemus and his brother in the display of verbal tricks in the dialogue named after him. He becomes involved in more important issues in *Gorgias*, first with Gorgias himself on the moral basis of rhetorical teaching and then, in the later conversation with Callicles, he faces up to and eventually refutes the maxim that "might is right", or, as it is put here, that "justice is the interest of the stronger". Another important work is *Protagoras*, which opens with an ironic tableau of different sophists surrounded by groups of devoted students in the house of Callias, but then moves into a dialogue with Protagoras himself. The subjects discussed include the merits of democracy, the unity of the virtues, virtue as knowledge and its possible mastery by pleasure (which involves an interlude on hedonism) and Protagoras' final doubts on virtue as a subject that after all might not be teachable. The "Socratic" works also include *Apology* and *Crito*. *Apology* is Plato's version of Socrates' defence at his trial on the charges of impiety and corrupting the young, and *Crito* is set in prison as Socrates awaits execution. Here Socrates puts forward arguments in favour of his refusal to attempt to escape, and shows that he is ready to accept his death as the law requires.

The next group of dialogues involve Socrates and Socratic biography but introduce two themes that appear to be Plato's own suggestions for solving some Socratic problems, namely his theory of forms and proofs and myths concerning the immortality of the soul. These occur in *Phaedo*, which starts and finishes with a straightforward account of Socrates' last day in prison talking with his friends, and of his execution by drinking hemlock. The dialogue has the sub-title "On the Soul", and, appropriately on such a day, the possibility of a future life is raised and agreed on through a series of proofs and a final myth. In these sections the character Socrates abandons the hesitancy he showed in the earlier works and, more as the spokesman for Plato himself, puts forward positive views.[14] *Symposium* is a similar case, in that the biographical details about Socrates are vivid: the invitation to the drinking-party, the "trance" on the way there, the speeches on the theme of love (*erōs*), Alcibiades' portrait of Socrates and his attempted seduction of the older man. But Socrates' own speech, which is attributed to the priestess Diotima, ends with an account of a Platonic "form", namely beauty itself, which is the true goal of the lover as he moves from the initial attraction of a beautiful body to the recognition of the beauty of the soul within. *Phaedrus* also brings in idealized forms in the myth of the journey of the soul in the company of the beloved to the heavens and the sight of the things "out there" that include the form of beauty "that was once ours to see in all its brightness" (250b).

The long *Republic* again has Socrates as principal speaker, here faced with the challenge of showing why we should follow justice for its own sake without regard to any adverse consequences now or after death. To tackle the problem Socrates first looks for justice in the city "writ large" as a guide to its presence in the individual. The investigation involves the theoretical construction of a city with its classes of philosopher-rulers, military executive and working population, corresponding to reason, spirit and desire in the soul, and concludes that justice lies in each part performing its particular function and the whole working in harmony. In the central books, three of the topics, called "waves", are faced and discussed in more detail, namely women as rulers, communal families and the education of the philosopher. It is here that Plato, through Socrates, gives the clearest exposition of the theory of forms. This is the subject of the climax of the philosophers' education, when they comprehend the realm of true being set against this world of opinion, and the unique position of the supreme "form of the good" in maintaining the structure of the whole. Although Socrates admits that this concept is extremely difficult to grasp, he offers three aids to understanding it in the accounts of the simile of the sun, the diagram of the line and the allegory of the cave. The following books then detail the degeneration of city and soul from the enlightened rule of philosophers in the state and reason in the soul to their opposites: political tyranny and psychological turmoil. The tenth book of the *Republic* acts as a double appendix to the whole. The first part gives a philosophical justification for the banishment of poetry, drama and art from the educational syllabus, and the second looks to the rewards of the just, which have been shown to be achievable in this life, and are now further enhanced by the description of after-death experiences in the famous Myth of Er.

Plato's later works

The remaining dialogues of Plato cover a variety of topics. *Timaeus* starts with a summary by Socrates of the growth of the city and the political reforms given in Books 2–4 of the *Republic*, and he asks for similar entertainment in return, in particular some account of his citizens in action. Critias obliges with an abridged version of the story of the island of Atlantis, involving events that happened nine thousand years ago. The noble citizens in action are the Athenians of a distant age, who defeated the powerful forces from Atlantis in their bid to take over the whole of the Mediterranean. Then in a single day Athens was destroyed in an earthquake and Atlantis completely flooded by the sea. The events were to be described in more detail in Critias' own dialogue, but this longer account stops in mid-sentence after a few pages on the origins of Atlantis, its political customs and complicated architecture, and its degeneration from its divine origins.

Before Critias' dialogue, however, and after the summary of the early books of the *Republic*, Timaeus, the main speaker in the work named after him, gives, also in mythical form, one of the most complex mathematical and scientific accounts to have survived from antiquity. It is a narrative that starts with the generation of the cosmos by a divine craftsman, who fits a world body (made of the four Empedoclean elements of earth, air, fire and water) into the revolutions of a world soul, in the likeness of an ideal model. But the elements are then found to be not basic enough. They themselves are composed of more fundamental mathematical units, and the whole is to be explained as the imposition of their mathematical form on to disordered space. Human body and soul are further imperfect replicas, and the opportunity is taken here for a comprehensive account of their structure and functioning, including an analysis of physical and psychic health and disease. The work ends with a eulogy of the cosmos as a perceptible divine object in the image of the intelligible: grand, good, most beautiful, unique and complete.

In the later dialogues Plato is often seen making a fresh start on topics that had been of interest to him earlier, but where his treatment of them now seems to him to be unsatisfactory. For example, he continually suggests proofs for the immortality of the soul, as he tries to show by reasoning that one's soul, inhabiting a living body, would survive the death of that body; *Phaedo* contains four such proofs, and *Republic* and *Phaedrus* two further attempts. The theory of forms, on the other hand, which had played an important part in the metaphysics of *Phaedo*, *Republic* and *Timaeus*, receives a devastating series of attacks in *Parmenides*. The spokesman for the theory here is a young Socrates, who is severely reprimanded by father Parmenides himself for not establishing a firm foundation for his reasoning. Parmenides recommends that Socrates should practise a series of exercises in the manner of Zeno's dilemmas for his philosophical training, and proceeds to give an extensive series of examples of what he means. Doubts expressed in *Parmenides* about the theory of forms, which had seemed to be a central Platonic tenet, reappear by default in *Theaetetus*. Here the structure is that of a standard Socratic definition dialogue: Socrates is the questioner, the search is for a definition of knowledge (*epistēmē*), and, after three attempts – (i) that knowledge is perception or (ii) right opinion or (iii) right opinion with *logos* (the means of defending it) – there is the resulting state of perplexity (*aporia*). The dialogue is extremely sophisticated, but the return to the earlier structure, the omission of "forms" that had previously been assumed as the object of knowledge, and the negative outcome show Plato as never satisfied, but always ready to rework earlier arguments in his lifelong practice of philosophy.

Philebus is another late Socratic dialogue where a definition of "the good" is under discussion, with two possibilities put forward: that "the good" is either (i) pleasure or (ii) reason. Arguments are produced for and against each position, and when there is no resolution the topic is re-cast: is the best human life one devoted to pleasure or to philosophy? But if taken to extremes neither alternative, on its own – to have pleasure with no consciousness of it or thinking with no pleasure in it – is acceptable, so it is agreed that the best life is a mixture of the two, but with more attention given to reason, since reason determines the quality and proportion of that mixture. The basic questions of a definition and classification of pleasures, true and false, their relation to pain and the arguments for and against the hedonistic life that had occupied many earlier dialogues are here resolved in a highly theoretical context. The involvement of number, measure, proportion, a hierarchy of precedence and the imposition of limit on the unlimited looks back to some Pythagorean concepts and forward to Neoplatonic adaptations.

Theaetetus was the first of a trio of connected works that continued with *Sophist* and *Politicus* (sometimes referred to as *Statesman*). Socrates, after failing to find a definition of knowledge in *Theaetetus*, hands over the discussion to a visitor from Elea (Parmenides' city) with the proposal that definitions should be found for "sophist", "statesman" and "philosopher". The project proceeds with *Sophist* and *Politicus*, but the proposed discussion of a definition of "philosopher" is indefinitely postponed. *Sophist* and *Politicus* are almost continuous expositions by the Eleatic visitor. There is little dialogue, and Socrates is mainly a silent figure; an unknown "younger Socrates", who was present in *Theaetetus*, now takes up the position of the yes-man, assenting in monosyllables to the main speaker. The ostensible aim of *Sophist* is to find the required definition of a term through successive divisions (similar to "division at the joints" from *Phaedrus*), and six attempts follow. The last of these definitions finds the sophist to be a producer of illusions or false opinions about the truth, and this leads into the main discussion on how false opinion is possible. It is here that Parmenides' famous denial of "is-not", with the consequent denials of generation, destruction, plurality and change, is finally answered. The confusions in negative and affirmative predication and in the different senses of "is" are clarified, and, in a battle between materialists and "friends of forms", five forms are found necessary to solve the inherent difficulties in the language, namely the forms of motion, rest, being, sameness and difference. These combine in judgements and are essential for their meaning, similar in some ways to vowels making sense of a syllable and allowing it to be pronounced. This whole digression, one of the most difficult stretches of Platonic argument, laid the foundation for scientific logic, and forged the link between Parmenides' *Alētheia* and Aristotle's professional treatises.

The *Politicus* looks for a definition of the statesman and an understanding of his particular expertise (his *technē*), again through a series of divisions that result in the statesman being named as a shepherd of the "hornless biped herd of humans", and his skill that of a cattle-drover or pig-farmer (265b–267e). This is obviously unsatisfactory, and the statesman as true shepherd is illustrated instead in a strange and complicated myth of alternating time cycles, which is indebted to Pythagorean precedents and Empedocles' ideas of recurring times. The dominant simile of the statesman as shepherd is here further modified to include the voluntary acceptance of his guidance by the flock. The example of weaving, the intertwining of warp and weft, is then introduced to show that the true statesman understands that vigour and aggression are the warp of society, peace and prudence the weft; both are needed in the various functions of the state, and it is the skill of the royal weaver to bring the two into a pattern of harmony acceptable to all. Plato's continual interest in political systems and the best type of rule shows a more moderate and feasible approach to government here than that characterized by the severity of the class scheme in the earlier *Republic* and the dogmatism of the later *Laws*. In this, Plato's last and longest work, an anonymous Athenian, the main speaker, discusses with a Spartan and a Cretan the legislation and constitution of a new settlement in Crete. The education of the citizens, religious practices, land ownership, trade, agriculture and the complete code of laws are all discussed in detail. The problems with democracy that troubled Socrates, and Plato's own tendency to put government into the hands of experts who work for the good of the citizen body, culminate in this blueprint for a stable and enduring state.

A. N. Whitehead famously said that European philosophy consists in a series of footnotes to Plato.[15] Whether this is true or not, we find Plato at the centre of Greek philosophy on all major issues, both in his modifications and adaptations of Presocratic theory and Socratic debate and in the effect he in turn had on subsequent thinkers in their reactions to his works. The fluidity of his method of presentation, the richness, originality and variety of his approaches and the constant reworking of possible solutions to key philosophical problems provoke responses that ensure his continuing relevance.

Aristotle of Stagira

The first and by far the most important of the ancient responses to Plato came from Aristotle. He was born in Stagira, a town in Chalcis in northern Greece, travelled down to Athens and joined Plato's Academy at the age of seventeen, where he stayed for twenty years, until Plato's death in 347 BCE. After that, perhaps ill at ease with subsequent changes in the Academy, Aristotle moved east to Assos and the facing island of Lesbos, and then north to Macedon, to be tutor to the young Alexander. Aristotle returned to Athens in 335, and established his own company of scholars there in the Lyceum, a gymnasium he rented outside the city boundaries; his followers were subsequently known as Peripatetics, from his habit of talking while walking up and down the colonnade (the *peripatos*) there. Twelve years later Aristotle left Athens for the second time when his connections with Macedonia made him politically suspect. He went back to Chalcis, where he died soon after, in 322 BCE, at the age of sixty-two. Theophrastus, from Eresos in Lesbos, took his place as head of the Lyceum.

Plato's completed literary products survive but we know little of his teaching; with Aristotle the reverse is true. His polished essays are no longer extant, except for a few fragments, but the vast number of works that are left are more like notes or research jottings. There is often a lack of organization, with numerous repetitions, many-pronged attacks on the same problem and arguments so terse as to be almost unintelligible. Clearly there are also many contributions from others, especially in the biological treatises, and many revisions of the material, either by Aristotle himself or those close to him. The fourteen books of *Metaphysics*, for example, cover a variety of disparate themes, and were only brought together by Andronicus of Rhodes in the first century BCE. This work starts with a history of Presocratic and Platonic theories of causation, followed by a book of puzzles and a lexicon of key terms. Four further books deal with questions of essence and substance, and the last two are on the philosophy of mathematics. The twelfth book, on god as prime mover and self-thinker, is the most polished, ending with the flourish of a Homeric quotation, but even here the eighth chapter is a later interpolation to take account of recent research by Eudoxus.

Aristotle's output is phenomenal.[16] He sets out to cover all aspects of human interest within a general encyclopaedic structure of: (i) *theoretical science*, which branches into theology and metaphysics, mathematics and the natural sciences; (ii) *practical science*, covering ethics and politics; and (iii) *productive science*, which deals with poetry, drama and rhetoric. Logic held a special place in being both part of theoretical science and the *organon* or "working tool" for all philosophy. Although Plato obviously had devised rules of argument in recording Socratic conversations, and in *Parmenides* and *Sophist* had analysed types of propositions, Aristotle gave philosophy its working methods. In a series of writings – *Categories, On Interpretation, Prior* and *Posterior Analytics, Sophistic Refutations* and *Topics* – Aristotle analysed the structure of propositions and the logical forms of proof, demonstration and definition; he showed what arguments are to be classed as necessary, possible or impossible, and the criteria of validity that lead to true or false conclusions.

Aristotle on natural science

Aristotle's *Physics* (along with the shorter work *On Generation and Decay*) deals with a series of problems in natural science that had troubled the Presocratics, and Aristotle gives his own definitive answer to them. He accepts the four elements of Empedocles as ingredients of natural substances, but because they have intrinsic opposite qualities – earth (cold and dry), air (hot and wet), fire (hot and dry) and water (cold and wet) – they can change into each other when one opposite is retained and the other transformed: earth becomes fire by heating, water becomes earth by drying and similarly with the actions of cooling and moistening. In another type of explanation, water is *potentially* earth when cold and wet, and *actually* earth after the drying process. In animal terms the child is potentially an adult and actually so on maturity. He or she can take on or lose various "accidental" attributes of height, weight and colour, for example, while keeping to the substantial nature of being human. Accidental attributes are transient, but if the *substance* is affected the individual no longer exists as such.

According to Aristotle, the Presocratics had some understanding of explanation (or "cause"), but they concentrated on the "material" one (except perhaps for the Pythagoreans and Empedocles), whereas there are actually four kinds. To understand something completely it is necessary to know not only what it is made of (the "material"), but also its shape or structure (the "form" that gives the definition), who made it (the "agent" or "efficient" cause) and what it is for (the "end" or "final" cause). Parts of plants and animals, for example, have final causes in that they function for the good of the whole – wings to fly with, eyes to see with – but the whole also has a final cause, which is to be the best possible of its kind, as the acorn grows into the best sort of oak tree, the cub into a courageous lion. This teleology (from *telos*, Greek for "end") implies not a divine purpose or a theory of evolution, but that natural laws, which govern change and growth, are always followed. When applied to the cosmos (which Aristotle discusses in his works on meteorology and the heavens), the natural movements of earth and water are to move "downwards", that is, towards the centre, and air and fire upwards. But the heavenly bodies (stars and planets) have their own element of *aithēr* (the "fifth element")[17] and its natural movement is circular, so that Aristotle's view of the universe, which persisted into the Middle Ages, was of a central earth, encircled by water, then by air and fire; these make up the sublunary realm of change, while the outer heavens, unchanging and eternal, move around them.

During his stay in Assos and Lesbos, Aristotle organized the material, much of it gathered by his students, for his zoological works, namely *Animal Studies* (*Historia animalium*, in ten books), *Parts of Animals*, *Animal Movements* and *Generation of Animals*. Here Aristotle literally brings us down to earth, urging us not to despise biology in comparison with celestial matters, since the material for such research is close at hand, and all animals, however humble, are worth studying: "If some have no graces to charm the sense, yet nature, which fashioned them, gives great pleasure in their study to all who can trace the links of causes and are inclined to philosophy" (*Parts of Animals* 645a6–7).

Animal Studies is mainly descriptive: an open notebook of observations covering a vast range of detailed material on hundreds of different species, their structures, organs and tissues. The other works in this genre concentrate more on two key issues. The first is the *classification* of the different animal types into full-blooded and bloodless, and then, through a series of divisions, into their ultimate genus and species. The second concerns the ways in which the animal and its parts are formed to achieve the best possible mode of life appropriate to it, as well as to ensure its own survival and its reproduction into the next generation. Related to these works is Aristotle's account of soul in the three books of *De anima*. Here again there is a hierarchy of function, in that the "soul" of a plant enables it to feed, grow and reproduce and an animal soul adds locomotion and perception to these functions, whereas the superior human soul is the "actuality" of the living body: the form of its organic material and the means by which it engages in rational thought. An interesting group of minor *Naturalia* deals with perception, memory and dreams.[18]

Aristotelian ethics and the productive sciences

One important area of Aristotle's philosophy is concerned with ethics, which is developed in two works: *Nicomachean Ethics* (dedicated to his father or son, both called Nicomachus) and the earlier *Eudemian Ethics*; three books are common to both works. His ethical theory is based on an exploration of the best human life: what is it that makes us truly happy? Rather than studying Plato's abstract form of the good, Aristotle argues that the best that we can do surely has to connect with what is most characteristic of *humanity*, and this would be the active life of reason (superior to animal nutrition, reproduction and perception), continued from maturity to death. So the life to aim at includes the regulation of feelings and desires that we have in common with other animal forms but, more importantly, it is concerned with the development and use of the exclusively human intellectual faculties. Contemplative thought therefore would be the most pleasant activity, most self-sufficient (being independent of external advantages) and closest to the divine. The result reflects the tripartite division of the soul in Plato's *Republic* into intelligence, spirit and appetite, for the successful and happy life, according to Aristotle, satisfies the whole person in its combination of intellectual reasoning, considered action and the enjoyment of external goods. It can be further enhanced by the company of a good friend, a "second self", who mirrors our actions and intensifies our appreciation of this life.

Furthermore, human beings are social animals with the gift of language, and are more likely to achieve the best life in the company of others like themselves in the community of the city-state, the *polis*. Aristotle therefore considers politics to be an extension of ethics and composed his eight books on political philosophy accordingly. He suggests that the *polis* starts as an extended village community formed to secure the means of survival, but, when this is achieved, its aims become no longer material or utilitarian but moral: to promote human development and the best life for its citizens. Aristotle discussed the different types of constitution most appropriate for this end; monarchy and aristocracy may be theoretically superior, but, in practical terms, a constitutional republic, in which a large middle-class predominates, is to be preferred. He also includes various provisions for family life, property holdings, education and law. As a corollary, Aristotle organized the reporting of various contemporary constitutions, 158 in all, of which just one, that of Athens, survives.

The two remaining works on Aristotle's "productive" sciences concern public speaking and poetics. *Rhetoric* is a practical handbook, giving guidance on composing and delivering a persuasive speech. Its message is summed up in the instructions for the composition of an epilogue, advice that might still find favour with politicians: "You must make the audience well-disposed towards yourself and ill-disposed towards your opponent, magnify or minimize the leading facts, excite the required state of emotions in your listeners and refresh their memories" (1419b10–13).

Poetics deals with poetic and dramatic composition and theory, and has long been influential in the history of literary criticism. Aristotle suggests that art and literature are not limited to mere copying, but idealize nature and complete its deficiencies. Tragedy in particular depicts emotions and crises in relation to all human life. The plot is all important, and should involve a central figure who is neither very good nor very bad but successful and of some standing, who is brought low through *hamartia*.[19] This downfall excites a corresponding pity and fear in the audience and so provides an outlet for these feelings in what Aristotle calls *katharsis*, a "purging" of violent emotion. History is written in prose, poetry in verse, but the important difference between the two is that history is limited to what actually happened, whereas poetry aims to depict the universal character in individuals and events. Famously, Aristotle concluded that "poetry is more philosophical than history" (*Poetics* 1451b5).

The development of Hellenistic philosophy

Plato and Aristotle are at the heart of Greek philosophy, and there was a time when it was thought that all that was needed to master the subject was a detailed study of Plato's *Republic* and Aristotle's *Ethics*. Now, however, there is increasing interest in the centuries following their lifetimes, and a recognition of the later achievements of those known collectively as "Hellenistic" philosophers, the most important of whom were the Epicureans, Sceptics and Stoics. Since Socrates himself wrote nothing, the method and content of his philosophizing had been open to different interpretations and were responsible for developments in directions other than those taken by Plato and Aristotle. Aristippus and his followers the Cyrenaics (so named after Aristippus' home town of Cyrene) interpreted Socrates' search for happiness and the best life as the search for the life of greatest pleasure. They thought that the function of reason was to control sense-experience by maximizing pleasure and minimizing pain to achieve a life of hedonism based on natural desires; in the practical calculations involved, however, there was still a role for Socratic independence and self-mastery. In their ethics they were forerunners of the Epicureans.

Contrasted with the Cyrenaics were the Cynics,[20] who followed Socrates in his asceticism, and in his emphasis on the moral life. For the Cynics the goal of human life was virtue, and this brought its own rewards. They opposed the Cyrenaics in despising pleasure, and deliberately courted hardship on the grounds that it provided an opportunity to assert their self-sufficiency and moral superiority. With a missionary zeal that was often taken to extremes, they attempted to impose their views on others by aggressive confrontation, continuous preaching and ostentatious poverty. The most famous Cynic was Diogenes of Sinope ("Socrates gone mad", according to Plato at Diogenes Laertius [hereafter DL] 6.54),[21] who lived the simple life of a wandering beggar, rejecting all ties of home, family and city, and the related conventions. One positive consequence of not belonging to any particular city was that he proclaimed himself a citizen of the whole world, and considered that all human beings, as well as gods

and animals, belonged to a universal community. Diogenes' immediate follower was Crates, who, with his partner Hipparchia, adopted
the minimalist way of life recommended by Diogenes, rejecting all
material comforts, and living together openly in the streets. Crates
was also a poet, and generally a kinder man than Diogenes. In his
humanism, and through his influence on Zeno of Citium, he mediates
between Cynics and Stoics.

Epicurus of Samos

Epicurus was born in Samos (as were the Presocratics Pythagoras
and Melissus), and came to Athens in 307 BCE, where he brought
together an informal gathering of like-minded friends in a "Garden".
This became a new rival to Plato's Academy and Aristotle's Lyceum,
which were both now well established as philosophical "schools". All
that remains from Epicurus' own extensive writings are three letters
that summarize his ethics, physics and cosmology, a handbook of pithy
aphorisms known as *Key Doctrines* (*Kyriai Doxai*; hereafter *KD*), some
fragments preserved in a Vatican collection (*Vatican Sayings*) and
others on papyri from Herculaneum. The major source for his views
is in Latin; it is a poem in epic hexameters by Lucretius from the first
century BCE, given the simple title *De rerum natura* ("On the nature
of things", or "How things are").

Among those who claimed to follow Socrates, the pleasure-seeking
Cyrenaics were the ones Epicurus favoured, but the sophisticated
hedonism that he developed was firmly based on the physics of an
atomic theory derived from Democritus, and supported with a *Kanōn*
or "criterion of truth". Since his physical theory demonstrated that
there was no divine government of the cosmos or any survival of the
soul as an individual entity after death, he concluded that happiness
had to be found solely by human endeavour and within the limits of
human potential. Looking, therefore, at human nature Epicurus found
that our basic instinct is to approach what is pleasant and avoid what
is painful. Since this is an instinct given by nature, it must be for our
benefit, and this means that pleasure has to be good for us and pain evil.
Although all pleasures may be good, however, not all are to be chosen;
they may not be if, for example, they are the product of unnatural or
unnecessary desires, such as for great wealth or power, or if, in the long
term, the consequence is greater pain. Practical wisdom (*phronēsis*) is

there to guide us in the moderate use of luxuries and the restriction of unnecessary desires, and also in the "hedonistic calculation". *Phronēsis* discriminates between pleasures and pains, evaluates and balances them, and then makes the decisions that will lead to the attainment of long-term happiness. Perhaps surprisingly it will be found that it recommends the traditional virtues, finding the life in which they are practised to be the best, since "wisdom, goodness and justice have grown up in close union with the pleasant life, and the pleasant life cannot be separated from them" (*KD* 5). What started as a theory of hedonism based on the most fundamental human instinct resulted in practice in the recommendation of a restrained and virtuous life that was proof against the vagaries of fortune. As with Aristotle, friendship was highly rated, and Epicurus considered philosophical conversations with friends the best of activities.

The Stoics

The Stoics were closer to the Cynics, and, like them, saw themselves in direct descent from Socrates. They approved his ascetic way of life, and continued his interest in the rigorous analysis of basic terms. Their logic was able to profit from Aristotle's work, while they based their physics on the divine fire that the Presocratic Heraclitus had made central to his philosophy. Their overriding interest, however, was in ethics, based on the twin Socratic foundations of care for the soul and the alliance of virtue with knowledge. This intellectualizing of virtue – the recognition of a fundamental connection between knowing right and doing right – was a distinctive feature of Greek ethics from its beginnings in Socratic dialectic through its developments in Plato and Aristotle down to the Hellenistic era. The Stoics adopted it whole-heartedly, made it central to morality and did not shrink from the consequences of believing that the supreme good is virtue, which alone has intrinsic merit and is to be desired for its own sake, and the only evil is vice. They claimed that this is where nature herself leads us, from the first basic instinct, which is for survival (and not for pleasure as the Epicureans supposed), through awareness and attachment to rational processes, to a consistent choice of what is appropriate and according to nature. It is only then, in practising virtue under the guidance of reason, that we shall realise our human potential and so be truly happy.

Whereas Epicureanism as a philosophy was a complete package, handed down in its entirety from the master, Epicurus himself, Stoicism had a continuous development from its foundation in mainland Greece until its arrival in Rome and growth through the Republic and Empire. Zeno of Citium in Cyprus came to Athens in 313 BCE, just before Epicurus. After investigating different philosophies, and spending some time with the Cynic Crates, he struck out on his own, discussing a new philosophy as he walked up and down the painted colonnade (the "Stoa Poikilē") in the main agora, and from this location he and his followers were known as Stoics. The main outlines of Stoicism, in their three divisions of logic, physics and ethics, were established by Zeno during his time in Athens, and further developed by his two immediate successors, Cleanthes of Assos (where Aristotle had spent several years), who focused on religion and wrote the powerful *Hymn to Zeus*, and Chrysippus from Cilicia in Asia Minor. Chrysippus restated Zeno's position, and in a vast range of writings (of which only a few lines remain) developed, emended and clarified the whole philosophy of Stoicism. He sharpened its logical tools and defended its orthodoxy against repeated onslaughts from the Platonists in the Academy and the Epicureans; on all aspects of Stoic teaching his word was the final authority. The later "middle Stoa" included Diogenes of Babylon and Panaetius from Rhodes, who settled in Rome with the group of intellectuals known as the "Scipionic circle". There was also the Syrian Posidonius, who stayed in Athens and visited Rome just once, but eventually established a school on the island of Rhodes that was on the itinerary of every educated Roman. These philosophers of the middle period were all influential in introducing Stoicism to the Romans. As they did so, they softened the ethical tone of the founders of the school by emphasizing the *progress* that could be made towards wisdom and virtue, rather than emphasizing the impossible ideal of the perfect character of the Stoic sage.

Academy, Lyceum and Scepticism

Aristotle's school had declined in importance soon after his own departure from the Lyceum, until there was a revival in the first century BCE by Andronicus of Rhodes, who initiated a series of commentaries on Aristotle's works. Plato's Academy had a divided history after the death of his immediate successors, his nephew Speusippus (who concentrated on mathematics) and Xenocrates of Chalcedon.[22] There was then a breakaway movement (known as the "New Academy") under Arcesilaus of Pitane and Carneades from North Africa, who were in sympathy with the Sceptics, especially their practice of finding counter-arguments to every proposal and so advocating a policy of "suspension of judgement". The last head of the Academy at this time, Antiochus of Ascalon, abandoned the Sceptic slant and reverted to the ways of the Old Academy. The Sceptics themselves followed the tradition of the Megarians, a group loosely centred around Euclides of Megara, a follower of Socrates and slightly older than Plato. The Megarians were particularly interested in critical arguments of various degrees of seriousness, including eristic attacks on opponents' conclusions and the generation of puzzles and paradoxes.[23]

Pyrrho of Elis was usually regarded as the founder of Scepticism, although here too the roots were traced to Socrates and even earlier. Pyrrho wrote nothing, and in the tradition he is portrayed as not trusting any perception or opinion about the world. Since for every argument there is a counter-argument, he thought it best not to be concerned with them, but to adopt an attitude of detachment and freedom from disturbance (*ataraxia*). One of the Sceptic sympathizers, Stilpo of Megara, who also believed in "detachment", "exceeded the rest in verbal invention and sophistry so that almost all Greece was drawn to him and began to 'Megarize'" (DL 2.113). Zeno of Citium, the founder of Stoicism, claimed to have learned his logic from Stilpo and his way of life from Crates.

The interaction between these different philosophies from all over the known world finally settled down in the first century BCE to three main centres: Antiochus and the old Academy in Athens, with Phaedrus heading the Epicurean Garden there; Posidonius supporting Stoicism in Rhodes; and Philo in the sceptical tradition and Panaetius with a modified Stoicism both working in Rome. Cicero had met with all these philosophers, as well as having Diodotus the Stoic living with his family.

Greek philosophy at Rome

The Romans were generally suspicious of philosophy as a Greek import, seeing moral dangers in some areas and distrusting the cleverness of the arguments. Two Epicureans were expelled from Rome in

173 BCE, and a general decree against philosophers was passed soon after. A turning point was reached when an embassy of three philosophers – Carneades the Sceptic, Diogenes the Stoic and the Aristotelian Critolaus – came to Rome in 155 BCE, with a petition from Athens for the senate, and while there they gave a series of lectures that made a profound impression. From then on most educated Romans would be familiar with the main strands of Greek philosophy, and it was Stoicism in particular, with its emphasis on the ascetic life, the practice of virtue, the sense of duty and service and its cosmopolitan outlook, that was especially favoured.

For mainstream Greek philosophy in the Republic, two authors writing in Latin are particularly noteworthy, especially as they provide source material in two key areas. The first is Lucretius, the Roman advocate of Epicureanism. He put difficult Greek concepts into a single Latin poem, explaining the principles of atomic physics, cosmology and psychology with the Epicurean aim of alleviating fears of divine interference during life and of punishments after death, and so promoting tranquillity of spirit. The second is Cicero, who also, as he said, provided a Latin voice for Greek philosophy. In this he is especially relevant in the philosophical writings that defend Stoicism, as in Cato's speech in the third book of *De finibus bonorum et malorum* (On supreme good and evil) and the exposition of Stoic theology in the second book of *De natura deorum* (On the nature of the gods).

A modified and politically charged form of Stoicism continued into the empire with the works of Seneca, Epictetus and Marcus Aurelius, but these are outside the scope of this volume. Instead we shall explore six topics that started at a high level of debate with the Greeks and are of enduring interest – cosmology, religion, psychology, epistemology, politics and ethics – along with the literary forms in which they were expressed.

2. Language, logic and literary form

Before exploring the six key topics, we should consider the linguistic and literary forms in which Greek philosophy was expressed and its logic developed. The search for truth, for an acceptable explanation of how things are, embracing the world and the relation of the state and the individual to it, was stimulated right from the start by the spirit of competition. This was aided to a considerable extent by the spread of literacy. Once new ideas were written down they could be published abroad, and were then available for analysis, criticism, defence, modification and improvement, in an extraordinarily fast movement of arguments and counter-arguments across the Mediterranean. We find, however, that individual philosophers chose and developed distinctive literary forms in both poetry and prose as appropriate to their ways of thinking. Not only do we have different dialects, especially Ionic from the coast and islands of Asia Minor and Attic for philosophers based in Athens, but prose could be answered with epic verse, and verse countered with prose, the verse sometimes prosaic and the prose in a variety of styles. Some set out their philosophy in enigmatic sentences, or as puzzles and dilemmas, or used the tricks and flourishes learnt from rhetoric. Plato, for the most part, preferred a dialogue form as closest to actual conversation, which could show an argument advancing step by step, but he also took great care in setting the scene, and, where the material was unsuitable for logical analysis, he used a narrative form in extraordinary myths. When Cicero gave Greek philosophy a Latin voice, his dialogues were more legalistic, comprising long speeches for and against different philosophical positions, whereas Lucretius reverted to the form of epic poetry, despite the difficulties of putting complex atomic physics into strict hexameter form. Others chose a terse, summary style, or wrote philosophic letters, or hymns, but three important figures – Pythagoras, Socrates and Pyrrho – left no writings, distrusting the written word for the very reasons that it was fixed and dogmatic.

Prose as the medium for philosophy

Thales, the first of the Milesians, was one of the "Seven Sages". As such he was cited as the author of many wise sayings, the most famous being "All things are full of gods", and "Stone has soul because it moves iron". Although he too wrote nothing his work was known, and Aristotle himself supplies arguments for the thesis attributed to him that water is the first principle. Thales provided the impetus for his fellow Milesians Anaximander and Anaximenes to respond with their own theories, which they did in the new medium of prose, Anaximander "somewhat poetically" and Anaximenes in "simple and unremarkable Ionic speech". Prose writing was being used in decrees and constitutions, in the first medical writings, in narratives (including Aesop's fables) and historical narrative in particular. Soon afterwards it appeared in the systematic geography and genealogies of Hecataeus, who was also from Miletus, and wrote in his own name "what I think is the truth". He was following the earlier Milesians in abandoning a verse form for that of common speech, which was suited to their new outlook on the world around them, as they deliberately countered the traditions of myth, ritual and religion on which the epic poetry of Homer and Hesiod had been based. Anaximander, for example, used the language of the law courts for the series of wrongs and reparations acted out by the elemental opposites, and Anaximenes adopted a mathematical ratio (as $a{:}b$ so $c{:}d$) to explain the relationship of breath and soul to air and cosmos.[1]

Philosophy in sound bites

Heraclitus also wrote in prose in a book that he deposited in the temple of Artemis at Ephesus as part of the city's treasure. He deliberately adopted the style of the Delphic oracle, using short, memorable but ambiguous phrases, often involving puns and wordplay: a style that, even in antiquity, gave him the title "the Obscure". The first fragment, however, is longer than the others: one sentence with a complicated syntax. It opens the collection with a literary flourish, devised to arouse the reader's interest and set out the main theme.[2] His aphoristic or "sound bite" method of expression is then used throughout. Here are some examples of his style: "unseen *harmonia* is stronger than seen" (DK 22B54); "way up, way down, one and the same" (B60); "sleepers are workers" (B75); "changing it rests" (B84a); "time is a child playing draughts" (B52); "immortals are mortals, mortals immortals, living the death of the one and dying the life of the other" (B62); "dry soul is wisest and best" (B118); and "a person's character is his destiny" (B119).

Similar pithy and enigmatic sayings are found in Alcmaeon – "we die because we cannot join the beginning to the end" (24B2) – and in Anaxagoras – "the seen gives a glimpse of the unseen" (59B21a) and "how could hair come from what is not hair, flesh from non-flesh?" (B10). Over 120 moral sayings in this style are attributed to Democritus, including the following examples: "it is hard to be governed by one's inferior" (68B49); "the soul is the house of the divine" (B171); and "the whole earth is open to the wise, the whole cosmos the native land of the good soul" (B247). Epicurus adapted details of Democritus' atomic physics and ethics for his own ends, and gave detailed summaries of his own philosophy in professional letters to three friends, but for general teaching purposes he wrote *Key Doctrines*, again a collection of easily remembered aphorisms. On mortality, for example, Epicurus writes that "death is nothing to us, for what has disintegrated has no sensation, and what has no sensation is nothing to us" (*KD* 2), on possessions that "natural wealth is limited and easily obtained; the wealth defined by vain fancies is always beyond reach" (*KD* 15), on pleasure that "when once the pain caused by need has been removed, pleasures of the body will not be increased in amount but only varied in quality" (*KD* 18) and "of all that wisdom procures for lifelong happiness, by far the greatest is the possession of friends" (*KD* 27). The Stoics had a similar style for their "paradoxes": "all sins are equal"; "only what is right is good"; "the wise are free, even if slaves, handsome even if deformed".[3]

Poetry and philosophy

Xenophanes was more poet than philosopher and wrote various types of poetry in various metres, including the iambic metre of tragedy, the epic hexameter and elegiac couplets. The elegiac poems were suitable for a symposium or to celebrate an Olympic victory, but in this metre there is also a four-line skit on Pythagoras and transmigration.[4] He wrote satires (known as *silloi*, i.e. squints) in hexameters; in them he criticized anthropomorphic ideas of gods, and also put forward constructive observations on natural phenomena. Parmenides, Empedocles and, later, Lucretius preferred to make sole use of the heroic hexameter, which was the verse form of the Homeric *Iliad* and *Odyssey*, and of Hesiod's *Theogony*.

There are a number of reasons, in addition to personal inclination, that might explain Parmenides' and Empedocles' preference for the epic format for their philosophy rather than the now established prose medium. First, it offers a way in which the reader or listener is eased into an unfamiliar and complex message by way of well-known formulae, but then there is also the opportunity to subvert the familiar phrases and images in the interests of the latest innovative approaches to the phenomenal world. In addition, in a long and difficult exposition the verse structure itself acts as an aide-memoire, and it is less likely that stages in the argument will be omitted or distorted when the music in the metre of the line regulates the train of thought. It may also have been the case that the epic verse form was preferred because it was *public*, geared to a wide audience and open-air recital,[5] and it also adds a serious tone to the exposition. There is Lucretius' point too, that putting a complicated theory into traditional poetic form is like children being given honey with their medicine, where the difficulty of the subject matter is sweetened and made more palatable by the poetry.

In this use of epic style and metre, a linear development can be seen from Homer through Parmenides to Empedocles, as similar phrasing is reworked in different contexts. It was traditional, for example, to represent a divine female in a relationship to mortal man as teacher to student, in the roles of giving and receiving information in narrative form on the most important topics. Inspiration for the Homeric poems and Hesiod's *Theogony* comes from the Muses, as the Muse Calliope inspires Empedocles, and the goddess greets the young Parmenides (a pattern continued in Socrates represented as receiving instruction on *erōs* from the priestess Diotima in Plato's *Symposium*).

To such direct representation is added the symbolism of the chariot. A chariot features in Homer when Hera and Athena drive at speed to consult Zeus; it is found in Sappho's poem about Aphrodite, goddess of love, descending to the poet; and there is the chariot of justice in Simonides' first poem. Now, in Parmenides' poem, the Daughters of the Sun as charioteers drive the young man to meet the goddess and hear her philosophy, and the Muse comes down in a chariot to inspire Empedocles in his scientific discoveries. In another context the Homeric language of the suffering of "far-wandering people" being due to the gods is adapted by the philosophers to the physical structure of "far-wandering limbs" of human beings on the borderline between life and death. The philosophical cosmology in the poets also follows the epic formula: Homer's world masses come under the provenance of Zeus, Poseidon and Hades; Hesiod narrates the emergence of sky and sea from earth; Parmenides' *Doxa* gives an account of the emergence of earth, sun, moon, *aithēr* and stars; and Empedocles has a similar list.[6] More importantly, Empedocles takes a catalogue of deities from the fourth book of the *Iliad* as a pattern for the list of his own four deities: Zeus, Hera, Aidoneus and Nestis. These are not divinities in any recognizable sense, to be prayed to or appeased, but they have been recast as the four elements of fire, air, earth and water, essential to the structure of individual and cosmos in the design and mechanism of natural processes.

New discoveries about the moon are also set out in Homeric vocabulary. Three passages from the *Odyssey* – Odysseus looking all round at a high rock (*Odyssey* [hereafter *Od*] 12.233), the man who comes from another place (*allotrios phōs*; *Od* 16.102), birds passing under the rays of the sun (*Od* 2.181) – are taken over by the philosophers in their explanation of the moon[7] shining by reflected light, travelling round the earth always facing the sun, eclipsed when the earth intervenes, and, like the sun, being not a divinity but a rock made of compacted air. In another context Parmenides adapts the Homeric description of Odysseus tied tightly to the mast with bonds so as not to be seduced by the Sirens (*Od* 12.196) for the certainty of his proof of the eternity of being, and of Hector before Troy ("fate bound him fast"; *Iliad* [hereafter *Il*] 22.5) for the invincible strength of logic (DK 28B8.37–8). As a final example, Empedocles uses the format of a Homeric simile – "as a Carian woman colours ivory with purple, so, Menelaus, were your thighs stained with blood" (*Il* 4.141–7) – first to describe the mingling of elements to form compounds in the simile beginning "as painters take pigments of various colours" (DK 31B23), and then in more detail to explain the structure and function of the eye, in lines suffused with Homeric vocabulary:

As when a man who intends to make a journey prepares a light for himself, fitting linen screens against the winds, but the more diffuse light leaps through and shines across the threshold ... in the same way the elemental fire keeps back the surrounding water but lets through the more diffuse light.   (B84)

Argumentative prose

Anaxagoras and Democritus, who set out to adapt Parmenides' conclusions to a world of plurality and change, and Parmenides' supporters Zeno and Melissus reverted to prose. Few of Zeno's original words are extant, but from the sources we know that the difficulties he raised concerned with spatial extension, numerical series and infinite regress were expounded in the form of a series of terse dilemmas. If, for example, (in DK 28B3) a critic of Parmenides' theory says that there are many things, Zeno asks whether their number is limited or unlimited: if they are as many as they are, the number is limited; on the other hand, there will always be other things between the things that are, and again other things between them, so the number is unlimited. The conclusion to be drawn is that the number cannot be both limited and unlimited, therefore the initial hypothesis "there are many things" fails. The four puzzles on movement were so famous that they were simply referred to as "the stadium" (a set distance cannot be covered), "the arrow" (the flying arrow is at rest), "the Achilles" (Achilles cannot overtake the tortoise) and "moving blocks" (which shows how a set time can be equal to half itself). The *language* in which the dilemmas and puzzles are set out is a new form of Greek, with few verbs and a minimal vocabulary, but extensive use of grammatical particles to provide balance between alternatives and to emphasize the surprising conclusions.[8] Zeno himself does not resolve his puzzles, but they serve as a warning that critics of Parmenides' theory need to be careful about the system they would put in its place. In response to Zeno, Melissus partially adapted Parmenides' conclusions to take account of Zeno's approach. Anaxagoras chose one horn of the dilemma – that there is infinite divisibility in seamless matter ("you could not cut off one part from another with an axe"; 59B8) – and used that as the basis for his theory of matter, whereas Democritus chose the other – that there *are* absolute minima, and called them atoms (*atoma*, uncuttable units). These are prosaic responses to the series of arguments expounded by a goddess in Parmenides' epic verse.

Rhetoric and persuasion

Socrates and the sophists turned their main forms of argument away from physics and cosmology to politics and ethics as more relevant to human life in the bustling cities of fifth-century Greece. The sophists generally prided themselves on their skills in rhetoric and persuasion, whether in a long speech on a set theme, a counter-argument to a given topic or a short, cut-and-thrust question and answer to score a quick point. Plato is still the main source for their activity, especially in the verbal fireworks of the two brothers in *Euthydemus* and the serious confrontations with Thrasymachus in *Republic* 1 and Callicles in *Gorgias*.[9] In the dialogue named after Protagoras he shows him defending democracy in a set speech (which includes a myth), and also in argument; Socrates, when challenged, retaliates reluctantly with a long piece of literary criticism, and then reverts to his preferred style of short exchanges. The dialogue is especially memorable for the initial description of the sophists gathered with their students at the house of Callias in an ironic adaptation of Odysseus' visit to the world of the dead at *Odyssey* 11.582–601. Odysseus' sighting of Tantalus, Heracles and other famous figures is adapted to Socrates' first glimpse of the sophists: "there I saw Tantalus, for Prodicus of Ceos was in town ..." (*Protagoras* 351d).

Socratic dialogues and their settings

Socrates, as we have seen, has no writings reliably attributed to him. He distrusted the written word as dogmatic and fixed, and impervious to questions. His method of philosophy was to engage with one individual, argue with him, and try to make him examine more closely the views that he held and to think more seriously about their consequences. Some respondents were indignant at what often resulted in public humiliation and turned against him, but the more philosophically inclined stayed with Socrates in his search for wisdom. So in his exposition and development of the Socratic method of philosophizing, Plato chose the dialogue form as closest to a spontaneous discussion, reproducing, particularly in his early writing, the vivid cut and thrust of intellectual engagement. Dialogue was a literary *genre* "between poetry and prose", according to Aristotle (DL 3.37); the direct exchange of speeches is part drama and part literary prose, and recalls the interchanges between heroes in epic poetry and the *stichomythia* (line-by-line exchanges) of characters in comedy and tragedy. It was defined as "a discourse consisting of question and answer on some philosophical or political subject, with due regard to the characters of the persons introduced and the choice of diction", and was contrasted with dialectic in which a *proposition* is either established or refuted by question and answer (DL 3.48 [*Life of Plato*]).[10] Reproducing (or inventing) Socratic oral exchanges was a common exercise in the fourth century BCE, and several authors are mentioned. We have all of Xenophon's *Memorabilia*, *Symposium* and *Household Management*, fragments from other authors, and more than thirty works involving Socrates in the Platonic *corpus*. Plato classified dialogue as "mixed drama and narrative", and it may well have been that Plato's pupils acted out some of the dialogues in the Academy; we are told that Plato himself gave a public recital of the whole of the *Phaedo*.[11]

Some Platonic scholars are impatient with his literary bent and would prefer to ignore the details at the beginnings of the earlier dialogues and the final myths, and concentrate on the hard philosophy in between, but in Plato's works the range of styles elaborates the philosophy and cannot be separated from it. This can be shown by the care he takes in setting the scenes of his dialogues, introducing the characters, varying the exchanges, bringing in the poetic language of simile, allegory and metaphor, and using the narrative of myth to complement the argument. Aristotle, in contrast, in the extant *corpus*, presents his most important work in the form of continuous prose notes: difficult, concise and candidly exploring possible variations in the vast range of subjects he undertakes. Whatever the topic, his style is consistent.

Most of those dialogues of Plato in which Socrates is presented as the main speaker have finely wrought settings, with characters that suit the topic to be discussed.[12] The definition dialogues, for example, are carefully staged. When the subject is courage, the main speakers are two illustrious military experts, Laches and Nicias; there is a graceful compliment to Socrates' presence of mind in the retreat of the Athenian forces before the Boeotians at Delium, and the dialogue starts with the pros and cons of recruits training in full armour. The virtue of *sōphrosynē* ("temperance", a virtue combining modesty and self-control) is discussed in the palaestra, the wrestling ground where the youth of Athens gathered, and the star of the gathering is the young teenager Charmides; the atmosphere is erotically charged, and even Socrates is affected. Charmides and then his guardian Critias become the respondents in the search for the definition. The portrait of the attractive young man, however, is subverted by the awareness in the reader of his subsequent history. Far from being a possible model for the virtue in question, Charmides was later appointed with Critias as one of the hated Thirty Tyrants, whom the Spartans put in charge of Athens in 404 BCE, and started a reign of terror; both men died in the fighting that restored the democracy. Similarly, the dialogue studying the virtue of piety is coloured by future events. Only two characters are involved: Socrates, who is on his way to the archon's office for the preliminary enquiries concerning the charge of impiety brought against him, and Euthyphro, who is just leaving, having laid such a charge against his own father. The one who is innocent and professes ignorance is to be instructed on matters concerning the gods and what is due to them by the expert, but at the end Euthyphro's definitions of piety fail, he leaves in embarrassed haste, and Socrates expresses his disappointment at not receiving the wisdom he expected to help him in his defence.

Two other dialogues with only two characters are quite different, in keeping with the contrast in their subject matter. *Meno* is unusual in beginning directly with no scene-setting, but with a tirade of questions from Meno, reflecting his impetuous character: "Can virtue be taught, Socrates? or is it the result of practice? or does it come by nature? or some other way?"; this inquisition easily, and with some irony, leads into the request for a *definition* of virtue before such questions could be tackled. In *Crito*, on the other hand, we have the picture of Socrates' friend visiting him in prison, sitting quietly by his bed and waiting for him to wake up, before launching into plans for Socrates' escape. Here Socrates is more serious than usual as he gives Crito the reasons for not escaping, ending with an extraordinary passage in which Socrates claims to have been addressed by the Laws of Athens personified. They spell out a version of the "social contract" to Socrates: the laws have legitimized his parents' marriage and educated and nurtured him, and, as with all citizens, in return for lifelong protection they can require his life, either in military combat in their defence or when found guilty in a court of law of an offence that merits capital punishment. Socrates says that the echo of these words resound in him and make it impossible for him to hear anything else.

Three further dialogues (out of many) may be mentioned briefly for the care taken in setting and character. The most beautiful is the opening scene of *Phaedrus*, where Socrates and his companion leave the city on a summer's day, paddle in the cool water of the Ilissus, and finally settle on a gentle grassy slope under a tall and spreading plane tree, reclining in the fresh sweet air to the sound of the cicadas; the heat and the seductive atmosphere have an uncanny effect on Socrates, which he attributes to Pan and the other strange powers of the place. The setting is recalled in the central part of the work in the interval between the discussions of love and rhetoric, and here the cicadas shame the human beings into engaging in dialectic rather than the long speeches. When it is time to leave, Socrates makes a sober prayer to Pan, whose presence in the rural setting had been palpable: "Dear Pan, and the other gods here, grant me inner beauty concordant with my outside world. Let me understand that only the wise are wealthy, and allow me no more riches than a moderate man would need or manage" (*Phaedrus* 279b–c).

The *Symposium* dialogue in contrast has an urban rather than a rural setting. Here Socrates is described as looking his best, having bathed and put on shoes. On the way to the drinking party he goes into one of his "trances", standing still and oblivious to his surroundings as he works out a knotty problem. When he arrives he finds that the entertainment is to be provided by the guests themselves, each giving a speech on *erōs* (sexual love). These speeches reflect the erotic currents present in the pairings of some of the guests and the character of the individual speakers: the doctor as long-winded, the comedy-writer Aristophanes interrupted by hiccups. Towards the end of the evening the young Alcibiades gatecrashes the party, half drunk, his garland askew and accompanied by a retinue of flute girls. He proceeds to deliver a portrait sketch of Socrates that shows him to be the ideal (and restrained) embodiment of that *erōs* which has engaged the whole company.

The third dialogue in this trio is *Phaedo*, set in prison, where Socrates speaks about death and immortality on his own last day, which will finish with his execution by poison at sunset. The opening and closing pages of *Phaedo* are straight biography, reporting the prison setting and the last gathering of friends, and, at the end, the farewells to Socrates and his courageous death. But the dialogue marks a turning point in that here Socrates engages with two topics that are particularly Platonic: the theory of forms and the immortality of the soul. When the theory appeared in *Symposium* it occurred in the context of Socrates being instructed by the priestess Diotima in the approach to absolute beauty, and in *Apology*, Socrates' speech at his trial, his personal view of time after death was thought to be either in the tradition of meeting other people who had died and gone to the shadow world of the dead in Hades or as a long and dreamless sleep. Plato, however, can now be found using Socrates as a mouthpiece for his own suggestions for solutions to problems that Socrates had raised but abandoned in perplexity, especially concerning definitions, essences, the philosophic life and *post mortem* rewards of virtue.

The same topics run through the ten books of *Republic*, where Socrates is presented as the main speaker throughout. The first book is a standard definition dialogue on the subject of justice, where confident definitions fail and the usual perplexity results. But when there is a fresh start with the plea to show that doing right should be pursued for its own sake in whatever situation and without regard to consequences, Socrates confidently takes control of the conversation with the other two, Plato's brothers Glaucon and Adeimantus, becoming more or less passive respondents. The earlier type of definition dialogue, with no Platonic forms, myths or talk of immortality, and ending in bewilderment, is found once more, in a late work, *Theaetetus*, where a definition of knowledge is required, but the suggestions made fail to survive the Socratic testing. This dialogue is set out as a narrative, read by Euclid the Megarian from notes he made earlier from Theaetetus' recollection of the conversation, with supplements and corrections from later meetings with Socrates. The format allows a move back to the direct narration of the earlier works, without the cumbersome indirect speech and constant use of "he said" that Plato had used throughout some of the middle works.[13] In the initial conversation here Euclid reports the tragic sight of Theaetetus carried in on a stretcher, dying from wounds and dysentery after the battle at Corinth. The whole dialogue is set out to compliment both Theaetetus, who was a teenage mathematical genius when Socrates met him and predicted a great future for him, and Socrates, shown in his old *persona* conducting an *elenchos* of extraordinary sophistication shortly before his own death.

Plato's poetic style

Theaetetus uses many literary devices in the course of the argument. During the examination of the first definition, the ghost of the dead Protagoras is supposedly raised so that he can join in the conversation and defend his thesis in person. In the second discussion the mind is famously compared to a wax tablet receiving impressions, and in the third Socrates uses the image of a "dream" about syllables and letters to distinguish knowing from apprehending, and the simile of catching and mistaking birds in an aviary to explain error. Such devices pervade *Republic*, but there is a curious grouping of five similes in a few pages (488a–501a), which reveal a bitter attitude to the ordinary people of democratic Athens. The subject under discussion is the desirability of having a philosopher-ruler, given that most contemporary philosophers are either eccentric or decent people but useless. Socrates' answer to this is the simile of the "ship of state", where the ship-owner is ignorant of seafaring, the sailors, similarly ignorant, clamour to be put in charge, and the one who does understand the art of navigation is despised as literally a useless stargazer. Next the people are compared not to sailors but to a huge wild animal, and a sophist is like its trainer, who has learned how to handle it, calling what it enjoys good and what makes it angry bad, and the sophists pass on this so-called wisdom as the teaching of virtue. As a result philosophy is abandoned, and is taken up by the working class, who are unworthy of her, as a bald little tinker who has come into some money might smarten up and go courting the boss's daughter. The true philosopher is now like a traveller who shelters against a wall in a storm, content if he can manage to lead a blameless private life. What is needed is the introduction of philosophy into politics, and a drastic rewriting of the constitution. The simile here is that of a sketch by an artist on a clean slate (or a slate wiped clean), who starts from a blank surface to draw a new state, filling out characters for its citizens that would be pleasing to the gods. We find that Socrates, who in earlier dialogues was shown as engaging publicly in conversations in the market and gymnasium, accosting anyone, and claiming to know only that he knows nothing, is now the mouthpiece for a view of the philosopher as sheltering from the storms of public life; he has extreme anti-democratic opinions, definite ideas on constructing a political constitution and is an advocate of the theory of forms. The justification perhaps comes in the great allegory of the cave, where Socrates would seem to instantiate the prisoner he describes as released from his shackles and turned towards the light, but who is reviled and even killed by his former fellow prisoners when he tries to tell them about the real world above, the realm of truth contrasted with the cave world of false beliefs.

Platonic myth

The *Republic* finishes with Socrates again being un-Socratic, when he narrates at length and without interruption the famous Myth of Er (613e–21d), an eschatological myth: one that tells of *eschata*, the "last things", which involves the fate of the soul after its release from the body at death. Er is a soldier, apparently dead and being carried to his pyre, who comes to life and recounts what he saw in the other world. This includes a vision of the revolving spheres of the planets around the earth; as each planet gives off a different note of the octave in its revolution, he hears the "harmony of the spheres". He sees souls choosing their next life, whether human or animal; then they drink from Lethe, the river of forgetfulness, and are born again.

There had been eschatological myths before, at the end of both *Gorgias* and *Phaedo*, and, contemporary with *Republic*, in *Phaedrus*. The *Gorgias* myth (523a–27c) is first and simplest, telling how Zeus instructed Prometheus to take away from human beings foreknowledge of the day of their death, so they could no longer prepare for the judgement. The judges distinguished between the wicked souls, who would be improved by a time of punishment, and the very wicked, who were incurable, and whose eternal punishment would act as a deterrent. The good "who were shining in purity and truth" (and included philosophers in particular) were sent to enjoy for ever the Isles of the Blessed. In *Phaedo* (107c–14c) the myth follows the four proofs of the soul's immortality. The proofs could at best show an impersonal survival of soul as a general principle of life and reason. To give a *personal* history, and convince his companions that he will still be alive in some way after drinking the hemlock, Socrates replaces logic with myth. The narrative has a sophisticated geographical setting involving our spherical earth; above it is the real earth and the real sky, elaborated in an imaginative description resembling a traditional Elysium. At a meeting of underground rivers the souls come for judgement: neutral souls go to Acheron for appropriate rewards and punishments; the incurably wicked souls are sent to Tartarus; but those that repent and are forgiven by their victims are released from further suffering. Good souls are directed to the true earth's surface, but for the truly virtuous, named as those who practise philosophy, there are even fairer mansions. Socrates concludes that this is all "a reasonable contention" and "a belief worth risking", and, in the myth, he justifies his earlier surprising statement that the life of philosophy is a preparation for death.

The *Phaedrus* myth (246a–57a) also follows an immortality proof that treats soul as a principle of movement (rather than of life or reason), and comes between the two main subjects of the dialogue: love and rhetoric. The myth has a celestial setting with a cosmic vision of a chariot procession of Zeus and the Olympian gods encircling the outer heaven and contemplating the realm of truth beyond. Human souls follow them with greater or lesser success, but most fall, and are born on earth, to endure a round of lives. One who practises philosophy and survives three times without wrongdoing is then free of reincarnation, and rejoins the divine procession, whereas others are likely to degenerate through a series of human and animal bodies. The poetic (and persuasive) prose that Plato adopts in his myth makes the moral to be drawn all the more effective, as this passage shows:

> If the better aspects of their minds prevail, and guide them towards a well-ordered life of philosophy, they spend their time here in happiness and harmony. After enslaving the part of the soul that lets in evil, and allowing free entry to virtue, they are masters of themselves and at peace; finally, when this life is ended, winged and weightless they make their ascent.
>
> (*Phaedrus* 256a–b)

Socrates says that the story of the true nature of the soul is long, and only a god could tell it, but what it *resembles* a man might relate, as he has done, and in a shorter time.

These four eschatological myths, from *Gorgias*, *Phaedo*, *Phaedrus* and *Republic*, are recounted by Socrates as continuous narratives, and contrary to his *persona* in earlier dialogues, where he is distrustful of long speeches and ornate prose. He there recommends that philosophy is pursued not by lecture-type instruction, but by dialogue, two people proceeding together, with mutual agreement at each stage of the argument. It would seem that in these myths Socrates is being presented once more as an appropriate spokesman for Plato's own views concerning the survival of the soul after death, and the morals to be drawn from it now for pursuing philosophy and practising virtue. Throughout there is supreme contempt for the physical: this world is the world of the dead, the body is a prison or tomb and we are only fully free and alive when soul leaves the body.

Myth is the genre to be used here because the subject, after-death experience, is one that is beyond verification, and standard philosophical tools are not relevant. In Platonic theory opinion rather than truth is acceptable for day-to-day activity if it turns out to be right opinion (*orthē doxa*); it is this that guides non-philosophic thinking and is available to human beings generally. Given a complex subject such as the nature of the soul, Plato might in one context propose a psychological analysis of it (as he does in the explanation of its tripartite division), attempt various proofs for deducing its immortality or see its elucidation as a task too difficult to undertake, but what is less ambitious and possible for human beings is to give a right opinion and say what it *resembles*, and this can be the cue to launch into myth.

Like the nature of the human soul and what may happen to it after death, the early history of the human race is an area in which there is little scope for mortal wisdom or philosophical progress. In the absence of evidence, demonstration and means of verification, the only way to deal with the topic is to resort to myth, and then to draw a moral from it for present behaviour. Included here would be the myth of *Politicus*, which involves a strange description of backward-running time in a narrative of the world moving regressively from its original state of divine guidance to its present degeneration. The Atlantis myth, which appears at the beginning of *Timaeus* and in the unfinished *Critias*, is similar in that there can be no certainty about events that happened long ago, but a useful moral may be drawn now from the troubles the human race brought on itself as it moved further away from its divine origins. The attractiveness and vivid narrative of the Atlantis myth, even in its incomplete form, has made it a favourite through the centuries, both fascinating and intriguing for its readers. It has stimulated endless speculation on the exact location of Atlantis, even though there are many indications that it is only a story in the standard form of a "foundation myth": of a divine father, a mortal mother and a son who becomes the founder of a city and a dynasty.[14]

There is one more myth of the greatest importance, which is so far from Socrates' interests that, as with the *Politicus* and Atlantis myths, it would not be appropriate for him to be the speaker, but the narration is given to a visitor from southern Italy (a centre for Pythagorean science and cosmology) called Timaeus. He tells the tale of how the world body and world soul, and the human body and human soul, were constructed, and brings in all the related details from cosmology, astronomy, mathematics, medicine, biology and chemistry that make up the main part of the work named after him. Such scientific material is, perhaps surprisingly, said to be suited not to philosophy but to myth because its subject matter is set firmly in the realm of "becoming", and as such has no reality in the sense of timeless truth; a description of it can be no more than a "likely account". The heavens, with the circles of the fixed stars and planets regulated by number, imitate as far as possible the uniformity and eternity of the model that its maker used, but, in life on earth in the region below the moon, the resistance to the master plan results in a continuous struggle for permanence and order. Although it was thought that accounts of the natural world will never reach truth, it is agreed that progress is possible, and scientific advance can be made by the continuous replacement of one theory by another that is "more probable". Plato plays down his mythical narrative of the cosmos as merely entertainment, light relief from the hard work of metaphysics, while still giving his own interpretation of the latest achievements in the sciences as a contribution to the ongoing debate about the structure of the physical world and how it functions.[15]

Greek philosophy in Latin

Cicero translated *Timaeus* into Latin three centuries after it was written, and so ensured its survival into the Middle Ages. It might seem a surprising choice of text for a time of political upheaval in the civil conflicts between Caesar and Pompey when there would have been little interest in speculative cosmology, but Cicero sees his philosophical works in terms of timeless public service: "I began to interest myself anew in the study of philosophy", he says, "so that my mind might thereby be lightened of the burden of its cares, and I might serve my fellow citizens in the most effective way" (*On Divination* 2.7). Cicero was especially interested in Plato, translating *Protagoras* along with *Timaeus*, and, in his own *Republic* and *Laws*, he adapted to a Roman context Plato's philosophical interests in government, constitutional law and justice. In particular he found a new relevance and role for Plato's philosopher-king: the ideal guide and guardian of the body politic (*reipublicae rector*) might well be realized in the wise and persuasive Roman statesman. At the conclusion of his *Republic*, Cicero has his own Romanized "Myth of Er", which also includes the injunction against suicide from Plato's *Phaedo* and the proof for the soul's immortality from movement translated directly from his *Phaedrus*.

Although much of Cicero's *Republic* is lost, the myth survived in a separate form under the title *Dream of Scipio* (*Somnium Scipionis*). The narrative is structured as a dream reported by Scipio Aemilianus just before his death in 129 BCE, in which his adoptive grandfather, the famous Scipio Africanus, foretells the fall of Carthage, and then his father shows him a vision of the universe. Some of the details follow Plato's myth – a bounded universe with a central spherical earth, planets orbiting it in concentric circles and giving out in their orbits the different musical notes that make up the "harmony of the spheres" – but in this context of the whole heavens there is more emphasis on the comparative insignificance of the earth, the small size of the Roman Empire in just one quarter of the planet and the irrelevance of human glory in the context of the whole. In addition, an astral eschatology, the theory that souls return to stars, replaces the story of the spinning fates and the choice of another life. It is said that each human being has been given a soul from the eternal fires of the Milky Way and we are destined to return there. Plato's god, in a Roman context, becomes a political god, who gains the greatest pleasure from human assemblies and civil associations bound by justice; and it is the statesmen who direct, preserve and enrich these political associations who are assured a return to their native stars. Using a similar mythical form, Cicero adapts Plato's Greek intellectualism and the encouragement to philosophy to Roman practicality and the glorification of the political life.

As well as the myth form that he adapted in *Republic*, Cicero is also influenced by Plato's dialogue form in some of the philosophical works that he produced in his short retirement from the political scene just before the death of Caesar. Cicero's general approach is to present the theories of the great Hellenistic schools – Epicurean, Stoic and Sceptic – in speeches and dialogues set earlier in the century, and with parts taken by distinguished and cultured Romans, many of whom were his personal friends. As with Plato, some care is taken with the setting, and the characters are suited to the subject matter. Laelius, for example, famous for his long-standing friendship with Scipio Aemilianus, is the main speaker in the treatise *On Friendship*, and the elder Cato is the main speaker in the treatise *On Old Age*. These dialogues, however, are not characterized by the cut and thrust of Socratic dialectic, but owe more to Cicero's experience in the law courts. The usual pattern is to have one point of view given at length, and that to be refuted and in turn replaced by an alternative. *On the Nature of the Gods*, for example, has the views of three different schools on religion presented in turn: the Epicurean by Velleius, the Stoic by Balbus and the Academic by the Sceptic Cotta. In the debate on the best life in the five books of *On Supreme Good and Evil*, the Epicurean Torquatus defends Epicurean hedonism, and this is criticized by Cicero in his own character; then the younger Cato speaks at length on the Stoic ideal of virtue and wisdom, which is again, but more charitably, countered by Cicero; the last book, set in Athens in Cicero's youth, revives the ethical positions of Plato and Aristotle, and ends with a compliment on the skill with which the Greek ideas have been discussed in Latin.

Philosophic letters

One of the most popular of Cicero's works, *De officiis*, is on practical virtue and duties. It is in the form of an extended letter to his son Marcus, in the tradition of the philosophic letter, a popular form of writing from the fourth century BCE. Earlier than this, there are thirteen philosophy-type *Epistles* said to have been written by Plato, addressed to Dion and Dionysius in Syracuse, Archytas and others on a variety of topics, but especially concerned with Plato's own philosophic autobiography and his attempts to establish the unsuitable young Dionysius as philosopher-ruler of Syracuse. There is a question mark over the authenticity of some, if not all, of these letters, but they should probably all be rejected on two main grounds. The first is the widespread practice in the fourth century of schools of rhetoric setting student assignments on writing fictitious letters from philosophers in the style of Plato or Aristotle to appropriate recipients; within a short time anyone of any importance had philosophic letters attributed to him. Secondly, throughout his works, Plato is most reticent about himself, citing his name on only two occasions: once to say he was present at Socrates' trial (*Apology* 38b) and the other to say he was absent from the gathering of friends in prison on Socrates' last day (*Phaedo* 59b). He also never gives an explicit account of the theory of forms in any of the dialogues, but when it is mentioned it is taken for granted; Socrates alludes to them as "all these things which we're for ever talking about" (*Phaedo* 76d, 100b; *Timaeus* 51b). It would be quite contrary to Plato's general approach to philosophy to write out a proof for the theory, and uncharacteristic of his studied anonymity to reveal so much about his failure and disappointment at being unable to establish a philosopher-ruler in Syracuse.

Whatever the case here, when we move further into the fourth century BCE, prose letter-writing does begin to be an accepted medium for philosophy. Poetry had previously had an addressee: Hesiod dedicated *Works and Days* to his brother; lyric poets spoke directly to friends and lovers; Empedocles wrote as a professional physicist to his student Pausanias and in more popular terms to his fellow citizens. With Epicurus, however, the letter is his chosen way of summarizing his most important teachings. Three are extant, preserved in Diogenes Laertius' *Life of Epicurus*. The first, the letter to Herodotus, is a short version of Epicurus' teaching on nature, and he explains why he has chosen this genre:

> For the sake of those, Herodotus, who are unable to work carefully through each and every detail of what we have written on nature, and who lack the ability to comprehend my longer books, I have personally composed an adequate summary of the entire system, to make it easier to commit to memory the most general doctrines. (DL 10.34)

Although there is a specific addressee, Epicurus goes on to say that the content is meant for general publication "so that this explanation may be useful to others also". Similarly the second letter, to Menoeceus, although shorter, is crucial in its digest of the main Epicurean theories on the nature of god and human piety, the right attitude to death, the categorization of desires and the correct interpretation of hedonism. A third, to Pythocles, a young student, deals with "the things above the earth" (*meteora*), the only direct evidence extant for Epicurean ideas on celestial bodies (although Diogenes includes a work on *Physics* running to thirty-seven books in his list of the best of Epicurus' writing; DL 10.27). Epicurus wrote in notoriously difficult Greek, as he admits here, and the summary is more accessible, and a useful aid to memory. It is also possible in the summarized form to isolate and emphasize a significant point, such as the Epicurean claim "that knowledge of the things above the earth has no other purpose than peace of mind" ("Letter to Pythocles", DL 10.85), for their movements and effects follow natural laws and are not subject to interference by capricious sky gods. The genre of the philosophic letter, written to a specific individual but intended for a wider audience, was to have a long history, practised by Seneca in the early Roman Empire, by Paul to Timothy, for example, in the New Testament, and, in the letter-diary format of "meditations to oneself", by the emperor himself, Marcus Aurelius.

Lucretius as poet and Epicurean philosopher

As well as the letters, only the epigrammatic set of *Key Doctrines*, also preserved in Diogenes Laertius, and the collection of *Vatican Sayings* (found in a manuscript in the Vatican library) survive from the vast output of Epicurus' own writings.[16] There are summaries of Epicurean theology by Cicero in his first book *On the Nature of the Gods* and on ethics in *On Supreme Good and Evil*, but these reports are admittedly biased, as Cicero, along with most Romans, distrusted Epicurean teaching, especially on the encouragement to avoid taking part in politics and to pursue a private life of pleasure. The main source for Epicurean teaching, however, is Lucretius' poem *De rerum natura*, from the last century of the Roman Republic, which may have been prepared for publication by Cicero. The work has a dedication to an obscure Roman official called Memmius, as if it were a private correspondence, but the message is for the general public, to restore tranquillity and to open the way to a happy life by explaining the true nature of the world and our place in it.

De rerum natura is composed as an epic poem in five books, written in a Latin form of the Homeric hexameter. It is a didactic work, aiming to instruct, in the tradition of Hesiod's *Works and Days* (which was basically a farming manual in verse), and so providing a pattern for the Latin genre that would be used in Vergil's *Georgics* and Manilius' *Astronomica*. In parts it is also satirical in its denunciation of folly, following the Cynic tradition and the example of the earlier poet Lucilius, who had fixed the hexameter as the medium for Roman satire, which would be continued by Perseus and Juvenal. But above all it is a *philosophic* poem, reverting to the genre of Parmenides and especially Empedocles, as the medium for removing error and passing on intact the complete system promulgated by Epicurus. Greek had hitherto been the language of philosophy in Rome, the preserve of the educated elite (who were fluent in Greek), but by writing in Latin Lucretius made the message – that peace of mind and present happiness are possible for everyone – directly accessible, and by putting it into verse (however difficult this was with some of the technical terms) he improved its attraction, comparing it to honeyed medicine for children. His invective against ignorance, error and superstition is of general application, that against other philosophies admittedly more technical, but there is also a direct relevance for the Roman aristocracy in his tirades against rampant avarice and political ambition, which he calls *vulnera vitae* (the running sores of life). He understands that there is a desperate search for a false security in wealth and power that leads to personal vice and unhappiness, and in the state to civil wars. There are some direct Roman touches, in, for example, the use in illustrations of state rituals and soldiers exercising on the Campus Martius, but, more than this, he brings the dull, crabbed Greek of Epicurus to life with the poetic devices of simile, metaphor, imagery and wit.[17] As with Plato, some have seen a conflict in Lucretius between the poet and the philosopher. Lucretius' work has at times been denigrated as passages of superb poetry interspersed with long discourses on atomic theory, but it is his intense conviction in the rightness of Epicurus' philosophy that drives the poetry, giving it power and beauty, and an enhanced seriousness.

The philosophic hymn

Lucretius' poem also contains two examples of the last literary form to be discussed, the philosophic hymn. Praises in hexameter verse to various gods have survived from earliest times under the general title of *Homeric Hymns*; they were composed for individual recital rather than for an assembly or choir. Their content would include an address to the god under various titles, an account of myths relating to his or her birth, travels and honours, and a final prayer. The Stoic Cleanthes was probably the first to adapt the genre to a philosophical context, using the format of an independent address to a god to develop a new theology. In his *Hymn to Zeus* the conventional figure of Zeus as the all-powerful sky god was recast, according to Stoic theory and in the tradition of Heraclitus, as intelligent and perfect *logos*, steering the whole and maintaining it in the best possible state. The hymn opens with the lines: "Greatest of immortals, Zeus of many names, ever all-powerful, / first principle of nature, master of the universe, all hail!" It continues in this vein, praising Stoic divine providence in its aspects of eternal reason and universal law, permeating the cosmos and welding good and evil into an ultimate justice. A shorter fragment from Cleanthes, addressed to Zeus and Fate combined, goes to the heart of Stoic ethics in a prayer quoted by Epictetus: "Lead me Zeus, and you, appointed Fate, to whatever place you have assigned me; / I shall follow eagerly; and, should my will grow weak and fail, still shall I follow" (*Enchiridion* 53).

Lucretius replies to this Stoic theology with an Epicurean version of the philosophic hymn. He opens his work with a complex (and beautiful) song of praise to the goddess Venus, founder of the Roman race through her son Aeneas, who, as patron of pleasure, will give charm to his poetry. Lucretius hails her also as the personification of Empedocles' spirit of Love and conqueror of Mars, the god of war and strife, but above all she represents the creative force of nature and the spirit of its regeneration. The titles and functions of the Romans' patron goddess are thus taken over as the basis for an account of the laws of atomic physics and of an ethics that rejects divine intervention and encourages a fearless hedonism. The second example is from the opening of the third book, which addresses Epicurus in heroic terms:

> You who were the first to be able to lift high so bright a torch
> in the deep darkness, casting light on the blessings of life,
> you I follow, O glory of the Greek people.
> You are our father and guide us with a father's advice ...

This repeats the theme from the first book:

> The vital force of his mind prevailed,
> and he marched far beyond the flaming ramparts of the world,
> travelled the vast universe in thought and spirit,
> and victorious brought back for us the knowledge of what can
> and what cannot be,
> the limit and boundary of individual power.   (lines 72–7)

As Lucretius, through the means of the philosophic hymn, replaced the stern Stoic deity Zeus with laughter-loving Venus, so too the Stoic hero Heracles, symbol of duty and perseverance, born mortal but made immortal for his great deeds, here gives way to Epicurus, the new hero, who is worthy of immortality for his intellectual gifts; in his mind he travelled vast distances and brought back as booty a new philosophy.

3. Cosmologies

Physicists through the ages have looked for an explanation for the behaviour of fundamental particles and forces within a single framework that would reveal the simplicity and power of the principles on which the functions and structures of the universe are based. There are a number of assumptions underlying this ongoing search, and their origins can be traced to the beginnings of Greek philosophy. The first is that there is a *basic structure* to the universe embodied in "laws of nature". Secondly, these are *accessible to human reason*, so that the solution to the problem of finding a theory that would unite so much diversity, and account for what is permanent through change, is within our grasp. Thirdly, *progress is made through criticism and adaptation* of what has gone before, and with these continual advances an ever more accurate story is told. Finally, however, there is the "*axiom of undecideability*": that there may be an ever closer approximation to certainty but, given our impermanent and contingent state, the struggle cannot succeed. Scientific advance is achieved by the continual replacement of one theory by another that is more probable than its predecessor, through a combination of brilliant intuition and the careful application of research (which the Greeks called *historia*). The results at each stage provide the stimulus for subsequent achievements in an ongoing and open-ended exploration of what exists now, and how such things came to be.

A theory of everything

From the beginning the Greeks were ready to find a "theory of everything", and, in a spirit of extraordinary optimism, they set out to interpret "the whole": the formation and present structure of the universe, its underlying laws and the role and function of its parts. It was thought that the bewildering array of phenomena could be pared down to an explanation in terms of simplicity, unity and order; such an explanation would be within the range of human intelligence, and the subject was worthy of the effort required to reach an understanding of it. At the beginning of philosophy, the Presocratics, in their creative thinking, and stimulated by the competition with earlier and contemporary theories, speculated on such subjects as the reduction of matter to basic elements, forces of attraction and repulsion at work on them, the mathematical structure of things, continuous flux and regeneration in the cosmos, the possibility of a constantly expanding universe and an initial version of atomic theory.

Hesiod's *Theogony*

The first attempt to explain everything came with Hesiod's poem *Theogony*. The most obvious way in which one entity comes from another is in the process of birth, and this model, of a succession of generations, was the one that Hesiod used to explain the emergence of the natural world. Night and day, earth and sky, hills, seas, rivers and springs, sun, moon, stars and winds, were all said to take their place in a long, complex genealogy of a family emerging from an original *chaos*, which was thought of as something like a featureless "gap". Mostly these entities are little more than named personifications, put in place to indicate the formation of the cosmos and then its main features. The emergence of the human race appears first in a series of ills listed as the children of Night (such as famine, pain, old age, deceit, strife and murder), and then of blessings. Order, peace and justice, given as children of Themis (who represents universal law), are followed, with the advance of civilization, by memory and the Muses. But Hesiod's comprehensive account also seeks to explain myth and ritual, so that, for example, Earth and Sky become players in the violent succession myth of Ouranos, Kronos and Zeus, in which Kronos subdues his father (with the connivance of his mother, Earth), and is in turn deposed by his own youngest son, Zeus. The ascendancy of Zeus is finally achieved after he and his sibling gods are victorious in a mighty cosmic battle against his father's generation of Titans. A succession of matings by Zeus produces the next generation of divinities, and the various histories and attributes of these, the "Olympians", are given briefly. There is nothing about the first human men, but a great deal about the first woman, Pandora, her jar of evils and her role as a punishment sent to earth by Zeus in retaliation for Prometheus' theft of fire, in a story not immediately reconcilable with the earlier account of human ills as part of the natural order of things. Hesiod's great achievement was to bring together all this material, which comes mainly from the traditions of early Greece and the East, and to weave it into a comprehensive account, in the epic style of Homer, of the ways in which the natural world and its standard features arose, and to include also early stories of the gods and the establishment of cults. Along with the Homeric poems, Hesiod's *Theogony* set the traditions of myth and ritual, but the genealogy model that he used for his cosmogony was soon challenged.

First principles

Anaximander, the first philosopher for whom there is reliable evidence from both secondary sources and his own words, started with two crucial changes from the *Theogony* story. First, Hesiod's initial "chaos" becomes for him *apeiron* (the limitless);[1] this is the vast, characterless origin of all things, extending endlessly in time and space. Anaximander is said to have called it the *archē* (first principle) (Simplicius, DK 12A9),[2] primary to such opposites as hot and cold, dry and moist, and separate from them. The reported argument is that if one of these opposites (or material related to them, such as Thales' "water") were the first principle and limitless, it would eventually overwhelm and destroy the rest, so the *archē* must be different from the opposites, and have no characteristics itself. It is the *source* from which the opposites arise and to which they return when they are destroyed for, as Anaximander says in the surviving fragment, "They suffer punishment and make reparation to one another for their injustice according to the assessment of time". The opposites are represented here as quarrelsome neighbours. At some time or place one encroaches on its counterpart, and that in turn, at another time and place, makes good the loss and itself becomes the aggressor. Gains and losses balance out overall in a cosmic equilibrium, exemplified in the repeated sequences of bright days and dark nights, hot, dry summers and cold, wet winters.

Anaximander's second correction of Hesiod's generation story was the claim that the stage of the emergence of the perceived cosmos is due not to a gendered, personified individual producing a child, but to "something capable of generating hot and cold" coming out of the eternal limitless, in a process that combines an automatic separation with biological growth. He went on to explain that the hot and cold that were then generated became defined as a sphere of flame and dark mist; part of the mist was compacted into earth, and this was surrounded by a layer of air, which in turn was enclosed by the fire "like bark round a tree". The earth at the centre was thought to be cylindrical, its depth a third of its diameter, and, in a brilliant deduction, Anaximander maintained that it would stay stable in its central position because it was "freely suspended", with no reason to move in one direction rather than another. The earth was eventually encircled at proportionate distances by sun, moon and stars, described as three rings that had broken off from the original fiery "bark" and were enclosed by part of the dark mist; these had openings, one each for the sun and moon rings and several for the stars, which allowed the inner fire to shine through. Winds and sea emerged as the result of the sun then affecting the mist about the earth. Since the shape of the earth was cylindrical, it was thought possible that there could be creatures living in the "anti-podes", which is the other surface of the cylindrical earth, with their feet literally opposite to ours. Finally, Anaximander suggested that the human race itself had its origins in the protection of the warm sea rather than the more barren and dangerous land: "There arose fish or fish-like creatures, inside which human beings grew and were retained until puberty; then these creatures broke open, and men and women emerged who were capable of feeding themselves" (DK 12A30).[3]

Anaximander's more cautious fellow townsman Anaximenes concentrated, in his cosmology, on studying the notion of *apeiron* (the limitless), agreeing that it was neutral and indefinite, but he gave it a character, that of atmospheric air, which is necessary for life and also a boundless source of that life. He noted that in itself air has no apparent character, but if compressed it becomes colder and misty, and, conversely, if thinned, it is warmer and drier. Anaximenes then proceeded to derive all things from this one principle according to a difference in *quantity*. He claimed that "thinner" air appears as fiery, in condensing it appears as liquid (as water and sea) and it could then thicken further to produce solids: ice as frozen water, but also earth and then stones. Temperature changes accompany the process, condensation bringing an increase of cold, and rarefaction more heat. The doxography (again originating with Theophrastus; DK 13A5–7) shows how Anaximenes based his cosmogony on this first principle: the air was initially compacted at the centre, where it formed the earth; parts of the earth then "thinned" into sea, and exhalations arising from the sea become still thinner and fiery, and so formed the celestial bodies. Rejecting Anaximander's cylindrical earth "freely suspended" in equal directions from the circumference, Anaximenes envisaged a hemispherical model in which the earth, once more assumed to be broad, flat and shallow, was the base, supported on a cushion of air to keep it stable. He thought of the fixed stars as nailed to the cover of the crystalline hemisphere, whereas the sun, moon and planets floated "like leaves" in the atmosphere. Despite some obvious errors, Anaximenes' achievement is remarkable for showing how a range of problems could be tackled once change was understood to be a *process* of quantitative alteration of one comprehensive substance.

Although, for these early thinkers, the cosmos is alive and connected with what is essential for life – as with Anaximenes' assumption of all-pervasive breath and, earlier, Thales' emphasis on the importance of water – the means by which the different features emerge is more mechanistic, and there is a tendency to assume an elementary *mathematical* structure, certainly for Anaximander in the ratio of the earth's diameter to its height, and in the comparative distances of his encircling rings. Sun, moon and stars are thought of as in no way divine, but produced from the reactions of basic entities of hot and cold, light and dark, rare and dense in their constant motion. Xenophanes continued the trend, deliberately challenging Homer and Hesiod (DK 21B11). Earth for him is not the great primeval mother, giving birth to starry heaven, hills and sea, and Titans, but simply that "from which all things come and into which they have their end"; its upper limit is in contact with air, and it stretches indefinitely below our feet (B27–9, B33). In Hesiod's *Theogony*, Iris, the rainbow messenger of the gods, was said to be the daughter of Thaumas and Electra, and sister to the Harpies, but Xenophanes counters this in the new language: "the one they call Iris, even this is by nature a cloud, / appearing purple and crimson and yellow" (B32).

Xenophanes was recognized as belonging with the Milesians in his non-mythical view of the natural world, and formed a link between them and Parmenides in paring down multiplicity to a basic unity.[4] Heraclitus, however, criticized Xenophanes, along with Hesiod and Pythagoras, for having learned a great deal without reaching understanding (22B40). But Heraclitus was sympathetic towards the Milesians in their more subtle explanation of the world in terms of one principle underlying its diversity, itself without beginning or end but responsible in some way for all else that is generated and destroyed. Like air for Anaximenes, Heraclitus' own first principle was in constant movement, and active in the cosmos and the individual, but he assigned to it the physical aspect of fire: "This cosmos, the same for all, no one of men or gods has made, but it was and is and will be ever-living fire, kindling in measures and being quenched in measure" (B30).

Fire keeps a local identity, but in itself can never be still, since its preservation depends on the continual intake and transformation of fuel. This perpetual motion was summarized in the tag *panta rhei* (everything is in a state of flux).[5] Fire in the cosmos (and also in the individual *psychē*) takes its place in the cycle of the changes or "turnings" of the world masses, from fire to water to earth, and back through water to fire. It is an ingredient in the changes but also controls them, "as goods for gold and gold for goods" (B90). The proportion or *logos*, according to which all these amounts are measured and balanced at different times and places, maintains the equilibrium of the cosmos, and the continual movement of the parts ensures the permanence of the whole, so that "changing it rests" (B84a). The sun plays a crucial part as a primary concentration of fire, controlling the lengths of the days and the seasons, and the distance of the solstices. And here Heraclitus goes straight back to Anaximander, in the belief of temporal and spatial gains and losses found in hot summers and cold winters, parched deserts and flooded fields, balancing out in a cosmic equilibrium controlled over time.

Elements

In relation to his predecessors, Heraclitus, as we have seen, was in sympathy with the Milesians, but criticized others for their lack of *nous*. He himself, however, was open to Parmenides' subsequent attack on those who accept plurality and change, described as: "dazed, uncritical crowds,/who consider to be and not to be the same and not the same,/and that for all things there is a path turning back again" (28B6.7–9). But Parmenides, in addition to his arguments against generation, plurality and change in the *Alētheia* (On truth), himself offered a cosmology in the last section of his poem known as *Doxa* (On opinion). It is prefaced by a warning that the account is deceptive, but is included as a dialectical device, to outstrip anyone else's thinking, and to win the competition on all counts. Its great contribution is to lay the foundations for a theory of elements that would be developed further by Empedocles and eventually enter the mainstream of scientific discovery. Parmenides concedes that if the denial of plurality (which was the basis of his main argument) were breached by a minimum addition, and *two* entities were allowed, then there would be interaction between them, and a (wrongly) perceived world of many things constantly changing could be constructed. In language both poetic and technical, Parmenides struggled to express this idea in his description of the primary duality:

> On the one hand aetherial flame of fire, gentle, tenuous,
> the same as itself in every direction but not the same as the other,
> but the other is on its own and the opposite,
> dark night, thick in form and heavy. (B8.56–9)

Here is the first characteristic for an element: to be self-identical and not like anything else. And the second is that it can be part of a seemingly quite different entity without losing its identity, so that in this case: "the whole is full of light and unclear night, both equal, since nothing is without either" (B9).

If this basic pair were understood to be permanent and unchanging, so the argument goes, with inherent and separate characteristics, then there might be a way, mistaken but plausible, of accounting for plurality and change throughout the cosmos. The proportion of the two in any particular compound would give that compound its particular character, and a preponderance of one or the other would be particularly noticeable, as for example with the sun and moon. The sun is mainly bright, and the moon mainly dark, but (and here Parmenides is the first to understand the phenomenon) the moon gets its light from the sun: "a borrowed light shining in the night wanders round earth" (B14). Individual forms of life would similarly be combinations of light and dark in this scheme, even including the human mind, where the more intelligent would have a greater proportion of light and know more, whereas lesser intelligence would be due to a preponderance of dark (B16).

Empedocles, following Parmenides, doubled his two elements to four. A group of four (the first square number, and signifying justice for the Pythagoreans) appeared to be the minimum number that could account for all the variety of the perceived world and allow for mutual activity regulated by patterns of balance and equilibrium. Empedocles indicated the vitality of the substructure by calling the elements "roots", and stressed their importance and permanence in the divine names he assigned them: Zeus, Hera, Aidoneus and Nestis for fire, air, earth and water respectively. These are obviously present as the natural masses characterizing a coastal town in Sicily – the earth below, the sea at its edge, the air above, and fire pouring from the volcanoes and shining in the bright sun, and parts of these same four could combine to generate mortal things. To show how such a wide diversity of phenomena could be generated from just these four elements Empedocles used the simile of a painting (at B23), which displays in two dimensions a variety of plant, animal and human life, although it consists basically of pigments of a few primary colours in particular arrangements.

The causes of change

The four elements were considered to be basic, unchanging, corporeal entities, forming temporary arrangements as their parts were brought into compounds with different forms, but not subject to any alteration themselves. But Parmenides had raised the question of *how* there could, logically, be movement, and to answer this Empedocles posited opposed principles of attraction and repulsion, which he called *Philia* (Love) and *Neikos* (Strife or Hate). These forces, which are so powerful in human affairs, were projected on to a cosmic scale, where Love could be seen as constructive and unifying, and Strife as destructive and separating.

Empedocles was following the Milesians in paring down plurality and diversity to a minimum number of basic substances, but Anaxagoras, his contemporary, countered this tendency by supposing that maximum plurality and diversity were there from the beginning: "all things were together" (59B1). Anaxagoras claimed that it was only because *everything* was and is in everything that change could be explained, "for how could hair come from what is not hair or flesh from what is not flesh?" (B10). In any object, great or small, all possible ingredients would be present, some imperceptible, but others would dominate to give the object its particular appearance. With "mixing" and "separating" (the terms for "birth" and "death" also used by Empedocles) there is a rearrangement of the parts and a preponderance of different ingredients with a resulting different appearance. The cause of the mixing and separating are not opposing forces, as with Empedocles, but pure cosmic *Nous* (Mind) which knows and controls all things, now and in the future, and caused the initial rotation in the original mixture.

Anaxagoras is unique among ancient cosmologists in writing about an expansionist universe, attributed to this power of Mind: "Mind controlled the whole rotation, so that it began to rotate in the beginning. And first it began to rotate from a small area, but now rotates over a wider area, and will continue to rotate ever more widely" (B12). As a result of the "swirl" or vortex (*dinē*) initiated by Mind, the denser part came to the centre to form the earth, what was less dense made up the sea around it, and the lighter air and fire formed an outer covering. Anaxagoras, however, recognized that with the vortex there would be a counter-tendency for heavy bodies to be swung outwards, and posited sun and stars as red-hot stones hurled from the centre and now carried round in revolutions in the *aithēr*. There was a beginning to the cosmos in its generation from the original mixture, but now the rotations continue outwards indefinitely into the future.

Atomic cosmology

The early atomists started their cosmogony, like Anaxagoras, with a vortex, but in their case it was a swirl of atom clusters that collected together. These clusters (or "molecules") were then caught up in various rotations and separated off on the principle of "like to like". A spherical earth emerged from those molecules of atoms brought together at the centre, to be surrounded by structures that were "moist and muddy". When these dried out they were carried by the vortex of the whole, and then ignited to form the stars and planets. A description of the whole process, common to different world-systems, including our present one, is preserved in Diogenes Laertius; it derives from Democritus, but also quotes some of Leucippus' more exotic original vocabulary:

The *kosmoi* are generated in the following way. Many bodies (i.e. atoms) of all sorts of shapes are "cut off" from the infinite and move into a great void. There they come together and produce a "whirling", in which they collide with one another and revolve in different ways and begin to separate out, like to like. But when there are so many that they can no longer rotate in equilibrium, those that are fine go to the surrounding void as if "sifted", while the rest stay together and become entangled, and, while they move together, they form a spherical structure. It is like a "membrane" which contains all sorts of bodies, and, as the atoms, packed together, keep flowing round in the whirl, the centre solidifies, and the surrounding membrane thins out. So the earth is formed when the atoms that had been brought to the middle stay together there, while the surrounding membrane expands as it attracts bodies from outside, drawing in whatever it touches as it whirls around. Some that get entangled form a structure that is at first moist and muddy, but, as they revolve with the whirling of the whole, they dry out and ignite to form the substance of the stars. (DL 9.31–2)

With an infinite number of atoms moving through an endless void, it was obvious that our present world would not be the only one to emerge, but over time, and in different areas, an indefinite number of other worlds would be forming, maturing and disintegrating. The whole passage has a modern ring, with the concepts of "whirls" starting up randomly in space and attracting more and more matter, of initial density and a cooling from a great heat, and of cosmic clumps being transformed into galaxies.

The vivacity, originality and constant interplay of the cosmologies of these Presocratics were eventually sidelined by the new interests of Socrates and his companions in fifth-century Athens. The study of the natural world and the problems it posed were seen as irrelevant to the paramount concerns of ethics and political theory. The important questions were now more intimately connected with daily life in its social and cultural contexts, and focused on the pursuit of excellence and the criteria for success for the individual and the state. Aristophanes, in his comedy *Clouds*, satirized Socrates as a cosmologist, portraying him swinging in a basket studying meteorological phenomena, as well as running a school and teaching pupils how to win unjust arguments. But the Socrates in Plato's early works, especially in his defence at his trial, denies having any expert knowledge and teaching anyone anything, but recognizes the damage the caricature has done to his reputation. In *Apology* (18b) and *Phaedo* (98a–c), for example, Plato shows Socrates' initial interest in problems about "things of sky and earth", and then his rejection of them as too difficult, and not of immediate concern to the human predicament. In particular, Socrates was disappointed to find that although some of the earlier scientific explanations might be correct as far as they went, they did not tackle the critical questions about what is best for humanity and the greater good of the whole.

Macrocosm and microcosm

The model for most Presocratic cosmologies was biological, that of the living animal, whereas for the atomists it was mechanistic, based on the random movement of atoms through the void. It was Democritus who first used the term *micros kosmos* (DK 68B34) for the individual, seeing a human being as an ordered system in miniature, comparable to the whole in its composite matter and ordered structure. The macrocosm–microcosm link, however, was common to most of his predecessors; it is found for example in Anaximenes' air as human and cosmic breath, Heraclitus' *logos* in the form of fire as controlling intelligence for the whole and the individual *psychē*, Empedocles' elements as world masses and constituents of animal parts, and Mind, for Anaxagoras, providing the same guidance and understanding in the universe and in some of its creatures.[6] In the *Timaeus* Plato sees the individual as a miniature cosmos in the way in which the cycles in the soul strive to be in harmony with planetary movements. The model he uses for his explanation of the cosmos is neither biological nor mechanistic, but that of a craftsman constructing an artefact from shapeless material. In his myth of the world's construction Plato is indebted to many of the advances made by his predecessors in the areas of cosmic intelligence and human intelligence, elemental material, Pythagorean number theory and the distinction between knowledge and belief, but he transforms and transcends them all in an account that became one of the most famous and influential of all texts to come down from the Greek world.

Was there a beginning of things?

The theme of the main section of Plato's *Timaeus* is the myth of a divine craftsman who fashions a world with body and soul by imposing order on disorder in the likeness of an eternally existing model. The first question raised is a crucial one: did this world have a beginning? For Anaximander and Anaximenes the world was generated in the past from the limitless surround; for Anaxagoras it was started by the action of Mind on an initial mixture. Heraclitus' fire was "ever-living" and successive generations arose from it as it was kindled and quenched in measures, Empedocles believed that the elements separate and come together in repeating cycles, whereas for the atomists the movement of atoms in the void is without beginning or end. Later, Aristotle would claim a "steady-state" theory of a world that ever was and will be as it is, the Epicureans would follow the early atomists with numerous worlds continually being generated, maturing and disintegrating through the void, and the Stoics conflated cyclic time with Heraclitean fire to give a periodic *ekpyrōsis* (a burning-up), followed by another beginning.

Plato is only too aware of the problem of a beginning in time, and solved it with a "two-world" theory. "What is" is the perfect world of being – eternal, unchanging, complete, incorporeal, independent and uncaused; it is the object of certain knowledge, reached by intelligence and reason, and acts as a *model*. Against it is set the imperfect world of becoming, which is changing, incomplete, corporeal, dependent and caused, the object of opinion and perception concerned with what is at best probable or likely, and it is a *copy* of eternal being. In saying that "it has become",[7] Plato is not giving this perceptible world a beginning in time, since it coexists with time, but he is classifying it as "becoming", and so imperfect and changing, in contrast to perfect and unchanging "being". An appropriate account of what is true and permanent is called *logos*, but for the probable and temporary a *mythos* is appropriate. It is not that an imaginary story is a substitute for science, but a recognition that science is inexact, that is, that science, while aiming at results that are as precise as can be, can always be improved on or superseded, and a narrative is here an appropriate medium for an explanation of it. Furthermore, the fact that the narrative about the perceptible world has a beginning does not entail a beginning to that world itself, but merely that a description of it as an artefact requires a starting-point.

The living world

The craftsman god in the *Timaeus* is good, and, because he has no envy (*phthonos*) in him, he produces the best possible world, alive with soul and intelligence, a unique copy of a unique model. As Timaeus concludes:

> We may say that we have now reached the end of our account of the whole, for this cosmos has now received the full number of mortal and immortal creatures. A living animal, visible itself, it contains all that is seen; a perceptible god, it is an image of the intelligible, supremely great and good, most beautiful and as perfect as possible, this one uniquely generated heaven.   (92c)

The Stoics, starting with Chrysippus, took over this theory of the cosmos as alive, and with a rational soul. He had an argument to support it:

> The cosmos is a living animal, a being ensouled and capable of perception, for animal is superior to non-animal, nothing is superior to the cosmos, therefore the cosmos is a living animal. And it is ensouled, as is clear from our souls being fragments of it.   (DL 7.143)

In this Plato and the Stoics deliberately set themselves against the atomists and their soulless, non-perceptive, non-intelligent plurality of worlds, which were composed from lifeless atoms moving randomly through void.

The world *body*, according to the *Timaeus* myth, is made of the four Empedoclean elements, with water (cold and wet) and air (wet and hot) as the mean proportion between the two extremes of earth (dry and cold) and fire (hot and dry), the detailed proportions given owing much to Pythagorean mathematical theory. This body is described as spherical and smooth, engaged in circular motion, free from disease and old age (another blow to the atomist theory of worlds deteriorating before their final disintegration), complete and self-sufficient. The world *soul* is described as intermediate between eternal being and temporal becoming, having both knowledge of the eternal and true opinion of the temporal, the eternal being expressed in the circle of the Same (at the outer edge of the fixed stars) and the temporal the circles of the Different (which give the orbits of the planets). World body and soul are put together through their centres, the soul directing the movements of the body and providing it with a divine source of unending and rational life.

Basic mathematical structures

From the myth at the end of the *Republic* (617b–e) it is found that Plato in this context adopted the Pythagorean theory of the "harmony of the spheres", which was an imaginative combination of principles of mathematics, harmonics and astronomy. After experimenting on a single string with a moveable bridge, Pythagoras himself, or one of his early associates, discovered that the separate notes that were produced corresponded to the length of the string from the bridge, and that the octave, and the ratios of fourth and fifth, were precisely determined by these mathematical intervals. Since a large body moving through space was assumed to produce some sound, and the planets were such bodies, they would be producing sounds as they rotated; and, since they were thought to move at speeds in proportion to their distance from the centre, it is likely that they would continually give off sounds related to the ratios of their orbits. At the circumference were the fixed stars, and then, in order, the seven planets Saturn, Jupiter, Mars, Venus, Mercury, Sun and Moon, with earth at the centre. The proportionate distances and speeds of the planets correspond to the ratios of octave, fourth and fifth, "and on the top of each circle stands a siren, which is carried round with it and utters a note of constant pitch, and the eight notes together make up a single scale" (*Republic* 617b).[8] We are not aware of this beautiful music because it is in our heads since birth, in the same way that those who live near the noise of a blacksmith's anvil or by the cataracts of the Nile are deaf to such sounds.[9]

Plato also adapted Pythagorean mathematics in two sections of the *Timaeus* myth. In the first (36a–c), he describes the complicated harmonic intervals marked on the inner and outer bands of Same and Different, which make up the world soul and regulate the movements of the stars and planets. In the second passage (54a–55e) he corrected his earlier assumption of Empedoclean elements, stating that earth, air, fire and water were not absolutely basic but derivative, and depended for their structure on "elements of elements", that is, geometric patterns that are imposed on random matter. These patterns are made from two basic types of triangles, isosceles and equilateral, which build up into five solids: a cube to form earth, a pyramid for fire, an octahedron for air and an icosahedron (twenty-faced) for water; and the craftsman-god makes the sphere of the whole (like a football) from twelve pentagons (dodecahedron). The complexities of the triangle compositions are due in part to the need to have the strict form of a *mathematical* structure, but with algebra not yet discovered, and arithmetic no longer satisfactory once it was realized that some numbers are "irrational", the mathematics focused on geometry. It was also possible to explain the visible transformation of air, water and fire into each other by the break-up and reassembly of their constituent triangles.

The self-regulating universe

Plato's magnificent cosmology was soon challenged in all its main features, and the first reaction was from his pupil Aristotle. Aristotle's own theory of nature (given in his *Physics*, i.e. the study of *physis*, the Greek word for "nature") laid down general principles governing causation, change, time and place. These were applied to individual studies in other works, especially of the heavens and meteorological phenomena, within the framework of a "steady-state" self-regulating universe; in the realm of change "beneath the moon", they were relevant to human and animal biology. He agreed with Plato that Empedocles' four elements of earth, air, fire and water were not absolutely fundamental and immutable, but he substituted for Plato's basic quantitative mathematics a qualitative theory that went back to the Milesians. Aristotle gave to each of the so-called elements a term from the pairs of the opposites of hot and cold, dry and wet. Fire, therefore, is hot and dry, atmospheric air hot and wet, water wet and cold and earth cold and dry. Elements could then change into each other directly by losing one of the contraries and acquiring its opposite (air for example losing its wetness, acquiring "the dry" and becoming hot) or indirectly via an intermediary (fire, which is hot and dry, transforming into cold, wet water via hot, wet air). A basic substratum, however, was still needed, and Aristotle called this "prime matter" (*prōtē hylē*): indeterminate and impossible to isolate. In Aristotelian terms this was "potentiality alone", which means it was just something that could receive form. It would be then actualized, and emerge into the range of perception, once it had acquired the characteristics of one of the "so-called" elements. Any

77

individual entity would therefore be a combination of form imposed on matter, rather than, as in Plato's theory, *participating* in a separate ideal form, and reproducing it to a greater or lesser degree of accuracy.

The movements of earth, air, fire and water, according to Aristotle, were determined by their weight or lightness, which were seen as primitive properties of these bodies, like the opposites hot and cold, and wet and dry. Earth, as heavy, has a natural movement "downwards", towards the centre, and takes its place there; fire, as light, has the opposite natural movement "upwards", towards the circumference. Water and air were thought to be *relatively* heavy and light, so that water, heavier than air but lighter than earth, tends to take its position around the earth, and the place of air is between water and fire, but there is never a complete separation into these four masses because of the constant reaction of the different temperatures and other contrasting properties of their constituent parts. The external activity of the sun and moon causes the divisions of day and night, the months and the seasons, which in turn are responsible for the birth, maturing and passing-away of the organisms on planet earth. The whole system has neither beginning nor end but is ever-existing, the outer spheres rotating in their perfect circles eternally, and life "beneath the moon" continuing indefinitely according to the physical laws that control the balance of generation, change and decay.

A fifth element

However, the system of rectilinear movements to and from the centre, which Aristotle thought obviously characterized earth, water, air and fire, could not explain the movements of planets and stars, which turn in circles. The tendency of earth and water to move downwards was seen as contrary to the upward tendency of air and fire, but circular movement has no contrary, so that which engages in circular movement could not be composed of or related to earth, water, air or fire. Aristotle therefore concluded that circular movement belonged to a *fifth* element, which he called *aithēr* (in Latin later *quinta essentia*, "quintessence"). Since this does not move up or down it would not be heavy or light, or subject to generation, corruption or change, but was to be understood as engaged for ever in its circular motion, immutable and impassive. Being above the world of change it has greater honour and purity and is therefore linked with the divine. The related cosmological pattern of a central, static, spherical earth, with water, air and fire engaged in linear movements in the mortal world of change beneath the moon, and above it the clear, unchanging region where *aithēr* rotates for ever, and bears in its rotation the divine spheres of planets and stars, was the most influential to survive from the ancient world.

Aristotle was famous for saying "god and nature do nothing in vain" (*De caelo* 271a33). This teleology, however, was not that of Plato's craftsman-god, who, in constructing the artefact that is this world, put every part in its place with a function related to the good of the whole, but for Aristotle individuals in the terrestrial regions are trying to realize the form imposed on their matter as closely as possible. Every acorn is striving to be a perfect oak tree, every lion cub a brave lion, every child the best possible human being, but the different levels of living things are each hampered internally by the constituent parts of

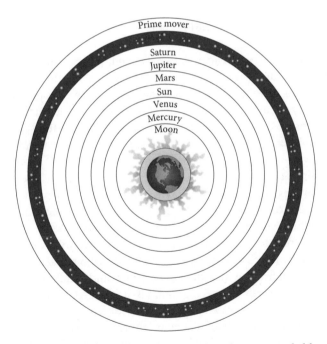

Figure 1. Aristotle's cosmic system. The central earth is surrounded by water, with air and fire above them in the sub-lunar region. The spheres of the planets and the circle of the fixed stars rotate perpetually under the ultimate control of the prime mover.

form at odds with the underlying matter, and externally by the outside forces of constant change. In the region of the upper sky the endeavour to reach the perfection of the divine results in the faultless rotation of the heavens.

This simple pattern, however, was to some extent undermined by Eudoxus, working in Plato's Academy, who observed that the motions of the planetary spheres had to be independent of each other to account for the phenomena of their "wanderings". To counter this, a complex system of interactive spheres would be needed, and this is what Aristotle eventually conceded (in the later insertion of chapter 8 into *Metaphysics Lambda*). He thought there that for the mechanization of planetary movement to succeed it would be necessary to posit fifty-five concentric spheres, thirty-three to produce the observed phenomena, and a further twenty-two to act as "reagent" spheres, nullifying the effects of one planet's sphere on the next.

The revolution of earth and planets

The notion of a static earth was challenged, perhaps from a hint in Plato's *Timaeus* (40b–c), by Heraclides Ponticus in the mid-fourth century BCE. He maintained that the earth revolves approximately once every twenty-four hours while still keeping its place in the centre of the cosmos. He also contradicted the notion that the spheres of the planets are concentric with the earth, and instead set Venus and Mercury as satellites of the sun. In this he paved the way for the later developments of the introduction of equants, deferents, eccentrics and epicycles into Greek mathematical cosmology, which culminated in the work of Ptolemy, in his great *Almagest*, in the second century CE. A natural corollary of Heraclides' work would have been to move the earth from the centre of the system. This seems to have been first suggested by the early Pythagorean Philolaus, who replaced the earth with a central fire, the "hearth of the cosmos", and had the earth (and a dark "counter-earth") revolving round it. It was Aristarchos of Samos, in the third century BCE, who argued that the earth, as well as revolving about its own axis, also simultaneously turns about the sun along the circumference of a circle. But his heliocentric theory did not have the influence it deserved, partly for the sheer daring of the hypothesis, but also because it diminished the importance of earth, and the central position of the human race that inhabited it.

Epicureans on limitless space and innumerable worlds

The Epicureans went further and denied any centre to the universe; nor could there be an absolute "up" and "down" in space, but only relative to an individual. The universe, by definition, is all that there is, and they denied that it had any boundary, for what is on the other side of the boundary would be included in what there is; this meant that, from any position in it, the universe stretches away, equally infinite in all directions. To give some idea of this infinity, Lucretius takes the movement of lightning, the fastest known phenomenon, and says that the dazzling flashes, racing through an interminable tract of space, could not traverse it, nor even shorten the distance still to be covered (*DRN* 1.1001–7).[10] In this context, Lucretius also introduces the "spear" puzzle, which, in the original, perhaps going back to Archytas, referred to stretching out an arm at the supposed boundary, but was given a Roman touch by Lucretius in the spear hurled into enemy territory as a declaration of war:

> Suppose you allow that space is finite, and someone runs to the very edge and throws a spear, do you think that it would fly on straight ahead or meet an obstruction? It must be one or the other, but either answer would have you admit to a limitless universe. If the spear continues on, then there is no boundary, if it is stopped I shall go after you and ask you to throw from there, and so on *ad infinitum*. (1.968–76)

According to the argument, if an obstacle impedes the spear then the stand was not taken at the very edge, and should be further out, which leads to the same question being asked: if there is no obstacle, what happens to the spear? It must travel on indefinitely. So whether there is or is not an obstacle, the conclusion abolishes any firm boundary to the cosmos as a whole, and space therefore has to be limitless.

The Epicurean theory following from this, which has a modern ring to it, was of numerous galaxies forming and disintegrating through the vastness of space. Hesiod's initial "chaos" had been the first attempt to name what was there before anything else, and the concept evolved into Anaximander's "limitless", Plato's "receptacle" and Aristotle's "prime matter". Parmenides had argued that there could be no "is not" in either time or space, and Empedocles followed him with the further step of identifying "is not" spatially with emptiness (*kenon*) before dismissing it. Only Leucippus and Democritus accepted the reality of empty space as such, claiming that "is not" is as valid an existing entity as "is". The "empty" (*kenon* as void) and the "full" (solid atoms) are all that there is. The Epicureans developed this further, pulling out the implications of limitless material in limitless space for numerous worlds:

> When there is a quantity of material in readiness, space is available, and there is no impediment, then there must be resulting activity.
>
> If at this moment there is a supply of atomic molecules too great to be counted, and if the same natural force abides, to hurl the seeds of things together in the same way as here, then you must admit that there are other planets earth in other places, with a variety of human and animal life.   (2.1067–76)

Our present world is one of those that had been generated from clusters of atoms and continually expanded until it reached maturity, but inevitably the composite structures will fall apart, the whole complex disintegrate, and its constituent atoms move out into space, some perhaps to reform into other worlds. Now our world is past its prime, and, as it is subject to internal decay and external blows, its end is unavoidable. The description of the process by Lucretius at the end of his second book foretells global warming, the exhaustion of the parched earth and gradual widely spreading decay until the "*moenia mundi*", the mighty walls of the world's citadel, attacked on all sides, crack and completely collapse (2.1144–74).

Stoic cosmology and recurring time

Stoic cosmology adopted from Plato and Aristotle the pattern of a central spherical earth with the stars and planets rotating around it. The whole was thought to be self-regulating and self-contained, with void, which the Epicureans understood to be all pervasive, banished to the exterior of the outer circumference, from where it extended indefinitely in all directions. The enclosed cosmos was thought to be made of continuous matter, which had two aspects: as an active and a passive principle. The passive aspect was the material of earth and sea, while the active one, which worked on these, was termed *pneuma*, originally fiery, but then described by Chrysippus more as a combination of air and fire in "warm breath", the essence of life. This theory followed that of Heraclitus, in that *pneuma* for the Stoics was also viewed as the rational organizing principle, divine (called, as it had been by Heraclitus, both *Zeus* and *logos*), pervading the cosmos and its organic parts, and holding it all together by means of its tensile energy. Here too there is a macrocosm–microcosm pattern, with the individual organisms not only replicating the whole in miniature but all being interconnected as animated matter.

Since the cosmos for the Stoics, following Plato in the *Timaeus*, was a living thing, an "animal", they expected it to have a life cycle. Its birth was from fire and air, which was then partially transformed into earth and water to give the elements of the organisms that subsequently emerged. But then, as an animal, the cosmos would grow, reach maturity, decline and eventually pass away; this "passing away", according to the Stoics, would be as a re-absorption into the original fire in a massive cosmic conflagration called *ekpyrōsis*. Then the cycle started again. There had been earlier suggestions of such a notion of recurring time cycles, in particular in the alternating dominance of Love and Strife found in Empedocles' *Physics*, and the story of a succession of repeated cosmic eras in Plato's myth in *Politicus* (268d–274e). It was also a reasonable assumption that, as the days and months and seasons of the year recur with the turnings of the sun and moon, so there might well be a "Great Year", when all the planets return to their earlier position. This "Great Year" would have its own great summer of conflagrations and its winter of floods, and natural disasters of this kind had been preserved in the myths of Phaethon, in which the chariot of the sun crashed to earth causing a conflagration, and of Deucalion and Pyrrha, the only human beings saved when once the whole earth was flooded. The Stoic Chrysippus finally combined these precedents into a version of cyclic time dominated by Heraclitean fire in the theory of *ekpyrōsis*. This meant that, at specific periods of time comparable to a "Great Year", there would be a conflagration and destruction of the cosmos, and then a regeneration and return to the former state of affairs:

> When the stars are brought back to the same position everything that happened in the previous cycle is repeated in exactly the same way. There will again be a Socrates and a Plato and everyone else along with the same friends and fellow citizens; the same things will happen to them and they will do the same things

again, and every city and village will return. The restoration of the whole occurs not once but many times, indeed without end into infinity ... There will be nothing strange compared with what happened before, but all will be exactly the same down to the smallest detail.   (Nemesius, *On Human Nature* 38.111)[11]

In their cosmology, as with their ethics, the Stoics did not shrink from taking their theory to its logical conclusion. Yet this is no more extreme than contemporary theories of parallel and successive universes.

4. Pagan monotheism

The existence of divinity was generally accepted in the ancient world, and one piece of evidence put forward for this acceptance was that over centuries, and throughout the known world, there was widespread agreement on this issue, as summarized by Cicero:

> Nothing but the presence in our minds of a firmly grasped concept of god could account for the stability and permanence of our belief in him, strengthened by the passing of time and maturing over the centuries. In other cases unfounded opinions have faded away over the years. Who thinks that the Hippocentaur or Chimaera once existed, what old woman is so silly as to be afraid of the horrors of the underworld that were once believed in? Time obliterates imaginative fiction, but strengthens innate judgments. So in our own country and elsewhere religious practice and acknowledgement of the divine grows stronger and is more widespread as time goes by.   (*On the Nature of the Gods* 2.5)[1]

Even the Epicureans approved in that they believed that images of gods sometimes appear in dreams, which would emanate from actual originals although from distant regions of outer space. The attitude to Greek religion adopted by the philosophers shows a criticism of traditional gods of myth and ritual, and their replacement by a "natural theology". The divine attribute of deathlessness was complemented by that of being ungenerated, and the concepts of intelligence, perfection, power and control were transferred to cosmic forces. Plato spoke of a creator god who was perfectly good but, in another context, claimed that goodness itself was the source of being, knowledge and truth. Aristotle interpreted the divine in terms of primary causation and the highest intelligence, whereas the Stoics embedded god in the world as energy pervading matter. As with cosmology, the philosophy of Greek religion shows a constant interplay of ideas and arguments on a subject that allows no definitive conclusion.

Against anthropomorphic gods

The historian Herodotus attributed the chief features of the Greek pantheon to a combination of Homer's *Iliad* and *Odyssey* and Hesiod's *Theogony*. In these poems the births and personal histories, appearances, powers and titles of the gods were set out, along with their fields of activity and interrelationships, and from then on these entered the mainstream of Greek religious tradition. According to Hesiod, from the first mingling of Ouranos and Gaia, the divine personifications of the heavens above and the earth beneath, came the generation of the Titans. To the youngest of these, Kronos and Rhea, were born six splendid children: "Hestia, Demeter and golden-sandalled Hera, pitiless Hades, loud-roaring Poseidon, the Earth-Shaker, and wise Zeus, whose thunder crashes over the broad lands" (*Theogony* 453–8). Hestia stayed at home and guarded the hearth, Demeter cared for the earth and its crops, Hera joined Zeus as his consort and, in a final separation of powers, Zeus took control of the sky and its weather, his brother Poseidon the sea, and Hades the dark world of the dead beneath the earth. In the next generation came the younger gods, vividly portrayed earlier in the Homeric epics, who would take their place on Olympus: laughter-loving Aphrodite, grey-eyed clever Athena, the twins Apollo and Artemis, the smith Hephaestus, the messenger Hermes and the dread Ares, god of war. Reinforced by painting and sculpture, the characteristics of these gods became so well known that, if they appeared undisguised, it was thought that they would be instantly recognizable, for they were presented as looking, speaking and acting like human beings, but taller, more splendid and more powerful; above all, they were *athanatoi* – they would never die.

But from the very beginning of philosophy the assumption that gods act like human beings was explicitly rejected. Xenophanes' criticisms set the tone, as in his fragment on their traditional immorality: "Homer and Hesiod have attributed to the gods / everything that is blameworthy and disgraceful among humans – / theft and adultery and mutual deception" (DK 21B11). He also understood the relativism underlying their depiction as human: "Humans suppose that gods have been born, / and wear clothes like theirs and have voice and body" (B14), and "Ethiopians say that their gods are snub-nosed and black, / and Thracians that theirs have blue eyes and red hair" (B16). In B15 comes the "reduction to the absurd": that if horses and cows could draw, they would draw gods looking like themselves – as horses and cows. Empedocles later had a similar message: "God is not equipped with a human head on a body, / two branching arms do not spring from his back, / he has no feet, no swift knees, no shaggy genitals" (B28, 29, 134).

But the criticisms were not all negative; Xenophanes, building on the work of the Milesians, produced a more positive concept of divinity:

> One god, greatest among gods and men, not at all like mortals
>   in body or mind.
> As a whole he sees, as a whole he thinks, and as a whole he
>   hears.
> And always he stays in the same place, not moving at all,
>   nor is it fitting for him to travel in different directions at different
>   times,
> but with no effort at all he keeps everything else moving,
> by the thinking of his mind.   (B.23, 24, 26, 25)

Heraclitus, like Xenophanes, was scathing on conventional religion and attacked its ritual:

> People make themselves clean and purify themselves by washing
> in blood, as if you could clean off mud by stepping into mud, but
> a man would be thought mad if anyone were to see him behaving
> in this way. They pray to their statues like someone talking to a
> house, not knowing the nature of gods and heroes.   (22B5)

There is however, for Heraclitus, as with Xenophanes, a contrast in that both negative and positive attributes of divinity are recognized, in particular concerning the chief god: "The one and only wise does and does not consent to be called by the name of Zeus" (B32). Heraclitus would here deny anthropomorphic features and familial relationships to Zeus, but the ancient epic attributes of immortality, power and knowledge are retained. His divinity understands the whole: "To god all things are beautiful and good and just, / but people have supposed some to be unjust, others just" (B102). In the god's physical manifestation there are no human characteristics, but he is elemental, appearing as "ever-living fire" (B30), "judging and constraining" (B66). Opposites are reconciled in him, and he takes part in the cosmic and human changes, while being their driving force: "God: day, night; winter, summer; war, peace; satiety, hunger; changing in the way that oil, when it is mixed with perfumes, is separately named according to the smell of each" (B67).

Natural theology

From Thales, the first of the Milesians, comes the dramatic and enigmatic saying that "all things are full of gods".[2] Homeric polytheism is here replaced with a kind of anonymous pantheism, involving a belief that life and movement are everywhere. Thales may have come to this conclusion from observing that a magnetic stone could move iron, a discovery attributed to him by Aristotle in this context (*De anima* 405a21), which may well have suggested that other apparently inanimate objects might have similar unseen powers. At the least the word *theos* has been stripped of connotations of ritual and myth, and given a new application in the world of nature.

Argument starts with Anaximander, who attacks not the anthropomorphism of traditional gods but the accounts of their various births and shared immortality. His premise is a sharp division between mortality (involving birth and death) and its opposite, so that *either* there is birth and death for individual gods, as with human beings, *or* there is neither start nor finish; the conventional assumption that gods are born, and then continue indefinitely, is illogical. Anaximander himself attributed divinity only to the "limitless", since that alone has no beginning, and (in his own words) is "deathless and indestructible" (DK 12B2). This limitless divine (which he called by the neutral term *to apeiron*) is without gender, and also without any defining character, but is to be understood as a unique entity extending endlessly back into the past and forward into the future, with no temporal or spatial boundaries. Surrounding and governing the whole, it provides an inexhaustible source for becoming, so that all that there is arises originally from it and duly returns to it in measured sequence over time.

This new understanding of the divine was then developed by Anaximander's colleague Anaximenes with two innovations, shown in the original wording of his one extant fragment: "As our soul (*psychē*) which is air maintains us, so breath and air surround the whole world". First, the soul is introduced as that which holds together, strengthens and controls the individual, and this is analogous to the divinity, without birth or death, which encloses the cosmos and is its source. Secondly, this divine source is not indefinite, as with Anaximander, but is now assigned a specific yet invisible character: that of living breath. These Milesians find that it is in the workings of nature that the truly immortal – what is birthless, deathless and limitless – is to be found, as both the origin of life and its support and control. This first principle (or *archē*) names what there was before anything else; it has a role in providing a causal explanation of the world and its phenomena, but does not itself have to be explained. Similarly it is a "beginning" for other things, but without having a beginning itself, and, since there is no end to its continuing existence, it is also "deathless", *athanatos*, the Homeric synonym for a god. There is in addition the concept, developed in Xenophanes and Heraclitus, of an intelligent divinity that surrounds and "steers" everything, containing the whole and in some way responsible for its movement and activity. But the emergence of this idea of monotheism in nature has nothing to do with morality, even though Anaximander used the concept of justice (*dikē*), and Heraclitus that of law (*nomos*). These terms are a way of expressing the principles of order, measure and limit regulating the workings of the cosmos and the patterns of movement of the celestial bodies within it.

Cosmic divinities

Empedocles is working along the same lines when he adapts the traditional divine attributes of power, privilege and deathlessness to the functioning of nature in his forceful introduction of the four elements: "Hear first the four roots of all things – / bright Zeus and life-bringing Hera, Aidoneus / and Nestis, with whose tears the world's streams flow" (DK 31B6). Using Homeric metre and style (similar to the catalogue of gods in Agamemnon's oath at *Iliad* 4.275), Empedocles subverts the Homeric context. The fragment lists four gods, two male and two female, one pair (Zeus and Hera) belonging to the upper realm and the other (Aidoneus, god of Hades and darkness, and the water-nymph Nestis) to the lower. But these are no longer divinities in any recognizable conventional sense, to be prayed to or appeased, with known appearances and histories: they have been recast as the eternal unchanging elements of fire, air, earth and water. In this exploration of what it means to be a god, the immanence of divinity is now shown in the workings of the universe, in the inherent designs and mechanisms of natural processes. In addition, according to this new view of the natural world, the eternal, unchanging basic ingredients of life (which Empedocles calls "roots", the botanical term indicating their vitality) are set up as worthy of the respect and wonder with which the Olympians were traditionally regarded.

Parmenides built on Anaximander's denial of absolute birth and death, and hammered home the implications with forceful argument, presented as a speech concerning truth delivered by a goddess to a young man at the end of his journey to the ends of the earth. She starts by saying that the first pair of "signs" characterizing what truly is points to the denial of generation and destruction. There could not have been a beginning, she argues, for, before the beginning of what there is, there would have been what there is not, and how could what there is have come from what is not? And, with a question embodying what was later known as "the principle of sufficient reason",[3] she asks what compulsion would there be to start at one time rather than another in an expanse of nothingness. Similarly, to assume destruction would mean that after the end of what there is there would be "what is not", which again is unacceptable, so there can be no beginning or end to what there is. A fortiori there could not be a succession of starts and stops, so what there is is continuous in time, and also unaltered, unmoving and unchanging. Any alteration in the present state requires the end of that state and the beginning of another, but, since there is no generation or destruction, what is not the case cannot come to be, and what is true at one time cannot not be true at another. Tenses are therefore irrelevant to true being: "it never was nor will be, since it is now all at once, one and continuous", and it is also complete, since it has no need or deficiencies. In addition, with the rejection of "what is not" in any sense, there are no temporal gaps, and the goddess concludes that there can be no spatial ones either, so that there is no internal alteration, but what there is is equal to itself "all over", comparable to a spherical mass in consistency and equilibrium (28B8.1–33). Parmenides has deduced from the basic language of "is" and "is not" an entity that is birthless and deathless, spatially homogenous, changeless and unique. These attributes relate to the new natural theology, while the arguments that establish them are given authority and power according to the old formula of revelation from a goddess.

In response to Parmenides, Empedocles denied genesis, destruction and change to his elements, but he required a plurality, a minimum of four, with permanent and different characteristics, so that their intermingling could account for the apparent variety of perceived objects. Leucippus and Democritus would take this theory to extremes, first by rejecting any attributes beyond size, shape and position for their elemental atoms, and secondly by extending plurality to an infinite number. The Eleatic Melissus, contemporary with these philosophers, reverted to a monotheistic outlook in accepting a continuously existing unchanging entity. He followed Parmenides in supporting its uniqueness (30B4–6), adding the argument that, if there were two, one would be a limit to the other. Furthermore, in his long seventh fragment Melissus covered the denial of *any* alteration in arrangement or structure for what there is, ruling out any form of pain or distress as being a deterioration in the state of being, and an intimation of mortality. This would imply that the opposite condition, equivalent or analogous to health and pleasant feeling, is appropriate, developing Empedocles' hint of a single, spherical god who "rejoices in encircling stillness" (31B28.2). Melissus took the additional step of denying "body" (*sōma*) to true being, and maintaining then that what has no body or parts would also have no "bulk" (*pachos*; 30B9). This conclusion would seem to be indebted to Zeno's dilemma on *megethos*: either what there is has no parts and so is nothing, or, if there are parts that in turn need intervening parts to distinguish them, the result is to be indefinitely big (29B1). Melissus avoided the dilemma by stripping what there is of body and bulk, even if there would then be no shape to define it as a distinct entity.

Taking into account these Eleatic arguments, and still in sympathy with the deity of Xenophanes and with the "one wise" of Heraclitus, both of which had a crucial part to play in generating and sustaining the natural world, Anaxagoras then put forward the concept of a cosmic Mind that is all-powerful, all-knowing and all-controlling. As in the "sphere" fragments of Empedocles (31B27–9), and his concept of "sacred thinking darting through the whole cosmos" (B134),

Anaxagoras proposed an intellectual divinity of cosmic dimensions, from which this world of change and variety is derived. He described Mind as limitless, self-determining and with independent existence, the most rarefied of all things and the purest, with comprehensive knowledge and the greatest power. Furthermore: "All that has life Mind controls, and all that was going to be, all that was but is no longer, and all that is now and will be, Mind arranged in order, and this rotation too, in which now rotate the stars and sun and moon and air and aether" (59B12). *Nous*, the term that Anaxagoras uses for "Mind" here, is masculine, but he removes any connotations of gender or character by putting the descriptive adjectives "limitless" (*apeiron*) and "independent" (*autokrates*) in the neuter. The language of eternity, independence, purity, omniscience and omnipotence used of Mind is theological, but Anaxagoras is careful to avoid the word *theos* and its derivatives, for cosmic Mind is indifferent to the world it has generated, and has no moral purpose for it.

Anaxagoras is here in agreement with all the early concepts of everlasting, unchanging, all-powerful physical principles, which bypass the question of a general good in the generation and maintenance of the natural world, and explain causation only in material terms. This is the basis of Socrates' famous criticism of the Presocratics set out in Plato's *Phaedo* (97b–100a). Socrates is said to have studied Presocratic theories, bought Anaxagoras' book and and was ready to work through the details of the shape and place of the earth, the velocities and orbits of sun, moon and stars and the like, expecting in the end to find an explanation in terms of purpose and according to what is "for the best". He hoped especially that Mind in Anaxagoras would be shown to be working towards some universal good and was disappointed to find only physical reasons given for events, as if someone were to explain Socrates sitting in prison as a connection of bones and joints and the contraction and relaxation of muscles and sinews. Such a biological explanation would be not erroneous but inadequate, since the *primary* reason for his sitting there is that he thinks it right to stay and obey the orders of the state; otherwise his bones and sinews would have been off elsewhere long ago. Socrates' actions are done through choice and controlled by intelligence, and he wants to make a clear distinction between this causal explanation (the *aition*) and the physical conditions necessary for its operation.

The god of morality

In the *Apology*, Plato's version of Socrates' defence at his trial on the charges of impiety and corrupting the young, Socrates claims that the oracle at Delphi, in saying that no one was wiser than he, had laid on him the charge of testing the wisdom of others, and this became his mission. Although the source of the charge is officially the particular god Apollo, Socrates speaks throughout in terms of an anonymous *theos*. Socrates interprets the oracle as meaning that wisdom belongs only to god, and god has assigned him to Athens, like a mosquito buzzing around a great horse, to unsettle people and make them understand that those who think themselves wise are not so, and that the recognition of their ignorance is the first step towards true knowledge. Socrates claims that this examination of himself and others is the philosophic life appointed by god, and he will abide by it, even if it has made him poor and could now bring him to death, for "I owe a greater obedience to god than to you".[4] The "new" divinity that Socrates introduces, his *daimōn*, (the introduction of which was part of the charge against him) connects with this universal god, reinforcing his command in a negative way. Should Socrates contemplate an action that is contrary to his service to god then he is held back by the warning from an inner voice. But the higher divinity, called simply *theos*, that urges him to right action and the pursuit of the philosophic life against all odds, has no personal characteristics or historic features; it seems that a universal monotheism is introduced which now has a *moral* aspect.

The condemnation of the anthropomorphism inherent in the portrayal of gods and goddesses in Homer and Hesiod, was, as we have seen, pursued vigorously by the early philosophers and was taken up by Plato; in the education of the citizens outlined in the *Republic*, he notoriously dismissed the works of these poets from the syllabus. Hesiod himself had described his *Theogony* as a narrative of "lies like the truth yet including an element of the true", and Socrates, as Plato's expositor here, picks up the reference, explaining that there are two forms of narrative (*logoi*): the false and the true. In the pre-school education of infants, mothers and nurses should use fictions, but with some truth in them, to mould the souls of their charges in the best way. With the older child, however, there is to be a rigid censorship of the traditional stories to purge them of falsehood, for they are deceptive on the topics rated most highly, being capable of inflicting lasting harm on the soul, which is the most important part of ourselves, in its most important concerns (*Republic* 378a–e).

In the second book of the *Republic*, challenged to show that one should pursue justice for its own sake without regard to the consequences in life or after death, Socrates looks first for the nature of justice in the state as easier to recognize (because "writ large"); this leads into the discussion of how a state would be constructed, and the guidelines for the primary education of its citizens. It is said that the harm inflicted by polytheistic myth in the tradition of Homer and Hesiod lies in their appeal to emotion rather than to reason, and especially in the pernicious examples they present to their young audience of immoral behaviour: the stories are sacrilegious, false, unsuitable and dangerous in their effect. The Presocratics, led by Xenophanes, had been against attributing to gods and goddesses the image of their human worshippers, in appearance, clothing and physical features; Plato inveighs further against the wrong actions attributed to them. Violence of children towards their parents – as in Kronos' treatment of his father at the very beginning of Hesiod's genealogy – and battles between the gods, their jealousies and the unfair treatment of heroes that are found throughout the Homeric poems are condemned as misrepresentations of the true nature of divinity. In addition, lying and deceit ascribed to gods are unacceptable, as in Zeus sending Agamemnon a misleading dream, or Thetis' powerful accusation of the conduct of Apollo, who promised health and long life to her children: "He who joined in our feasting, he who said all this, he it was who killed my son" (*Republic* 383b). Plato, through Socrates, gives the corrections to these attributions in monotheistic terms. God must always be portrayed as he naturally is: as good and the source of good, ever truthful and with no grounds for deceit.

The last principle to be observed by the educators, in addition to justice and truth, is an Eleatic one: that god is changeless. The argument here is a deduction from the perfection of god: change comes about either from an external agent or internally, but strong and healthy bodies, and courageous and intelligent minds, stay constant themselves and are least affected by time or other external agents; god, therefore, as most perfect, would not be touched by outside events nor could change come from within. Any such change would necessarily be for the worse, and it is impossible for god to want to cause his own deterioration. The divine, again as in Presocratic language, "stays as he is, uniformly and for ever".[5]

The good as divine

In the central books of the *Republic* there is a reprise of the controversial view, put forward earlier in the discussion of philosopher-
rulers, that the smallest change needed to bring the ideal state into
being is for politicians to take to philosophy or for philosophers to be
in charge of the state. To justify this assumption Socrates, as Plato's
spokesman, says that it is necessary to understand how to define the
philosopher and the higher education needed for his or her training
for statecraft. This involves knowledge of the form of the good, the
highest knowledge of all, without which all other knowledge is useless
(*Republic* 505a). In the ensuing discussion of the form of the good
(also called "goodness itself" or simply "the good"), the language used
comes close to a philosophical monotheism. Socrates is reluctant to
define "the good" because it would be beyond the comprehension of
his audience. Instead he offers a simile that compares it to the sun in
the visible world, and then explains the similarity in one extraordinary
sentence:

> This then which gives truth to objects known and restores its
> power to the knowing subject, say it is the form of the good; and,
> since it is the cause of knowledge and truth, regard it as known,
> but, while these two – knowledge and truth – are fair, in thinking
> it other than and even fairer than these two, you will be thinking
> rightly; and knowledge and truth, as in the other world light
> and sight are thought of as as sun-like but not the sun, so here
> it is right to think of these two as god-like but not right to think
> of either of them as the good, but the state of the good is to be
> valued even more highly. (508e)

There is a further development:

> And I think you agree that, for the objects of knowledge, not only
> is there derived from the good their ability to be known, but their
> being and their reality is also given to them from it; for the good
> is not existence but is further beyond existence, exceeding it in
> dignity and power. (509b)

The sun, which is the cause of light and sight, corresponds to the
good, the cause of truth and knowledge, and, as the sun gives its objects

birth and nourishment, the good gives its objects (which are the other forms) their being and reality. The good is the cause of the being of the forms, of their truth and of our knowledge of them. Forms are to be understood in relation to their goodness and as a subordinate kind of goodness, whereas the good "is on the other side of being", a superior kind of reality, beyond definition.

In the allegory of the cave the sun is again used as an aid to understanding the good. The upward journey of the released prisoner to the visible world above the cave, and his final contemplation of the sun, is comparable to the philosopher's struggle to reach the good, and, when it is grasped, he realizes that it is the cause of all that is right and beautiful: of light in the visible world and of truth and understanding in the intelligible world. Here the form of the good is emphasized as the object of *knowledge*, as would be appropriate in the context of the education of the philosopher, but there is a similar panegyric of another form, that of beauty in the *Symposium*, as the true object of *love*. When the lover moves upwards from love of a particular body to love of soul, and from there to love of intellectual pursuits, it is said that he would finally reach beauty itself:

> It will not appear to him as face or hand or anything else that is of the body, nor in reason nor in science, nor as being *in* anything – living creature, earth, sky or anything else, but by itself, ever unique and eternal. All other beautiful things have a share in this in some way, but they are born and die, while beauty itself does not diminish or suffer change. (211a)

The form of beauty here, like the form of the good in the *Republic*, is described in the elevated language of earlier monotheism, and given the attributes of timelessness, unchangeability, perfection and uniqueness. Where the form of the good is made responsible in some way for the existence, truth and reality of what is intelligible, and, derivatively, for the phenomena of the visible world, the form of beauty is the goal of all human desiring.

Creationism

We have seen how Plato presented a primary divinity in terms of a traditional god stripped of imperfections, and also as the form of the good. In the generation myth of the later *Timaeus* there is a third interpretation: the divine in the character of a craftsman-god, a *dēmiourgos*. In this context our world is not represented as dependent in some unspecified way on the form of the good, but described in terms of a specific artefact constructed by a craftsman in the likeness of a perfect model. Imperfections in the copy are due to the recalcitrant material, which resists to some extent the imposition of the ideal form, much as a sculptor or carpenter has to deal as best he can with flaws in the marble or wood that work against the desired result. Plato elevates the *persona* of an ordinary workman in stone or metal to that of creator of the world, and then gives him divine attributes. He is described as eternal god, the one and only creator, and also the caring father, good in himself and also the source of all external good. Because he is free of envy,[6] this god, in contrast, wants all things to be as like himself as possible. So the world he creates is the best possible, being, through his providence, alive with soul and intelligence, a unique spherical world in circular motion, which is one only, but, because of its excellence, content with itself as companion and friend, and it too is called "a blessed god" (*Timaeus* 30a–c, 34a–c).

Two sets of secondary gods emerge in the myth of the *Timaeus*. The first are divinities in nature, including the fixed stars, "living beings, divine and eternal", as well as sun, moon and planets, with earth as the first and oldest of the gods (40a–d). This was in agreement with literary and religious tradition, which viewed the heavenly bodies as gods, and with earlier philosophy, which envisaged them as made of animate cosmic matter. There is a deliberate *riposte* to atomic theory here, for the atomists viewed the sky and its contents as inert matter, taking their cue from Anaxagoras, who was prosecuted on grounds of impiety for saying that the sun was a hot stone. The later gods of the second set in the *Timaeus* are listed as those from Homer and Hesiod – the Titans and Olympians and their children – and the stories and customs related to them are summarily accepted in this context, with some irony directed at those who claim descent from them. The *dēmiourgos* had sown the seeds of immortal soul in the various regions of earth, moon, stars and planets, and then entrusted to these lesser gods the task of providing bodies for the different forms of life that would inhabit the earth he had made. If he himself were responsible for them then human beings would be perfect, but the lesser gods were there "to control and guide the mortal creature for the best, except in so far as it became a cause of evil to itself" (42b–c).

The goodness of god is a key Platonic tenet. Xenophanes, as we have seen, had railed against the traditional acceptance of gods in human form, and against the immoral tales told about them by Homer and Hesiod, and the theme was taken up by Plato as the essential foundation of his education programme. Stories of wars and battles and plots among the gods were inadmissible, as well as any portrayal of moral weakness in the divine, which meant the rejection of both Homeric epic and tragedy. God is good in himself and the cause, not of all things, but only of what is good. If a man suffers then it must still be said that the god's acts were just, and that the sufferers benefit in some way from the suffering. The wording is very explicit:

> If a state is to run on the right lines, every possible step must be taken to prevent anyone, young or old, saying or being told, whether in poetry or prose, that god, being good, can be the cause of harm to anyone. Such opinions would not be respectful to god, beneficial to us or internally consistent.
>
> (*Republic* 380b–c)

The point is reiterated at the end of the *Republic* in the Myth of Er, where the soul alone is said to be responsible for the choice of the next life on earth, and any ills that it may contain: the *aitia* (cause, blame) is with the one who chooses, god is *anaitios* (blameless; 617e). The goodness and generosity of god as creator of the cosmos and human souls are also emphasized throughout the myth of the *Timaeus*, when, as has been seen, being devoid of envy he brings into being the best possible world. And there is one further occasion in the context of myth where the goodness of god is emphasized. In the *Theogony* Hesiod had told of how Kronos mutilated his father and in turn was overthrown by his son Zeus, which Plato's Socrates in the *Republic* calls "the greatest lie about the greatest subject". In the *Politicus* dialogue, however, Plato, with an anonymous "Eleatic visitor" as spokesman, recommends that Hesiod's tale in his other poem, *Works and Days*, should definitely be published, for there Kronos is an acceptable role model, in that he was said to have inaugurated a golden age of happiness on earth, securing for humanity peace, justice and law. Consequently the *Politicus* myth explains how order in the cosmos alternates with chaos, and all is well only when the Kronos-type god is in control, "for all the good there is in the universe stems from its constructor, whereas cruelty and injustice stem from the disorderly condition it was in previously" (273b).

Gods as allegories

One way of finding an explanation for the traditional role of the gods in human affairs was in the use of allegory, where the name of a god or goddess was used in the context of an action or attribute typically associated with them. Plato denounced this interpretation in his criticism of the poets at *Republic* 378d on the grounds that the inexperienced would find it difficult to distinguish allegory from reality, but such an understanding was familiar from earliest times. In the Homeric poems, violent and sudden happenings internal to a character could be attributed to the external activity of gods: for example a loss of temper accompanied by the urge to violence might be the result of the breath of Ares, the god of war; a bright idea that comes into one's mind unexpectedly is from Athena; and "the works of golden Aphrodite" is the euphemism for sex. In his tragedy *Trojan Women*, Euripides shows Helen attempting to excuse her elopement with Paris on the grounds that she was in thrall to this powerful goddess, but his mother exposes her guilt in the line "my son was fair and you desired him". In his *Encomium to Helen*, the sophist Gorgias pursued this question of her innocence or guilt in relation to the goddess: was Helen accountable for her actions, or had she been possessed by Aphrodite?

Empedocles took such allegorizing further, and redefined the function of traditional gods by giving his elements divine names: Hera for air, Zeus or Hephaistos for fire, Nestis for water and Aidoneus for earth. He describes the simple ratio in the structure of bones, for example, as two parts earth, two of water and four of fire as follows:

> The kindly earth received into its broad hollows of the eight parts
> two of the brightness of Nestis and four of Hephaistos, and these came to be white bones,
> held together by the gluing of harmony.   (DK 31B96)

Lucretius, who followed the Epicurean practice of placing the home of the gods in intergalactic spaces, far from human affairs, used allegory in two different contexts. He opened his poem with a formal invocation to Venus, winning over his Roman audience with her grand title *Aeneadum genetrix* ("mother of the descendants of Aeneas"), but then he immediately demythologized her in the manner of earlier natural theology, praising her as the spirit of bounteous nature, generating and cherishing the myriad forms of life. In his third book, on the mortality of the soul, Lucretius further allegorized, and here interpreted the traditional realm of Hades and its great sinners as human mental torments that are self-inflicted: Tantalus' fear of the falling rock is to be understood as superstitious dread of oppressive gods, Tityos' anguish is the gnawing of unrequited passion; Sisyphus' toil is the useless labour involved in unfulfilled ambition; the Danaids' collecting water in sieves represents the futility of insatiable desires; the whip lashings of the Furies are the stings of conscience – in sum, "the life of the foolish becomes their own hell on earth" (3.978–1023).

The Stoics adapted in a different way the Homeric polytheism that continued in Greek and then into Roman culture; they saw the benefits of nature in terms of individual presiding deities, exemplified in Roman literature, in which the name "Ceres" was commonly used for corn or bread, "Neptune" for water, "Vulcan" for fire and "Liber" for wine. Most importantly Zeus/Jupiter stands for or "is really" for the Stoics much more than the sky god, as in Euripides' words: "You see the high vault of boundless aither which surrounds the world with soft embrace, / This think of as the highest god, this understand to be Jupiter" (fr. 386, Nauck, quoted by Cicero, *On the Nature of the Gods* 2.65).[7] The implications of representing the traditional king of the Olympians in such monotheistic terms were first set out in an early Stoic text, Cleanthes' famous *Hymn to Zeus*, with its eloquent opening lines:

> Greatest of immortals, many-titled, ever all-powerful,
> Zeus, first moving principle of nature, directing all things according to law,
> All hail! … This whole cosmos spinning round the earth,
> obeys wherever you lead, and willingly is ruled by you.
>
> (Long & Sedley 54I)

Zeus' traditional thunderbolt was then interpreted as the "ever-living fire" through which the divine force of all-pervading reason achieves its ends in the justice of eternal universal law. In a further development of this theory Zeus/Jupiter was taken to instantiate the unique omnipotent divinity of the Stoics, to be understood as the physical force pervading the cosmos, the rational principle activating its matter and the moral foresight guiding all for the best, which was also called *pronoia* in Greek, *fatum* in Latin. In general, in Stoic theory, it then became possible to view individual gods not just as allegories for the bounty of nature but as various aspects of the one god; when this was properly understood, individual citizens could with a clear conscience join in the worship and reverence of these gods under the names that custom had bestowed on them, as Cicero explains in *On the Nature of the Gods* (2.71).

Anti-creationism and atheism

The creator god of Plato's *Timaeus*, as we have seen, devised the world to be as perfect as possible, and the Stoics followed this lead in the "argument from design". As the details of an artefact point to an intelligent artist or engineer, so the design of the whole cosmos, from the intricacies of planetary movements to the complexities of living organisms, indicate a designer: in modern terms the watch has a watchmaker. But against this was the anti-religious stand of the teaching of Epicurus, set out most vividly in Lucretius' poem. This attitude denied the existence of a universal, providential divinity from the clear evidence of a *lack* of intelligent design. How could an intelligent divine power have made the world when so much is wrong with it? Lucretius presents numerous examples of the earth's imperfections as testimony that there is no supernatural design: *tantā stat praedita culpā* (it has so many faults) is the phrase he uses (5.199). Two-thirds of planet earth are uninhabitable, because so much of it is too hot or too cold, or covered by water or drought-stricken deserts; the fruits of agriculture are ruined by heat, frost, winds and storms; the human child is naked and vulnerable; illnesses come with the changing seasons; and untimely death stalks abroad. Not only are there no designer gods producing the best possible world, but fear of gods and their vengeful punishments in this world and after death is to be explained as a device used by influential men to subdue the people, and so achieve their own ends. A famous example was the sacrifice of the young and innocent Iphigenia to further military ambition, summed up in Lucretius' famous line: *tantum religio potuit suadere malorum* (so much evil was wrought by the powerful persuasion of religion; 1.101). The whole poem is a defence of the position that an omnipotent divinity involved in what happens on earth is not a primary principle in the formation and maintenance of the cosmos, but a social construct developed subsequently in the history of the human race, which "caused tribulation for generations to come" (5.1194–7).

The Epicureans admitted the existence of gods as the source of images in dreams but banished them to intergalactic space, remote from the workings of the cosmos and unconcerned with human affairs. Their undisturbed existence was an example to imitate, and this, rather than the futility of conventional prayer and sacrifice, was the true piety. Praise was due to the marvels of nature, based on the physical laws of atomic theory, and to Epicurus as the true hero, who freed the human race from the burden of superstitious fear of gods interfering in life now and imposing tortures after death. This fundamental atheism, however, developed in such detail by the Epicureans and brilliantly expounded by Lucretius, had its roots much earlier, in the work of the first atomists and the fifth-century sophists, and was recognized as widespread: as Plato put it, "an illness from which the world is never free" (*Laws* 888b).

In this context, in the tenth book of Plato's *Laws*, comes the classic passage on the dangers inherent in the atheistic position and the need to counter it.[8] There the whole fabric of the constitution that is being established in great detail by the Athenian visitor for the best possible state is threatened by the priority given to nature and chance by some philosophies, along with the denial of divine existence, rational design and providential care for all aspects of the cosmos, including human life. The Athenian deals with this serious opposition by imagining a bright young atheist as its representative, and himself as presenting the counter-argument in a calm and orderly fashion, beginning "my child, you are still young and your opinions will change with time" (*Laws* 888a). The young man holds that the basic elements of earth, air, fire and water owe their existence to nature and chance (as the result of random atomic conglomerations) and that the secondary bodies, the stars and planets, arise from the natural movement of the elements. The consequent interaction of opposites then produces plant, animal and human life. The gods are fictions, found not in nature (*physis*) but as a result of human construction (*technē*).

In response the Athenian sets out the argument to reverse this conclusion, wishing to convince his young opponent that soul (*psychē*) is prior to matter rather than emerging later than it. Using an analysis of kinds of motion first raised in the proof for immortal soul in the *Phaedrus* and to be taken up later by Aristotle in *Metaphysics Lambda*, the Athenian traces the chains of movement and alteration back to an original "self-mover", which is not dependent for its life and activity on any external cause, but is itself responsible for subsequent generation.

Consequently soul as self-moving is prior to matter, and the spiritual order of things is older than the material; this means that the attributes of soul – reason, will, calculation and memory – antedate the attributes of matter, such as length, breadth and depth. It is then possible to see soul as initiating and controlling the movements of the cosmos, "caring for the entire universe and directing it along the best path" (897c). Belief in such a world soul brings with it belief in a rational divinity, who, perfect in virtue, cares for all aspects of the cosmos, even to the welfare of each individual human being.

The unmoved mover and thinking about thinking

Plato himself, as we have seen, came to the recognition of a primary divine principle by two routes – by exploring the perfection, independence and uniqueness of the form of the good in the *Republic*, and by proposing, admittedly in mythical terms, a cosmic father-creator in the *Timaeus* – but it was Aristotle who developed pagan monotheism most fully, and so successfully that his assumptions and arguments were taken up by the Christian fathers, and most notably by Thomas Aquinas in his *Summa Theologiae*. After the analysis of the "unmoved mover" in the *Physics*, and with arguments further developed in the twelfth book of his *Metaphysics* (generally known by its Greek numbering as *Metaphysics Lambda*), the study of the divine for Aristotle became "first philosophy", that is, the primary, ultimate and most important object of enquiry, and its pursuit the highest human activity.

In the first chapters of *Metaphysics Lambda* there is a summary of the distinction between perceptible and unchanging entities, and then of the four kinds of change: (i) generation and passing-away; (ii) alteration; (iii) increase and decrease; and (iv) locomotion. All such change is from the potential to the actual, involving form and matter. Then, in the sixth chapter, Aristotle reverts to a study of different kinds of entities and proceeds with a tighter development of the distinctions previously made. The opening section of this chapter establishes first that there is an existing entity that is eternal and without change or movement, and secondly that the only *continuous* movement is spatial and circular. The problem of the generation of this movement is then raised. In agreement with the Presocratics Empedocles and Anaxagoras in recognizing the need for an actual cause of change, and with

Leucipppus in realizing that change is eternal, and following on from his own earlier work in *Physics, De generatione* and *De caelo*, Aristotle concludes that the perpetual circular movement of the outer heaven, the *prōtos ouranos*, is the causal explanation of continuous uniformity in the movement of the stars and planets. The sun is dependent on the region above it, but, in virtue of its daily and annual movements, is itself responsible for the continuous variety of phenomena that occurs by night and day and through the seasons on the earth below. This is all argued in neutral, mechanistic terms, but there comes a surprising change in the account, at the beginning of chapter 7, of the cause of the movement of the outer heaven itself. There has to be an unchanging entity that is responsible for this movement by being "the object of desire and the object of thought" (*Metaphysics* Λ 1072a26), bringing about movement without being itself being moved. In the rest of this chapter and in chapter 9 Aristotle comes to grips with the implications of the coincidence of physics, teleology, knowledge and desire for the nature and activity of the divine,

In *Physics* 7.1 and 8.4–6, Aristotle had argued from causation for the existence of an unmoved mover to account for constant change in this world. Since everything here is "moved" (i.e. in a state of constant change and alteration), there must be an intermediate entity that "moves the moved" and, to avoid an infinite regress, there would be some primary entity that is ultimately responsible for the chain of movement, but is itself unmoved. This notion, of an impersonal, first "unmoved mover", which starts as an explanation for physical alteration, is taken as a theological premise in chapter 6 of *Metaphysics Lambda* for deducing the nature of the divine. Given the necessary existence of an unmoved mover, simple, actual and immaterial, and without spatial extension or internal division, the movement it imparts cannot be that of an agent applying force; it can be explained only in terms of final causation. Because the unmoved mover would be "beautiful and best", it is desired for its own sake, and, whereas all other things cause motion because they are in motion themselves, the good that is the end of action causes movement because it is the object of love (*Metaphysics* Λ 1072b2–10). The conclusion of the argument is that the outer heaven is moved in its eternal circular motion not by being pushed but by thinking of, desiring and loving the first substance. As it rotates in this state of thinking, desiring and loving, it imparts movement physically to the intermediate region below it, and from there to the natural world. Of necessity, the unmoved mover exists to account for change, as the *archē*, the ultimate first principle, and is fine and good (*kalon*). It is in this context that the primary substance is called "god" (*theos*) for the first time, and given the masculine pronoun, at the point when life that is eternal and most good is attributed to him.

But what does god *do*, as pure actuality? What kind of life is his? According to Aristotle, our life is best and happiest, however briefly, when we are engaged in contemplative thought. It is to be expected then that what is best for us sometimes would belong to god for ever in his everlasting existence, and, since "thinking in itself belongs with what is good in itself, and the highest thought with the highest good" (1072b18), god is a thinking being. But the thinking has to be *of* something, it needs an object. Now it was endemic in Greek philosophy to assume that subject and object are mutually affected in awareness and understanding of the external world. Individual human beings are limited in their range of knowledge by their internal condition, and that condition constantly changes as it is made better or worse by stimuli that are external to it. We can improve our abilities through effort and practice, but never reach higher than those abilities allow, so that the external object of perception and thought is always more powerful than the subject. For a divinity that is supreme, unchanging and engaged in thinking, there is only one object appropriate, or even possible, for its thinking. The object of thought cannot here be more powerful than the thinking mind, for nothing is more powerful than the divine mind; and it cannot be less powerful, for then the object, by its influence, would cause an inadmissible deterioration in the divine thinking subject. The object of thought therefore has to be identical in power and substance with the subject, which means that the only available object for the god's thought is himself, and his thinking is indeed called "thinking about thinking" (1074b35). This activity is best and happiest, but there is no further clarification on what such self-thinking could mean, and Aristotle does not raise the issue again in the extant works. Towards the end of *Metaphysics Lambda*, however, there is a suggestion as to the way in which god as supreme and ultimate being, inwardly focused on the pure activity of self-contemplative thought, eternal, unchanging and apart from the visible cosmos, is still responsible for what is beautiful and good in it. Not only is he the cause of the unending rotation of the heavenly bodies through their desire to emulate his perfection with their own perfect circular movement,[9] but the order in the whole cosmos is compared to that of soldiers in an army in proper formation or of the individuals of different rank in a well-managed household, where success depends on each fulfilling his or her role and so working towards the good of the whole. The teleology in nature, in the hierarchy of living forms reaching towards the realization of their potential, is another way of regarding divinity, and human beings at the top of the scale, in their own thinking about thinking, become god-like.

5. Souls and selves

In Homeric epic the human soul only featured at the end of the life of the individual. Heroic action was finished when the warrior lay slain on the battlefield while his soul (his *psychē*) had an endless shadow existence in Hades. The very opening of the *Iliad* sets out the distinction when it states that the wrath of Achilles sent many mighty souls of heroes to Hades, but left the men themselves (*autoi*) to be carrion for dogs and birds. In the *Odyssey* the souls going down to Hades are compared to dreams taking wing (*Od* 11.224) and to twittering bats (*Od* 24.6–9). They keep their recognizable features ("he was wondrously like the man himself", says Achilles of Patroclus' ghost; *Il* 23.107), but generally they have no meaningful speech unless they drink sacrificial blood or appear to mortals with a specific message. Their consolations are in the memory of their own past heroic deeds, the preservation of their name among men, and their joy in the record carried on to the next generation, as, for example, the ghost of Achilles strides gladly through the fields of asphodel after hearing from Odysseus of his son's great achievements (*Od* 11.538–40, 24.93–4). With the exception of the prophet Teiresias, who is permitted to keep intact his understanding (*nous*) and his thoughts (*phrenes*), the greatest loss for the departed is to be deprived of the power of reasoning. Physically and mentally the life of the Homeric hero is over. It would take Plato, with Socrates as his spokesman, to overturn this strong tradition, and make the opposite claim. Instead of the time on earth being seen as the only true life, and the time after death as a shadow existence, he would view our existence here as a kind of imprisonment or living death, and real life, the life of reason, which is akin to the divine, would come with the release of immortal soul from mortal body.

Between Homer and Plato an understanding of the complexities in the nature of *psychē* was developed, and the question of its relationship to the body was explored in depth. After the Homeric epics, which were for public recital, came the flowering of lyric poetry, composed for a small audience and a more intimate setting. The lyric poets looked inwards to scrutinize their personal feelings and emotions in their daily involvement with others, so that there arose awareness of an inner life, continuous psychic activity that could have an immediate physical effect. Sappho provides a famous instance of this in an explicit analysis of the results that conflicting emotions of joy, love and jealousy had on her senses at the sight of her beloved with another: her tongue became paralysed, her eyes were blinded, there was a drumming in her ears, and her whole body suffered from tremors, perspiration and increased temperature (fr. 31). This exploration of mental trauma and its physical effects was continued by the tragic poets, and by Euripides in particular. In Phaedra's great soliloquy, for example (*Hippolytus* 373–430), the queen reflects on the inner torment that has brought on her fever and caused the weakness in her limbs as unrequited love conflicts with shame and guilt; she concludes that the only honourable option for her is to keep silent about her passion, and to waste away in a self-inflicted death. In contrast, in Euripides' presentation of Medea's passionate analysis of her feelings towards Jason and the dishonourable position she finds herself in, the result is not silent submission, but wild looks, hysterical behaviour and eventually violent infanticide (*Medea* 1–46, 214–66, 764–93). In *Ion*, Creusa's weeping is the physical expression of her soul's inner sorrow, as when she says: "My eyes stream with tears, and my *psychē* grieves, / the target of wicked plotting by men and gods" (876–7). The whole force of lyric poetry and tragic drama rested to a great extent on the depiction of strong emotion overpowering dispassionate decision-making, and the physical effects of that conflict on the characters involved.

Soul as living, thinking self

The theory of *psychē* in philosophy combined these two approaches. In one respect it followed the connection with life in the Homeric manner, but understood soul to be active throughout one's time, and not just at the point of death. In another, *psychē* was also taken to be responsible for the inner life of thought and decision-making as analysed by the lyricists and tragedians, but there was a tendency to view emotions that hamper these mental processes as belonging to the body or as characterizing an inferior part of the soul. The early philosophers also linked the human *psychē* both with cosmic forces in structure and substance and with the life of simpler animals. Aristotle summed up this latter interest in his "ladder of life". This was a grada-tion of soul-types that started with the most primitive forms with at least a vital principle to keep them alive, then progressing through plants that, in virtue of this vital principle, grow, feed and reproduce their kind, to more complex animals that are also capable of move-ment and feeling. At the top of the range are human beings, who, in addition to sharing the achievements of the lower levels of life, have the soul, characterized by rational thought, which gives form and life to the material structure and, more importantly, actualizes human potential.

This way of linking living creatures and locating them in the cosmos characterized much of Presocratic thought. Clearly they participate in the processes of nature, but it was some time before the soul was connected with the human being acting as a *moral* agent. Anaximenes' fragment is important in this context as the first comment on soul as an integral part of the human being; it marks the beginning of psych-ology (which means literally an account of the *psychē*): "As our soul (*psychē*), which is air (*aēr*), maintains us, so breath (*pneuma*) and air (*aēr*) surround the whole world (*kosmos*)". First, there is the new use of the word *psychē*, not in the Homeric sense of that which leaves the living at the moment of death, and continues as a flitting shade in the realm of the dead, but as the enduring principle of life, which holds together, strengthens and controls the individual.[1] Then there is the connection established between *psychē/aēr* in the animate individual and *pneuma/aēr* in the whole world order, so that the same substance keeps both structures alive, maintaining and controlling them through the act of breathing. Air in itself is not accessible to the senses – it cannot be seen or heard or tasted or handled – but it is a "thing" (as experiments with balloon-like gourds and inflatable swimming-aids were showing), and its intake in breathing is essential to life. So *psychē* now is human breath, keeping us alive and holding us together, with the characteristics of the atmospheric air, which is the breath and life of

109

the whole cosmos. Before Democritus gave us the word "microcosm", the idea is already here, that the cosmos is like a large-scale animal, and the individual a world in miniature.

Heraclitus similarly linked the individual to the cosmos, but for him it was in the workings of *logos* and its instantiation as fire. At the very opening of his work he states that "all things happen according to *logos*", and in another fragment explains that "although most people associate with it closely, they are separated from it, and what they come across every day seems to them strange" (DK 22B72). We need to realize that there is one divine reason (*logos*) that "steers" everything, in a way comparable to Anaximenes' theory of breath controlling the cosmos, but for Heraclitus this is more than just a natural process, because knowledge and purpose are involved. The physical transformations of fire are according to reason, since the mutual exchanges of sea, earth and fire are measured in proportion, and the fire, although it is part of the exchange, still sets the measure, as gold sets the standard in barter and is also part of the transfer.

These simultaneous and antithetical "turnings" of fire are repeated on a small scale in the individual. The specific place of fire here is taken by *psychē*, and is close to being identified with it: "It is death for *psychē* to become water, for water it is death to become earth: from earth arises water, and from water *psychē*" (B36). *Psychē* as *logos* in the individual is the principle of life and controls the material structure as it does in the cosmos, but it is also, for the first time in this context, a principle of reason and choice. The individual has some control over the physical process in that the indulgence of desire and anger results in an increase of moisture, which is a weakening of *psychē*'s powers. To be drunk is literally to have a wet *psychē* (B77, 85), with the consequent sacrifice of coherent language and control over the body: the drunk slurs his speech and needs help to get home (B117). Conversely, it is in the individual's power to dry out his soul by resisting impulse (*thymos*), and best of all is to choose glory, gained by those who die in battle, honoured by gods and men (B24).

It would seem then that for Heraclitus the souls of the young war-dead are in the best state: fiery and "dry". But in a non-military context the dry *psychē* is also the one that is wise, for, as the soul becomes drier and more fiery the further removed it is from dampening desires, so its *rational* side correspondingly increases. This can continue without limit, for the soul's capacity for understanding is inexhaustible: the more it knows the more there is available for it to know – "You could not in your going find the limits of soul though you travelled the whole way, so deep is its *logos*" (B45). As well as being roused to an increasing realization of the true nature of the external world, and of humanity's part in it, when awake and working, and even when sleeping (as B26 and B75 indicate), the individual is encouraged to engage like Heraclitus in self-searching, drawing on the soul's limitless resources for continuing enlightenment.

Much of Heraclitus' enigmatic interpretation of the role of *psychē* is taken over by Anaxagoras in his more explicit explanation of the role of *Nous* (Mind) in the cosmos and in the individual. This all-pervading Mind for Anaxagoras has the characteristics of *psychē* developed earlier – knowledge, power and control – and is the continuing motive cause for the present structure of the whole and its future expansion. But, in attempting to define the nature of Mind itself, Anaxagoras stretches the language available to him to the limits, preparing the way for a subsequent shift of terminology from the material to the immaterial. Anaxagoras was in agreement with Heraclitus in maintaining that cosmic life and mind are related to the universe as individual life and mind are to each human being. The *nous* he describes however is not air (as Anaximenes proposed) or Heraclitean fire, but the most rarefied of all things and the purest: unlimited, independent and, above all, not mixed or tainted with anything else. If it were, its purity, knowledge and power would be at once diminished as it became physically involved with the immediate mixture, and eventually with the totality of things. Here are Anaxagoras' words on cosmic *Nous*:

> Other things have a portion of everything, but Mind is unlimited and self-determining and mixed with no other thing: it alone has independent existence. For if it were not independent, but mixed with some other thing, it would have a share in all things, if it had been mixed with any one ... It is the most rarefied of all things and the purest, and has knowledge of each thing, and the greatest power. All that has life, whether larger or smaller, Mind controls, and Mind controlled the rotation of the whole, so as to make it rotate in the beginning ... Mind knew all that had been mixed and was being separated and becoming distinct. And all that was going to be, all that was but is no longer, and all that is now, and will be, mind arranged in order, and this rotation too, in which now rotate stars and sun and moon and air and *aethēr*, as they are being separated off. (59B12)

The rational life of the individual human being is similarly explained: "In everything there is a portion of everything except of Mind, but some have Mind as well" (B11).

Anaxagoras connects the Mind (*Nous*) in us with cosmic *Nous* in its independence, its control of the physical and its capacity for understanding, but in neither appearance does *Nous* seem to be in any way a *moral* agent. The amount of *Nous* in an individual appears arbitrary, and the role it plays in moral decisions is nowhere explained. Socrates famously criticized Anaxagoras for interpreting *Nous* as mechanistic (*Phaedo* 97b–98d), and, since, on this evidence, Anaxagoras provided no explanation for cosmic *Nous* as an agent working for good, it seems unlikely that he thought of ethical considerations as relevant to the workings of the human mind.

In his theory of mental activity regulated by the amount of cosmic *Nous* present in the individual, Anaxagoras was more in agreement with Parmenides' lines on the physical basis of intelligence given in the *Doxa*, the deceptive account of opinion:

> According to the nature of the mixture of the wandering limbs
>   that each one has,
> so does thought stand for each; that which thinks,
> the natural structure (*physis*) of the limbs, is the same for each
>   and everyone;
> and what there is more of *is* that thought.   (DK 28B16)[2]

Here the proportion of cosmic light and dark in the physical structure of individual human beings determines the nature of their thinking. The spectrum ranges from total light, which gives complete knowledge, to complete darkness, the state of the unknowing corpse. Although Anaxagoras introduces *Nous* as an additional factor, neither he nor Parmenides explains (as Heraclitus had attempted to do) how individuals are responsible for their given level of understanding, or whether they have the means to improve or diminish it.

Democritus and the early atomists also had a mechanistic theory of the *psychē*. They claimed that only atoms and void exist; a world is composed of just these two, and so is the individual, the microcosm (and it was Democritus who first called the individual the *mikros cosmos*). The physical human body was thought to be a coherent structure composed of various atom-groups moving in the body's empty spaces, and soul (*psychē*) and mind (*phrēn*) had a similar material basis. What keeps individuals alive and provides for the quality of their thought are groups of fine, spherical atoms interspersed throughout the molecules of body atoms and the intervening void. These spherical atoms react to other atomic movements internally, and to the impact of external forces, which means that psychic and mental events would be non-moral, and out of the individual's control. This is made explicit in a quotation of Democritus from Sextus Empiricus: "In fact we have no certain understanding, but it changes according to the condition of the body, as well as the force of what enters in and presses against it" (68B9). Our ability to be aware of our surroundings is dependent on our physical condition, which continually changes as atoms from the external world push on the outside of the body, some penetrating inside. Accurate observation is therefore impossible, and true understanding is no more accessible than something at the bottom of the sea (B117). Such psychic activities as reflection and considered decision-making have no firm foundation, but are inextricably linked to random atomic motion.

The transmigrating soul

The Pythagorean view of *psychē* was diametrically opposed to any theories of soul being part of the physical structure of the body or linked to it or conditioned by it. The Pythagoreans agreed that soul was indeed the vital principle of the body, which contained it during that body's lifetime, but claimed that it had an existence separate from it, both before the birth and after the death of that particular body. Such a view of "transmigration" – that a soul enters a body at birth and leaves it at death to be born again in another body – is one of the few Pythagorean beliefs that can be attributed with some certainty to Pythagoras himself. There is the strong evidence of his near contemporary Xenophanes who tells this anecdote about Pythagoras:

> They say that once, as he was passing by when a puppy was being beaten.
> He took pity on it and spoke as follows:
> "Stop! Don't hit it! for it is the soul of a friend of mine,
> which I recognised when I heard its voice".   (21B7)

This fragment (in elegiac verse) is the first extant reference in Greek to transmigration, and three significant conclusions can be drawn from it: for the ironic humour to be effective, the theory would have been well known; the *psychē* was assumed to transmigrate not only between human beings but, in this instance at least, from human to animal form; and it could continue with the same voice, recognized by Pythagoras himself. As the theory developed, the soul was thought to have a completely independent and even everlasting existence, only temporarily consigned to any particular body. The Homeric view of the full human life lived by the hero in this world, with just a bare shadow existence for the *psychē* after death, is competing with the idea of life here being the shadow existence, and after-death experience the reality. This will be expounded by the Platonic Socrates, both in argument and in eschatological myth.

Before that there is a compromise position taken up by Empedocles. He calls the soul *daimōn*, and links it with his own personal history, having been born as boy, girl, plant, bird and fish (31B117), in exile from a divine state (B115.13), but now enjoying the best human life as poet, prophet, healer and leader, and on course to rejoin the gods (B112.4–6, 146, 147). But these fragments come from his popular address to the citizens of Acragas, and should be interpreted in the light of his technical treatise to his student Pausanias. There he follows Parmenides' *Doxa* in having thinking depend on the quality of the mixture of the ingredients that make up the body, two (light and night) for Parmenides (B16) but four (earth, air, fire and water) for Empedocles. Those who have the most harmonious mixture of elements in the organ of thought, which is literally the blood around the heart, are the wisest (B105), although (and here Empedocles anticipates atomic theory) the continual physical changes in the structure of the body as well as external influences alter the character of the thinking. But Empedocles, like Heraclitus, was ready to give some responsibility for the quality of the thought to the thinker, who could improve it by constant intention and effort. There was also a moral effect in that the individual was encouraged to align with the work of *Philia*, the universal power of unity and attraction, and reject the division and hate characteristic of the opposite Strife (*Neikos*).

On the cosmic scale it is inevitable that Strife will become dominant until, "as time goes round", it yields to *Philia* and the world returns to a state of unity that is identified with god (B27–9). When Empedocles says that he "trusted in Strife" (B115.14), this does not necessarily mean that he *remembered* what happened or that a choice was then open to him. He deduces that the parts of elements of which he is now composed have been used for different forms of life in earth, air, fire and water. None of these inferior forms of life were satisfactory because their mixtures were out of proportion (B121, 130, 136) or they were not properly constituted or cut off too early, but now Empedocles sees himself as a recognizable *ego*, who has attained the highest form of life on earth, with the best mixture of elements producing a pure *phronēsis*. He encourages his fellow citizens to follow his example by ceasing from quarrelling and slaughter and restoring the universal friendliness characteristic of an earlier age (B128). In particular he urges Pausanias to think the right sort of thoughts "with goodwill and unsullied attention", but if, like most men, his thoughts are trivial, his *phronēsis* will deteriorate, and eventually disintegrate to join the separating masses of earth, air, fire and water (B110.6–10).

Empedocles here found a way of reconciling the Pythagorean "wandering soul" with the materialism of the other Presocratics (including Parmenides' light and dark *noēma* in B16) in a personal *daimōn* made up of elements in as near perfect a ratio as possible, but which would disperse and the parts reform into further individuals. In such theories the soul was not in conflict with the body but a part of it, with a particular constitution that could, in most accounts, be made better or worse according to the motivation and lifestyle of the individual. Plato, on the other hand, in adopting and modifying the Pythagorean viewpoint, found divisions within the soul to account for a much more sophisticated psychology, but also set soul against body in a lifelong struggle between care for the soul and bodily satisfaction.

Care for the soul

It is difficult to know the extent to which Plato is indebted to Socrates' insight, but there is considerable support for the historic Socrates opposing "care for the soul" to the pursuit of wealth or power. A crucial sentence comes in the *Apology*, Plato's presentation of Socrates' defence at his trial, in the section when Socrates rejects a possible offer from his judges to be acquitted if he gives up his practice of philosophy. He says that he will never give up questioning his fellow citizens in his usual way:

> Aren't you ashamed of putting so much effort into becoming
> as rich as possible, and acquiring as much prestige and honour

as you can, and giving no care or attention to truth and understanding, and putting your soul (*psychē*) in the best possible
condition?   (29d–e)

Later he reiterates the point: "I spend all my time trying to persuade
you, young and old, not to care for your bodies or your possessions but
for your soul above all else, to make it as excellent as possible" (30a–
b). Here body (*sōma*) and soul (*psychē*), and the concerns of each, are
forcibly contrasted: wealth and honour belong with the body, but truth
and understanding with the soul.

The *Apology* is a public speech with touches of humour and irony,
delivered to a large and mainly hostile audience who, in the end,
impose the death penalty. In the *Crito*, in contrast, Socrates is talking
in the privacy of his prison cell to one friend only, explaining, in all
seriousness, why he must refuse the offer of escape and face death.
Here we are moving into new moral territory, and Socrates is most
reluctant to use the word *psychē* in this context. He elicits agreement
to a straightforward question: "Is there a part of us which is improved
by healthy actions and ruined by unhealthy ones?" This is obviously
the body, and so, Socrates continues: "What about the part of us which
is harmed by injustice and improved by justice? Do we think that this
part of ourselves, whatever it is, which is concerned with injustice and
justice, is inferior to the body?" Crito answers, "Certainly not". "But it is
more deserving of honour?" "Of course" (*Crito* 47e–48a). The cautious,
neutral wording which Socrates uses ("this part of ourselves, whatever
it is") would seem to be a way of conditioning us to accepting a new
duality, a strong body–soul contrast that ties the soul firmly to the
ethics of right and wrong action in its improvement or deterioration.

The dramatic setting of Plato's *Phaedo*, which was also known by the
title *On Soul* (*psychē*), comes immediately after the *Crito*, describing
events in the prison on the last day of Socrates' life. The beginning and
the end read as straight biography, with the news of the return of the ship
from Delphi that marked the day of execution, the gathering of friends,
the farewell to family, the last bath and the drinking of the hemlock. The
long conversation in the central part, however, draws on material that
is clearly Platonic rather than Socratic, especially when it deals with the
immortality of the soul and the so-called theory of forms.

In the *Apology*, Socrates had been reported as claiming that he was
uncertain about what awaits one after death (40c–e). Perhaps it is anni-
hilation and the dead have no consciousness of anything, and then that

is a blessing, for he says, somewhat surprisingly, that surely everyone would agree that there are few days and nights happier than the time spent in dreamless sleep, and, if death is like that, it is a gain. On the other hand, if the old stories are true and death is a removal to another place, then it would be a wonderful experience to meet and exchange views with those who had, like him, been unjustly condemned to death, and to continue philosophizing with the great heroes of the past. At the beginning of the *Phaedo*, however, Socrates is represented as taking a different line: "Is death nothing more or less than this – the body by itself separated from the soul, and the soul on its own separated from the body?" (*Phaedo* 64c). From this starting-point Socrates can then launch into his first "sermon". Since death is the separation of soul from body, then the best form of life consists in a preparation for death, which is achieved by keeping soul and body apart as far as possible to make the final separation easier. The way to do this is by neglecting physical demands and so lessening the hold of body over soul, and then by fostering the development and "purification" of the soul on its own in the pursuit of philosophy and the love of wisdom. Socrates' friends listen patiently to this, but Cebes voices the general misgivings about the soul being immortal at all:

> When it's released from the body it may no longer exist anywhere, but be dispersed and destroyed on the very day that the man himself dies, as soon as it is freed from the body; as it emerges it may be dissipated like breath or smoke, and vanish away, so that it will nowhere amount to anything.   (*Phaedo* 70a)

Socrates meets this challenge by embarking on four proofs for the immortality of the soul.

The immortal soul

In the first of these ("the argument from opposites") *psychē* is viewed as the principle of life. The proof starts from agreement that there are opposite *states* such as small and big, awake and asleep, and opposite *processes* for the transition from one to the other, namely increasing and decreasing, and falling asleep and waking up. In the opposite states of living and dead there would likewise be opposite processes, the familiar one of dying and the corresponding one of coming to life

117

again; souls therefore exist in some place after death from which they return to life in a body again. Furthermore, if there were not these corresponding cyclic processes, then everything would end up at one extreme, as being enormously large, or being asleep or being dead, which is not the case (70d–72e).

The second proof is an argument from recollection, considering the soul as intellect, and complementing the first proof, which took the soul as life principle. It uses the example of our being reminded by a portrait of its original, and assessing the likeness; however close the likeness, it can never be exact, and we can make a judgement on its shortcoming from our acquaintance with the original. Similarly if we look at a couple of sticks of roughly the same length or at an apparently beautiful object they will remind us of the originals, perfect equality and real beauty. We can assess the deficiencies in the particulars and rank them as more or less close to the originals because we have an understanding of the paradigm (or form) in each case. We could not have this memory and understanding from this world, where nothing is absolutely perfect, and so we must remember it from a previous existence. The remembering soul therefore existed before the body's birth, and, from the previous proof, where opposites were shown to succeed each other, it must also exist after the body's death (72e–77e).

The third proof, from "simplicity", involves certain characteristics of the soul, as well as a reaffirmation of the existence of perfect "forms". It is said that there is a basic contrast between what is *simple* and constant, that is, which has no parts, and so does not disintegrate into them and is therefore eternal, and the *complex* and variable, composed of parts, and therefore destructible and mortal. Forms belong in the first category, being simple, eternal and constant, the invisible objects of knowledge, whereas a body belongs with the composite, being mortal and changing, and the visible object of perception. So where does soul belong? It is not a "form" but similar to it in being invisible and connected with knowledge, and, since it has many of its attributes, it is more likely that it also belongs with the simple and eternal, rather than the complex and mortal (78c–81a).

Socrates' friends are uncomfortable with these proofs, and offer counter-examples that would refute them. First, the soul might be a "harmony", which would disintegrate with the body at death, in a similar way to the cessation of an invisible and beautiful melody, when the instrument that has produced it breaks. And secondly there could be a series of transmigrations, which would be in agreement with the recurrence of opposite processes and states, the ability to recollect perfect paradigms from a previous existence and the simplicity of soul; however, as a tailor might wear out several coats yet the final one outlasts him, so the soul might enter a limited number of bodies, but what assurance would there be that this present one is not the last body? The soul could be long-lived but not immortal, continually expending energy, and, without compensation, it would be eventually exhausted. Entering into a body is the beginning of the end, "as it lives its lives in increasing weariness, and finally perishes in what is called death" (95c–d).

The fourth proof of immortality, which is set out to meet this objection, requires an understanding of the difference between essential and accidental predicates,[3] and also an acceptance of the theory of forms. Forms give explanations (the "safe, silly answer" that beautiful things are beautiful because of beauty), and they stay themselves (Simmias is tall next to Socrates, and short next to Phaedo, but tallness is never shortness nor beauty ugliness). If soul is taken as the principle of life rather than the agent of thinking, then it is possible to make certain comparisons. Fire is always hot and never cold, snow is always cold and never hot, three is always odd and never even, and, comparably, what partakes of soul is alive and never dead. *Importing* forms (fever, fire, soul) bring with them the relevant *imported* forms (illness, heat, life), and exclude the opposite forms (health, cold and death), which retreat. In other words, soul can no more be dead than three can be even, fire cold or snow hot (102b–107b).

But Plato was still not satisfied. He continued his search for a watertight proof for the immortality of the soul, and made two further attempts, one in the *Republic*, which again takes soul as the life principle, and the other from the *Phaedrus*, which views it as the source of the body's movements and activities. In the last book of the *Republic*, Plato has Socrates arguing once more for an immortal soul (*psychē*), to the astonishment of his respondent Glaucon. Socrates looks at what it is that is essentially (rather than accidentally) destructive of anything and finds it in the evil, the flaw or the disease that is specific to it. For example, when the eyes are attacked by ophthalmia, the body by illness, grain by mildew or iron by rust, the specific evil in each case eventually causes the destruction of the related object. Should there be anything that can be marred by its specific evil but not destroyed by it, then nothing else could do so, and it would be indestructible. Now the specific evil of the soul is injustice, with its accompanying vices of

119

cowardice, indiscipline and ignorance. The soul has never been killed by these, nor has it been destroyed by any evil specific to the body, and so, if it is immune to its own evil and to any harm to the body it inhabits, then it is indestructible (*Republic* 608d–611a). The argument is clearly unsatisfactory in its question-begging premise of only one specific evil in each case (and the Epicureans later argued at length that destruction of the body *involves* disintegration of the soul). In addition there are also problems with the soul being taken here as a simple entity, whereas a great part of the psychology and politics of the *Republic* as a whole depend on it being complex, made up of the three parts of reason, spirit and appetite.

Plato could not rest in his search for a rational basis for the soul's immortality, and attacked the topic for the sixth time, in the *Phaedrus* (245d–e). As presented by Socrates, soul is now regarded as more sophisticated than the principle of life for the body; it is also the source of its movement, change and general activity; as such all soul is deathless (*pasa psychē athanatos*). The proof has three stages. First, what is always in movement is immortal, but that which is a source of movement to something else but is itself moved would stop living when it stops being moved. Only what moves itself, the self-moving, never stops moving (for that would be to abandon itself). Secondly, the original principle, the *archē*, of movement has necessarily and by definition no beginning and would not end (or else everything would perish). Thirdly, since soul moves the body and is the source of its own movement, when the body that is kept alive and moved by the soul is destroyed, soul abandons the body but not itself, and continues eternally in its self-movement. Cicero was so impressed by this argument that he translated it into Latin and linked it to his own eschatological myth at the end of his *De republica* (in the section surviving separately as *Somnium Scipionis*, "Dream of Scipio"); he also introduced it, naming its source in Plato's *Phaedrus*, in the first book of *Tusculan Disputations* (1.53–4) in a general discourse on soul.

After-death experiences

In all three Platonic dialogues *Phaedo*, *Republic* and *Phaedrus*, and in Cicero's *Somnium Scipionis*, the proofs for an immortal soul are followed by eschatological myths: stories of what might happen to the soul when separated from the body at death. One reason for this is that, however valid the proofs might be, they have dealt with soul in a generalized way, as principle of life or intelligence, and offered little reassurance to Socrates' friends that the *individual*, whom they have loved and conversed with, will still in some way be in existence after drinking the hemlock. When Crito asks Socrates how he wishes to be buried (*Phaedo* 115c), Socrates replies that it does not matter what happens to his body, for the *real* person, who is talking to them and marshalling all these arguments, will be up and away: the antithesis of the Homeric position where the man himself (*autos*) lies dead on the battlefield and only a shadow existence awaits his *psychē*. The eschatological myths combine some traditional literary features with Pythagorean ideas of transmigration and cyclic time. They also involve a *judgement* in which injustices in this world are redressed and the unjust suffer punishment, and also a *moral*, on how life should be lived now. Despite disclaimers of their truth status they round off their dialogues to drive home, in imaginative narrative, the philosophical themes.

The myth that ends the *Gorgias* (523a–27c) is the simplest: unconnected with an immortality proof, not involving transmigration and having the traditional features of a judgement. The good are sent to enjoy the Isles of the Blessed; the wicked, if curable, have a limited time of punishment, viewed as medicine for the soul to improve it and restore it to health; but the lot of souls who are beyond help is to suffer eternal torment in atonement for their crimes, and to act as visible deterrents. Socrates finds the account persuasive, and true as far as he is concerned. It summarizes his long argument with Callicles that we should seek the reality not the appearance of goodness (for the judgement will be of naked judge on naked soul), and replaces Callicles' principle, that justice is the interest of the stronger, with the Socratic position, first in argument and then in myth, that it is worse to do wrong (which harms the soul) rather than to be wronged (which, whether by robbery, violence or even murder) only affects the body.

The *Phaedo* myth (107c–114c), which follows the four proofs for immortality, sets up a complex geography of underground rivers and an exotic "true earth", as high above this one as this is above the ocean, having *aithēr* equivalent to our air, with a landscape abounding in colour and riches. There is a judgement, where souls may be released if they are forgiven by their victims and return to our world; but again, if they are incurable, there is an eternity in Tartarus. The good dwell in the splendour and light of the true earth, and the most excellent, the philosophers who have spent their lives in preparation for death, go

121

to even "fairer mansions", beyond description. Socrates admits that he has allowed himself some poetic licence as he was carried away by his interest in the details, but basically he is reasonably sure that the story is true, and, more importantly, it provides the incentive to lead a philosophic life, which, in keeping soul as far as possible from contamination with the body in this life, will ease its final separation.

At the end of the ten books of the *Republic*, and after the new proof for the soul's immortality, comes the famous Myth of Er, presented without comment as the personal experience of Er the Pamphylian, who came back to life after being killed in battle, and recounted his experiences (*Republic* 613e–21d). There is first the traditional meadow where judgement takes place, and a crossroads where the just are sent to the right and upwards, and the unjust to the left and downwards. As in the *Phaedo* there is a return after a thousand years, here back to the meadow after tenfold rewards for good acts and tenfold punishment for wrongs done, while the excessively wicked, most of them tyrants, are punished without remittance in Tartarus. Much of this is extremely crude, and the straight division of the souls into the good and the bad trivializes the subtle analyses of the wide varieties of human character, psychology and motivation that had been skilfully expounded in the previous books, yet it is said that "we shall be saved if we remember the story".

The second part of the myth moves to a cosmic setting with a description of a complex model of the universe, the orbits of the planets, and the harmony of their spheres. The souls come before the three seated Fates, the daughters of Necessity, where lots are cast for the order in which they are to choose the next life, and an interpreter explains that the individual is responsible for what will happen as the result of that choice and "god is blameless". Here the moral is emphasized that "we must know how to choose the middle course, and to avoid as far as we can, in this life and the next, the extremes on either hand, for in this way one becomes most happy" (619a). The wisest choice was made by Odysseus, when he chose the uneventful life of an ordinary man; this is commended, but is not compatible with the main thrust of the *Republic* and also the *Phaedo*, that the best life is that of the philosopher, devoted to the pursuit of reason and contemplation of the good.

Cicero's version of this Platonic myth comes at the end of his *De republica* (in the section preserved as the *Somnium Scipionis*), following the Latin translation of the proof of the soul's immortality taken from

Plato's *Phaedrus*. It keeps many of the features of the Myth of Er in the description of the celestial setting, the orbital movements of the planets and the harmony of their spheres, but it is an *astral escha-tology*, that is, a belief that souls come from the stars and return there. It is also very Roman in involving as the supreme deity a *political* god, who finds most acceptable "the gatherings and assemblies of men who are bound together by law, in the communities known as states", and in having a moral lesson for humanity that is related to politics rather than philosophy:

> Every man who has preserved or helped his country, or has made its greatness even greater, is reserved a special place in heaven, where he may enjoy an eternal life of happiness ... so cherish justice and *pietas*, owed to parents and kin, and most of all to one's country. That is the life which leads to heaven, and to the company of those who have completed their lives in this world, and are now released from their bodies, and dwell in that region which the Greeks have taught you to call the Milky Way.
>
> (6.13–16)

The mortal soul

After defining death as the parting of soul from body, Plato had attempted to prove the immortality of soul in general as the pervading principle of life and reason, and then to account for the survival of individuals in the myths of the journey of their souls after death. In this context he modified earlier Pythagorean ideas of metamorphoses and assimilated them to literary traditions of *post mortem* judgement and places of reward and punishment. He was directly opposed here as elsewhere by the Epicureans, who were influenced by the Presocratics Leucippus and Democritus, and argued for the dissolution of the soul along with the body at death. They rejected Pythagorean and Platonic dualism and maintained that soul has a material atomic structure like everything else, and is as vulnerable to disintegration as the body which houses it. This position is set out most forcefully by Lucretius in the third book of his *De rerum natura*, which is concerned with the substance, structure, function and mortality of soul, and is a key text in ancient psychology, both for its anti-Platonic polemic and its posi-tive argument.

The Greek word *psyche* is used for both the principle of life and of reason; in Latin the two senses are split into two words – *anima* (for life) and *animus* (for mind). They are, however, one soul substance: *animus* concentrated in the heart where, it was supposed, are thought and feeling, and *anima* spread through the body. In his Latin presentation of the Epicurean Greek position, Lucretius first insists that the soul (as *anima*) is material, and as much an integral part of us as the hand or foot. Soul and body, far from being in conflict, work together, as can be seen in the physical results of mental disturbances (we may blush at a memory, or go pale and shake with fear), and in the mental results of physical disturbances (in fainting from pain, for example). The soul wakes the body up and generally pushes it around, making it do as it wants, and the body in turn affects the soul with reduction of willpower and distraction in thought. Such reciprocal movements can only come about by touching and pushing, which involve material objects on both sides; both therefore have a material, atomic, structure, but the soul atoms are smaller, smoother and rounder than those of the body and have more surrounding void, which makes for swifter movement. These soul atoms form clusters, or molecules, with the characteristics of breath, air, heat and a fourth element, the "soul of soul" (*anima animae*), deeply hidden in the heart, the most fundamental part of us, which is responsible for our thinking but also for consciousness and ultimately life itself. As an eyeball can be damaged but the eye still sees, whereas, if the pupil is pierced, sight is lost at once, so the *anima* may be affected (if an arm or leg is injured, for example) but we still live but, if the *animus* is struck (as happens with a blow to the heart), the patient dies (3.94–257).

Once the structure of the soul and its close involvement with the body had been established, Lucretius proceeded to counter Pythagorean theories of transmigration and Platonic proofs for the immortality of the soul, on the basis, long accepted in Greek philosophy, that change indicates mortality (a beginning and an end to life) and changelessness immortality. He first tackled the non-existence of the soul after death, showing that, because the soul substance is flimsy, it flows out, like water in a jug, when the body no longer holds it. Soul and body grow, mature and age together and are therefore likely to die together, and the soul has its own ills, which presage its mortality. In fever, drunkenness and epilepsy the body clearly affects the soul/mind (*animus*) for the worse, and in the case of creeping paralysis the body gradually destroys the soul/life (*anima*). Furthermore the soul as *animus* cannot have thoughts, emotions or sensations without bodily organs, nor can it be separated from the body when they are so closely interlocked, nor does the soul exist before birth, as the Pythagoreans held and as portrayed in Platonic myth, for we have no memory of life before birth. In addition, if a soul, keeping its identity, came into a body of the same kind, then there would be wise babies, which is ridiculous, and violates the parallel growth of mind and body; if, on the other hand, a soul is modified and weakened to adapt to a baby's body then it is so different as to be a new soul. If a soul came from a body of the same kind, it would have to be so rearranged as to be starting again, and, if it came from a body of a different kind – a lion-soul in a deer, for example, or a thinking-soul in a plant – this too would be ridiculous, and violate the character and development of the species. And, finally, a squabble among souls for particular bodies is also absurd, for the soul works with and in the body, and disintegrates at the body's death. A mortal–immortal union is incredible, and, in sum, soul satisfies none of the criteria for immortality that characterize solid atoms, intangible void and the sum total of the universe. Traditional *post mortem* suffering and punishments, described in literature and taken over in Platonic myth, are to be seen as allegories for everyday mental torments that are self-inflicted here and now, as the foolish make their own "hell on earth".

A three-part soul

Platonic myth, as given especially in the *Phaedo* and *Republic*, and the proofs that precede them, which concern the soul either as life principle or agent of reason and memory, take the soul as a unit: a single entity that is joined to the body at birth, struggles with it through life and separates wholly from it at death. However, in books 2–4 of the *Republic*, Plato, through Socrates, argues for a soul with three parts that are parallel to three classes in the state. The struggles within this tripartite soul are vividly portrayed in the figure of the charioteer and his two horses in the myth that comes in a central section of the *Phaedrus*, and, in the non-Socratic myth of the *Timaeus*, the functioning and relationship of the three parts of the soul to the three related areas of the body are explored. In these passages the focus is not on soul as life principle or self-mover but on the mental conflict arising from the *separation* of rational functioning from spirit and appetite, and its resolution in the governance of reason when it is supported by spirit over the demands of appetite.

The problem arises in the *Republic* when Socrates is challenged to show why we should act rightly if we could be free of any dire results of wrongdoing in this world or the next. Socrates suggests looking at the soul "writ large" as a *polis*; if justice can be defined and understood on this larger scale, then it would be easier to grasp its nature in the individual *psychē*. This leads to the account of the logical growth of an ideal state and the intertwining soul–state analogy. A simple community is therefore described, with a division of labour among the various tradesmen; then luxuries are introduced and potential leaders emerge, who are divided into military and executive "guardian" classes. Wisdom characterizes the guardians, courage the military and temperance runs through the whole civic body. Justice emerges as the harmony that results from the citizens "doing their own thing", that is, the guardians ruling, the soldiers supporting them and the people obeying. When the structure is applied to an individual it is found not that soul as a whole is opposed to the appetites of the body and tries to suppress them as far as possible (the emphasis in the *Phaedo*), but that the soul is divided into a rational part and, in opposition to it, an appetitive part that craves indulgence, as for example in wanting a drink when reason says no. To find a soul-part corresponding to the military in the state, Plato takes the case of *thumos* ("spirit", "status-seeking", almost "a sense of honour"). This is separate from appetite, on the one hand, in the phenomenon of "self-disgust", shown in a conflict to look or not look on something shameful (and there is a Homeric precedent for *thumos* rebuking indulgence), and separate from reason, on the other hand, in that it is found in children and animals, who were not thought to be rational. The virtues of the parts of the soul, corresponding to the classes in the state, are then *wisdom* for reason, the ruler, *courage* for spirit, its adjutant, *temperance* in accepting one's place, and *justice* as pervasive harmony, which results when reason rules, assisted by righteous anger and a sense of honour, and the appetites obey.

The relationship of the three parts to each other is given a vivid representation in the *Phaedrus* myth (246a–257a), which follows the proof of the immortality of the soul as a whole, based on its function as self-moving cause of motion and change in the body. In the myth the rational part of the soul is compared to a charioteer trying to control two horses. One is white and handsome, tempered by self-control, the ally of true glory, needing no whip, and this corresponds to the spirited part of the soul. The other horse in the traces, representing the part of the soul driven by appetite, is black, crooked, "a haphazard jumble of limbs", and can scarcely be controlled by the whip and goad. When charioteer and horses come within sight of the beloved, the black horse is said to get out of control, and the charioteer has to wrench the bit from its teeth, splashing its tongue and jaws with blood and painfully pinning its legs back on to the ground. Only after several such attempts does the horse finally calm down, and the charioteer, assisted by the white horse and with the black horse now subdued, approaches the beloved in reverence and awe. Then:

> If the better aspects of their minds prevail, and guide them towards a well-ordered life of philosophy, they spend their time here in happiness and harmony. After enslaving the part of the soul that lets in evil, and allowing free entry to virtue, they are masters of themselves and at peace ... and neither human prudence nor divine madness can offer any greater good than this.   (256a–b)

Like this description in the *Phaedrus* of the soul as charioteer driving two horses of conflicting temperaments, the narrative of Plato's *Timaeus* is in the form of a myth, recommended as a "reasonable contention" to be accepted, an account as likely as any other on a subject where certainty is beyond human reach. The *Timaeus* myth deals with cosmology, the movements of stars and planets, the construction of world body and soul and their human counterparts, the mathematical basis of phenomena, and the working of reason and necessity in the functioning of the individual. As with Anaximenes, Heraclitus and Anaxagoras, a relationship is set out between cosmos and individual, but the system is more complex in Plato, as he links soul with both life and reason, but also takes account of Pythagorean theory. In passages in *Timaeus* dealing with the human soul, the narrator explains that it is made up, as the world soul is, of intermediate being, sameness and difference, so that it too can calculate sameness and difference, and therefore access the realm of the unchanging with knowledge, and the changing world with opinion and belief; because the composition of the human soul is less pure, however, its abilities are correspondingly more limited. The joining of soul to human body at birth is a traumatic, confusing experience, and it is some time before the immortal soul can control the circuits of its movements and gain control of the body (*Timaeus* 41d–43c). In the human soul's future after death an astral eschatology is here combined with a theory of transmigration, which means that each soul comes from its native star, and, after a virtuous life on earth, returns there, unless there is a failure in virtue, in which case the soul is then sent through a round of human and animal lives.

In the third part of the myth the lesser gods take over from the supreme divinity and fashion the individual human. Given the immortal soul as the principle of reason they place it in the globe of the head, separated from the rest of the body by the isthmus of the neck, and they add two mortal parts: appetite beneath the diaphragm, and spirit in the heart area to mediate between reason above and appetite below. Among all the ancient philosophers (with the exception of a hint from Alcmaeon), only Plato understands that we think with our heads rather than the heart area, which had seemed the more obvious candidate, given its central position, and the feelings of anger, fear and the like that are found there. Plato's explanation, however, seems to rest on the *distance* of the head from the belly, which would keep it undisturbed, "and so leaving the highest part of us to deliberate quietly about the welfare of each and all" (*Timaeus* 71a).

Soul as self

Aristotle's discussion of soul, mainly in the three books of his *De anima* (About *psychē*) disagrees with Platonic theories of soul on several counts: as non-material, as having parts, as primarily the principle of reason, and as surviving the death of the body. In this treatise Aristotle takes *psychē* more generally as the source of life and movement, and extends the discussion to cover all forms of life, but with particular emphasis on human beings and animals, where there is a relationship between function and movement. At the start he disarms criticism by recognizing the difficulty of the subject, saying: "In general it is one of the hardest things about which one could have any conviction on any aspect" (402a). He then, as often, surveys the opinions of his predecessors, to see what is of use, what can be discarded and what problems are raised that require a solution. Aristotle finds support for the view that soul is in some way a source of movement in most of the Presocratics, starting with Thales, who claimed that a (magnetic) stone has soul because it causes iron to move, and Alcmaeon who attributed divinity to soul because, like the planets, it is in continuous motion. He is also in sympathy with Anaxagoras, for whom *Nous* (Mind) is responsible for cosmic and human movement, with Democritus in that soul is in continuous movement (although disagreeing with its atomic structure), and Plato because of the soul movements described in the *Timaeus*.

But is the connection of soul with body that of mover and moved? Aristotle would think not, for he does not regard them as two separate physical substances. Nor does he accept that soul is in some way dependent on bodily parts or an arrangement of them. Empedocles had suggested that soul is to be interpreted as the *ratio* of the component elements, as bone is bone because the ratio of its elements of earth, water and fire is 2:2:4 (DK 31B96). Ratio is particularly important for the elements in the heart area "for the blood around the heart is thinking (*noēma*) for humans" (B105.3, 110.5), and the closer the ratio is to a perfect proportion, the better the thinking and the more superior the individual's character (*ēthos*) and nature (*physis*). This is taken as a more sophisticated version of a theory of soul as "harmony" of bodily parts, which had been propounded by Simmias in Plato's *Phaedo* as a counter-example for Socrates' earlier "proofs" of the soul's immortality, and may well go back to the adaptation of a Pythagorean idea by Philolaus:

> We believe the soul to be something like this: our body is in a sort of tension, held together by hot and cold and dry and wet and other things of this sort, and our soul is a blending and *harmonia* of these same things when they have been finely blended in proportion one with another.   (*Phaedo* 86b–c)

As the tune stops when the instrument is broken, so soul would cease to exist when the body dies. Socrates answers this by saying that a harmony cannot act contrary to its parts or admit of degrees, so that there would be no explanation for more or less evil in the soul. Aristotle's criticism is that an explanation of soul in terms of harmony, ratio or proportion does not account for soul initiating movement in the body, whereas a spontaneous source of movement and change is common to all animal functions. This objection is relevant also in rejecting the contemporary view of Xenocrates: that soul is a "self-moving number", and any attempt to combine movement and number in this way brings with it further difficulties in mathematical theory (*De anima* 408b–409b).

Even so, understanding soul in some way as the adjustment of physical parts persisted, and found expression in Stoic psychology. The Stoics brought into their explanation of soul the five senses (sight, hearing, touch, taste and smell), and also voice, reproduction and the "governing" part (*hēgemonikon*), and these eight parts were all thought to have a physical basis in *pneuma* ("hot breath", a combination of fire and air). Through *pneuma* there is communication from the senses to the governing part, which is located in the heart area, and centralizes information from the rest. In animals any resulting action is instinctive, "according to nature", but in human beings the governing part is rational, and initiates appropriate action after deliberation and judgement on the information received. But the Stoics also see the soul–body relationship as a complete "blending" or mixing (*krasis*), and find the best "self" in that person where the tension (*tonos*) of the *pneuma* is at perfect pitch; then it is that right action always results and the individual may be termed "wise". Here the Stoics answer the objection that Socrates had raised in the *Phaedo* against Simmias' suggestion that the soul is a *harmonia*, related to the body as a melody is to the instrument that plays it. Socrates had said that there could not be degrees of *harmonia*, whereas the individual soul could be more or less good, or more or less evil. For the Stoics there were no degrees of virtue: either the *tonos* was exact and the individual was wise and virtuous, or it was out of tune and the individual was foolish and his actions wrong.[4]

So how does Aristotle view the relationship of soul to body? He claims that the connection is that of form to matter. This can be seen in the example of wax and the impression stamped on it. The two make a unity, and it would be as absurd to think of soul as incorporeal or immortal as to suppose that the impression is separable from the wax. As the essence of the stamped wax is to be found in the form of the impression, which gives it its individuality and meaning, so soul gives the body its true nature. In another example, Aristotle says that if the eye were a living creature then vision would be its soul; it is the "essence" of eye (for without vision there is no eye in the strict sense), and also its primary function and activity. As the pupil and vision make an eye, so soul and body make a living creature, in a hierarchy of complexity from plants to animals, culminating in human beings, endowed with reason as well as the lower psychic faculties of movement, perception and growth.

For Aristotle, therefore, soul is the explanation (*aitia*) and first principle (*archē*) of the body, form to its matter, the agent of its related

functions (life, growth, movement, perception and reason as appropriate to its complexity), but also in a sense the body's "final cause"
in that the body exists for the sake of soul (*De anima* 415b), and, in
Aristotelian terms, actualizes its potential. In the *Nicomachean Ethics*
(which is less technical than *De anima*) Aristotle's sympathies with the
earlier Presocratic theories are more evident. For him too the internal
psychic structure can be reinforced by applied intention and repeated
activity, and he goes on to claim that this (which he calls the actualizing
of potential) is in accord with the distinctively human soul-function
of reason: "Indeed, this would seem actually to *be* each man in that
it is the authoritative and best part of him, and it would be strange if
we were to choose not our own best life but that of something else"
(*Nicomachean Ethics* 1178a).

6. Believing, doubting and knowing

Oedipus notoriously brought on his own tragic end because of the driving force of his will to know his own identity, a grim illustration of the comment with which Aristotle opens his *Metaphysics*: "all humans, because of their very nature, yearn for knowledge". The word Aristotle uses here for knowing is *eidenai*, which has a root connection with the verb for "seeing": a knowing *that*, grasped by the rational mind. This contrasts with nouns *epistēmē*, a knowing *how*, connected with scientific understanding, and also *gnōmē* or *gnōsis*, recognition from acquaintance, *noēsis*, intellectual activity, and *phronēsis*, practical wisdom. These terms often overlap, and, in their multiplicity, we find that the Greeks continually raised questions about knowledge and the different kinds of knowing. They explored the contrast with doubt and opinion, the part played by perception, especially sight, in guaranteeing the validity of knowledge, the relationship of the subject (a "knowing mind") to the object ("what is known"), how knowledge should be defined, and the possibility of "knowledge of knowledge", a master science that would bring with it a "theory of everything". The recognition of such problems regarding the basis and validity of knowledge and the attempts to answer them, which relate to the branch of philosophy known as epistemology, were of central importance to the main Greek philosophers, and count among their greatest achievements.

Human ignorance

From the beginnings of philosophy, however, there was a tendency towards scepticism. In its non-technical sense this tendency leads to the conclusion that, despite the yearning to know, for human beings to achieve knowledge, and with it the understanding of the truth of things, is an impossible ideal. In the Homeric poems knowledge of the past belongs to the Muses, and *they* give the poet the authority to sing of bygone heroic deeds. Zeus, as supreme god, knows the future, which unfolds according to his design (his *boulē*; *Il* 1.5), or he interprets individual fates (as when he weighs those of Hector and Achilles to Achilles' advantage) and acts accordingly. But from the point of view of the mortals involved he is not always to be trusted, as when he sends Agamemnon a deceitful dream. Individual gods also mislead – Apollo, for example, disguised as the Trojan Agenor, diverts Achilles from the fighting, and Athena, impersonating Deiphobus, ensures the defeat of his brother Hector. When Apollo does benefit mortals with his gift of prophecy it comes at a price, as with physical blindness for Teiresias' foresight, and incredulity in the face of Cassandra's true utterances. Hesiod, following on from Homer, claimed to receive authority for his poem, *Theogony*, from the Muses at Mount Helicon, but here they themselves warn the poet that, as well as the truth, they speak lies like the truth (*Theogony* 26–7).

As we have seen, the early Presocratic Xenophanes inveighed against both Homer and Hesiod for attributing deceit to the gods along with "theft and adultery and mutual trickery" (DK 21B11). He set out to replace the traditional Olympians with a new type of divinity, unlike human beings in appearance and voice, who "sees as a whole, thinks as a whole and as a whole he hears, moving everything by the thinking of his mind" (B24, 26.2). Two immediate results arise from this new theology. The first is that mortals are cut off from knowledge, for: "If by chance we should happen to speak about what has come to pass, even as it is, still we would not *know*, but opinion (*dokos*) is stretched over all" (B34). These words set out for the first time the contrast between knowledge, which is certain but unattainable, and opinion or belief, which may or may not be correct, but is unverifiable; even if our opinions were true, we still could not be confident about them. But the second result is that *progress* is possible through human effort: "Gods of course did not reveal everything to humans at the beginning, but in time, by inquiring and searching (*historia*), they improve their discoveries" (B18).

Human progress

This theme of progress towards knowledge, despite the inherent difficulties that beset the normal human condition, is pursued further by
some of Xenophanes' immediate successors. Heraclitus was scornful
of Xenophanes' *polymathia* and lack of understanding, but he agrees
that advances can be made through human effort and strong motivation. His approach is through the community of thought (B113),
which reflects *logos* in both its universal and individual psychic functioning. Most people, however, act as if asleep, they do not know how
to listen or speak and are deaf to the truth even when they hear it. We
need to wake up, to use our eyes and ears aright, to be aware of how
things are and to recognize the unseen *harmonia* that is stronger than
the seen (B1, 19, 54, 73). The way to achieve these aims is twofold: to
make correct judgements about the external world, the world that is
common to all; and also, like Heraclitus himself, to search within. For
him the *logos* of the human *psychē* has hidden depths and "increases
itself", which would seem to mean that the more we understand the
more there is to know. Furthermore, those who would be philosophers (*philosophoi*, literally "wisdom-lovers") must be "inquirers and
searchers of many things", and Heraclitus uses the same root word here
(*historia*) as Xenophanes had done for the effort required in making
progress (22B45, 101, 115, 35).

Empedocles pulls together some of these threads. Like Heraclitus
he sees that people generally are very limited in their outlook and have
little or no understanding of how things are:

> Observing a small part of life in their lifetime,
> they are convinced only of that which each has experienced,
> as they are driven in different directions, yet all boast of finding
> the whole.
> These things are not to be seen or heard by men, or grasped in
> the mind in this way. (31B2)

Yet, with the authority of the Muse (and Parmenides also had presented
his philosophy as expounded by a goddess), it is possible to be confident in the truth of what the poet says, but it also requires concentrated effort on the part of the listener. The argument has first to be
articulated (B4) and then taken in and studied by the pupil, but, if
he is distracted by the countless trivialities that beset people and dull

their meditations, the true argument will be dispersed. Much effort is therefore required, and the resulting "onrush of conviction" may even be unwelcome (B110, 114). The universality of knowing and thinking, which Heraclitus had recognized as *logos* that exists externally in the structure of the cosmos and is accessible, with effort, by the individual *psyche*, is also adopted by Empedocles when he proclaims that "*all things* have *phronesis* and a share of thinking" (B110.10). Anaxagoras too was in sympathy with Heraclitus and Empedocles here with his theory of Mind (*Nous*), which is both a universal force responsible for initiating cosmic events, and present in individuals.

Sophistic relativism and verbal dexterity

But it was the earlier Presocratic view typified in Xenophanes that prevailed in the intellectual climate of fifth-century Athens. From what is known of the sophists and Socrates, we find an emphasis on the effort required in enquiring and searching for truth, and a reinforcement of the climate of doubt about reaching agreement or certainty on any subject. These views are forcefully set out by the two most important sophists, Protagoras and Gorgias. In his *Life of Protagoras*, Diogenes Laertius gives two striking quotations as the opening sentences of two different works by this sophist. One is a cautious statement on the difficulty of certainty in religion, which is in opposition both to popular tradition and beliefs, and to the new versions of natural theology propounded by some of the Presocratics: "Where the gods are concerned, I am not in a position to be sure whether they exist or not; there are so many impediments to such knowledge, including the obscurity of the subject and the shortness of human life" (DK 80B4). The second, and the most famous, is on Protagoras' "relativism": "Man is the measure of all things – of the things that are, that they are, and of the things that are not, that they are not" (B1). This was interpreted as meaning that all perceptions are true for the individual at the moment of perceiving, and there is no further authority or criterion to judge the matter. If opinions conflict (as in "the wind is cold for me and warm for you") then both are equally true. Here Protagoras takes to its logical conclusion Democritus' stand that truth is in appearances, reinforced by his statements that "nothing is true, or at least it is unclear to us" (Aristotle, *Metaphysics* 1009b11), "to know what anything actually is is baffling" (DK 68B8) and "in reality

135

we know nothing about anything, but for each of us there is the re-shaping of belief" (B7).[1]

Protagoras also claimed that there could be two contradictory arguments about any statement, both equally valid, in logic as well as in perception, and used the technique of defending contradictory premises as a teaching tool in the debating competitions that he instituted. When the sense of *aretē* shifted from "excellence in war" to "excellence in civic qualities" with the establishment of the *polis*, ambitious and wealthy young men were anxious to learn how to be successful in a democratic setting in which all male citizens were, in theory, of equal standing. This meant, in particular, that the skills of rhetoric and persuasion were needed to win over the assemblies of the people in decisions of policy and law, and to gain the consequent support and esteem. It was to supply this need, in providing something like a university education in politics and public speaking, that Protagoras and other sophists equipped to teach the desired curriculum were drawn to Athens. Protagoras himself worked in the city for over forty years, comfortably wealthy from the fees for his tuition, and enjoying a high reputation. In the two dialogues of Plato in which he plays a major role he is treated with courtesy even where Plato shows him forced to concede victory in the debates with Socrates. The dialogue named after him presents Protagoras as defending with myth and argument the position that every citizen is gifted with a share in civic virtue, so that the rule of the many is more justified in nature than that of the few. In the *Theaetetus*, Protagoras is dramatically brought back to life to defend his maxim that "man is the measure", which Plato interprets as a definition of knowledge that identifies it with sense-perception, so that in truth "seeing is believing", and all sense-data are equally valid.

The other distinguished sophist, Gorgias from Leontini in Sicily, specialized in rhetoric. He gave exhibition speeches at the Olympian and Pythian games, and also solo performances in the theatre, when he would speak spontaneously on any subject thrown at him by his audience. He first came to Athens on a diplomatic mission to gain allies against Syracuse, and then for a number of years from 428 BCE settled there as a successful teacher of professional oratory. He had many distinguished pupils and became so famous that a verb *gorgiazein* was coined, meaning "to speak in the manner of Gorgias". His skill with words was also shown in his writings. In one work, for example, he argued provocatively that Helen should not be blamed for causing the

Trojan War, and in another ventured into metaphysics with a treatise that seemed to be deliberately aimed at Parmenides' denial of "what is not". This had the title *On Nothing*, and argued: (i) that nothing exists; (ii) if anything did exist it would be impossible to comprehend; and (iii) even if it were comprehensible it could not be explained or communicated to others.

Whereas Protagoras openly claimed to develop civic virtue in his pupils, Gorgias concentrated more on the art of persuasion, which could override the opinion of an expert in any field, and so was all powerful in the assembly and the law courts. There was no area, it seemed, in which a proposition could not be attacked and defeated with the new skills. If the skill is put to a wrong use this should no more be blamed on the teacher than a boxer would be guilty if a pupil used the expertise he had learned to attack his father. This is the position Plato gives him in *Gorgias*, the dialogue named after him, although the appearance of the orator is much briefer than those of the other two respondents, Polus and Callicles. Gorgias, like Protagoras, is treated with respect, but his defence of the superiority of rhetoric leads into the much more morally dangerous position taken up by Polus, and then, more powerfully, by Callicles.

Callicles' claims in the dialogue are: (i) that "might is right"; (ii) that the powerful dominate the weak according to natural law; and (iii) that an extreme hedonism is justifiable. Socrates is represented as delighted with such a strong respondent who will act as a "touchstone", for: "You will never acquiesce from lack of wisdom or excess of false shame or from any desire to deceive me, as, by your own account, you are my friend. So then it will be no exaggeration to say that agreement between us is bound to result in truth" (*Gorgias* 487e, trans. Emlyn-Jones). Eventually, however, agreement between the two breaks down since Callicles refuses to answer when he is losing the argument, and Socrates consequently takes the parts of both questioner and respondent. The "truth" that Socrates ends with turns out to be a myth that he finds persuasive: a story that describes torments awaiting the unjust after death if they are not prepared to have their souls healed by punishment when alive.

Socrates was shown as recognizing the dangers of Callicles' position for political stability and individual flourishing, and being serious in his dialectical refutation of it, as he had been in his dispute with Protagoras. In a lighter vein in the *Euthydemus* he is portrayed in conversation with two more conventional sophists, the brothers Euthydemus and

Dioysodorus, who, like Protagoras and Gorgias (but with fewer scruples) introduced disputants to the tricks of their trade for a fee, teaching their students how to defeat any opponent on any subject, and to draw absurd conclusions from any set statement, whether true or false. The dialogue shows the brothers giving a dazzling display of their wizardry with words, succeeding in their eristic by seizing on a lack of precision in the use of terms, along with punning and equivocation. For example, the young Cleinias is asked whether his dog has puppies, and then, because the dog is a father, and is his, the dog is his father. More seriously he is discomfited by the question "Is it the clever or the ignorant who learn?", and Dionysodorus whispers to Socrates that whichever answer the lad gives, he will be proved wrong, for all the questions are designed as traps. Cleinias' reply that clever people do not learn, because they know already, is trumped with the counter-example that, with a specific task, previously unknown, it is the clever, not the ignorant, who learn (*Euthydemus* 275d–277c, 298e). This particular dilemma was to surface again in the *Meno*, when Socrates himself is faced with the challenge that the search for knowledge is pointless, for either one knows already, in which case the search is irrelevant, or, if one does not know, it would be impossible to recognize whether an answer found was the right one or not (*Meno* 80d–e).

Double arguments and scepticism

The general position – that for any argument there is a counter-argument – was illustrated particularly by Protagoras, Gorgias and Euthydemus, but, according to Aristotle, handbooks on this practice were written by a number of sophists (*Sophistical Refutations* 183b37). It was also the subject of the anonymous treatise, probably contemporary with the work of these sophists, known as *Dissoi logoi* (Double arguments). This treatise is an extreme example of rhetorical *antilogiai* (i.e. one *logos* set against another), but there are also echoes of Heraclitus' language on the identity of opposites based on relative viewpoints in such statements as "illness is both bad and good" and "the same thing is lighter and heavier", and of Zeno's dilemmas. Sections in *Dissoi logoi* on "Good and Bad", "Just and Unjust" and the like give opportunities to play with puns, paradoxes and apparent contradictions, but the most interesting comes under the title "True and False", where the ripostes highlight the problem of the relation of words to facts. It is shown that both true and false statements use the same words, but, if the words relate to what is the case, the statement is true, if not, then that same statement is false. An example given in this section is the statement "I am an initiate". If ten people were sitting in a row and each said "I am an initiate", this could be false nine times and true the tenth for the one who has actually been initiated, although the words are the same.[2]

The underlying principles of *Dissoi logoi* looked back to the methods of the Presocratics Heraclitus and Zeno, and were supported by a follower of Democritus, Metrodorus of Chios, who opened his work *On Nature* with the words: "None of us knows anything, not even whether we know anything or not". *Dissoi logoi* were embedded in the arguments of the sophists, but also looked forward to Pyrrhonian Scepticism, which was firmly established by the first century BCE. The claim here was that if the very attainment of knowledge is in doubt, and for every argument there is a counter-argument, then, in this climate of "equipollence", it would surely be preferable to support neither side, but to suspend judgement. Pyrrho, the acknowledged founder of Scepticism, wrote nothing himself, but through the writings of his pupil Timon it is clear that he was not a nihilist, denying existence or external reality, but rejected enquiry into such matters precisely because there was no possibility of a successful outcome. He was more concerned with a negative epistemology: knowing anything for sure is impossible. There is no statement, he would maintain, that can be true and not admit an equally valid negative, and no opinion or belief that did not have its opposite; this general attitude was summed up in the phrase *ou mallon* (no more this than that). Gorgias had argued that even if a statement was correct and correctly communicated, there would be no way of *identifying* it as correct and separating it out from its opposite, and, according to Protagoras, feelings could not be relied on, for the same phenomenon could have opposite effects on different individuals. For Pyrrho, however, there were also consequences for one's way of life: if nothing matters because there is no certainty and always an alternative possibility, then the state resulting from consequent suspension of belief is that of *ataraxia*, calmness and freedom from anxiety. In his *Life of Pyrrho*, Diogenes Laertius gives a vivid picture of his famous serenity and what this meant in practice:

> He led a life consistent with this doctrine, going out of his way for nothing, taking no precaution, but facing all risks as they came, whether carts, dogs or precipices, but he was kept out of

harm's way by his friends who used to follow close after him. ...
He was so respected by his native city [Elis, in the Peloponnese]
that they made him high priest, and on his account voted that all
philosophers should be exempt from taxation.   (DL 9.62, 64)

Socratic ignorance and the *elenchos*

In his comedy *Clouds*, Aristophanes had put Socrates firmly among the
sophists, for he showed him on stage teaching the tricks of rhetoric for
a fee, setting up contrary arguments, staging a confrontation between
Right and Wrong, questioning conventional religion, having strange
ideas on cosmology, engaging in hair-splitting eristic and making the
worse cause trump the better. But Plato's Socrates, as reported in the
Apology, the defence speech at his trial, claimed that Aristophanes
was wrong on all counts, and that this caricature contributed to the
prosecution's charge of corrupting the young. Socrates was especially
insistent that he never taught or accepted a fee, or troubled himself
with cosmological speculations. He recognized that he knew nothing
himself and indeed believed that knowledge was impossible for any
human being; it was for this claim that the Sceptics who came after
Plato in the Academy, and then Pyrrho and his followers, looked back
to Socrates as one of their number.

Socrates' mother was a midwife, and in a passage in the *Theaetetus*
Plato shows Socrates practising his mother's craft, not in helping to
give birth to children of the flesh but in bringing thoughts to birth:

> My patients are men, not women, and my concern is not with the
> body but with the soul that is in labour. And the highest point of
> my art is to prove by every test whether the offspring of a young
> man's thought is a false phantom or instinct with life and truth.
> Heaven constrains me to serve as a midwife, but has debarred
> me from giving birth. So of myself I have no sort of wisdom, nor
> has any discovery ever been born to me as the child of my soul.
> (*Theaetetus* 150b–c)[3]

Some of the early dialogues of Plato, which have Socrates as the
main speaker, give lively accounts of Socrates engaged in this testing
of other people's ideas, which was known as *elenchos*. In the clarification of the issues at stake, what was required initially was a *definition*

of the terms being used. The *Laches*, for example, named after one of the characters who is a military man, is a dialogue of this type. It starts with a discussion of the merits of fighting in armour, but soon turns to a search for a definition of courage. The first suggestion is an *example* of courage: "holding one's ground and not running away". The second suggestion, "endurance of soul", is an improvement on this (since it has a more general application); this in turn is modified to "wise endurance of soul", and finally to "knowledge of what is truly frightening". Similarly with the *Euthyphro*. Piety is first interpreted as "prosecuting the impious", but this is too narrow, so the next move is to suggest that it is "what the gods love" or, more explicitly, "what all the gods love", and, lastly, "knowledge of what is pleasing to the gods". In *Charmides* the first definition of the virtue of *sōphrosynē* ("prudence" or "temperance") is "quietness and modesty", then "minding one's own affairs" and, thirdly, "knowing oneself", ending with the interesting but unworkable definition as "knowing knowing" or "knowledge of knowledge".

The common pattern of these dialogues shows an expert, such as the general in *Laches* and the priest in *Euthyphro*, starting confidently with an answer to the question "What is *x*?", which is dismissed because its scope is too limited. Subsequent amendments broaden the issue, but the respondent becomes more and more uncomfortable as Socrates shows up flaws in the answers, and he finally gives up. The definitions, however, improve in the process, and end with knowledge being involved. Although the answers are clearly moving in a direction more acceptable to Socrates, they all still fail under examination, and the end result, for Socrates and the respondent, is a state of *aporia*, literally "no way out", which causes bewilderment and discomfiture in the respondent, and produces a confession of ignorance from Socrates. This claim by Socrates to know nothing (after a display of dialectical skill that silences the respondent) came to be known as his "irony", and is well described by Meno in the dialogue named after him:

> Socrates, even before I met you I heard that you are a perplexed man yourself and reduce others to perplexity. At this moment I feel that you are exercising magic and witchcraft upon me, and positively laying me under your spell, until I am just a mass of helplessness <as if stung by a sting-ray>. My mind and my mouth are literally numb, and I have nothing to reply to you.
>
> (*Meno* 80a)

In the *Apology*, Socrates explains how this reputation for producing perplexity came about. His friend Chaerephon went to Delphi and asked the Oracle if there was anyone wiser than Socrates, and received the reply that there was no one. Socrates set out to discover what this reply really meant. Since he was only too conscious that he himself had no wisdom, great or small, he went to look for a wise man. He first approached a senior politician and questioned him closely, and this was the result:

> I reflected as I walked away that I am certainly wiser than this man. It is only too likely that neither of us has any knowledge to boast of, but he thinks he knows something which he does not know, whereas I am quite conscious of my ignorance. At any rate it seems that I am wiser than he is to this small degree, that I do not think that I know what I do not know. (*Apology* 21a–d)

Socrates says that he then continued his search, which he compares to "a labour of Hercules", for a man who had some knowledge. He first interviewed politicians, who appeared to others (and especially to themselves) to be wise. Then he approached poets, but they did not seem to understand the poetry that they composed under divine inspiration. Finally he talked to skilled craftsmen, and found that, while they had genuine skills, they thought that this gave them the right to speak on matters of which they knew nothing. These conversations, with three sets of people who had a reputation for wisdom, all ended in the same way, with the expert deflated. Socrates concluded that the Oracle meant by its answer that real wisdom belongs only to god, that human knowledge has little or no value and that the wisest are those who, like Socrates, acknowledge their ignorance.

In one of his rare comments on the historical Socrates, Aristotle said that "with good reason he attempted to establish what a thing is", and that there are two innovations that can fairly be attributed to Socrates: "inductive argument" and "definition" (*Metaphysics* 1078b). How are Aristotle's positive remarks to be reconciled with Socrates' admission of ignorance? Socrates' method of examining what other people claimed to know, as was shown in *Laches*, *Euthyphro* and *Charmides*, required the clarification of the key term under discussion, whether courage, piety or temperance, before proceeding further. It is at this stage that Socrates used what Aristotle called "inductive argument". From a series of particular examples, Socrates was trying to pull out what it was that was common to them all, which would encompass a *general truth* that brought them under the same name, a *constant factor* in different situations and a *standard* for judging further instances. He gives two examples of what he is aiming at, in the definition of "speed" in the *Laches* as "the ability to do much in a short time" (192b), and of "shape" in the *Meno* as "the limit of a solid" (76a). In the moral sphere it was expected that, once the general truth had been crystallized in the definition and the process applied to a series of different virtues, then the set of definitions would build up to a body of moral knowledge; this could then be applied to a particular case and the right action would follow.[4] The "skill" (*technē*) acquired was comparable to that of medicine: the doctor amasses a definition of an illness from a series of individual instances, and, when a new case appears, he can make the correct diagnosis and act accordingly.

Knowledge and true opinion

Socrates' method, in the search for definitions through the accompanying *elenchos*, were, as we have seen, to examine traditional beliefs (one's own and other people's), to remove error (which was likely to involve raising doubts about previously held moral certainties), and so to reach an admission of ignorance. But such an admission should provide the stimulus to start afresh, for, if an assumed opinion no longer holds, then a sympathetic respondent would want to know where the truth is to be found, and how to reach it. Socrates is represented by Plato as finding no value in books as a teaching tool, for they say the same thing again and again, and cannot be questioned or argued with (*Phaedrus* 275a). Instead, he thought that the best method of progress in learning is a cooperative dialectic on a one-to-one basis, with the two participants reaching agreement at each stage, and then moving forwards from that position. In a rare positive moment Socrates (according to Plato) urged his respondent to keep on seeking the truth and not be despondent if arguments fail:

> One thing I am ready to fight for as long as I can, in word and in act: that we shall be better, braver and more active if we believe it right to look for what we don't know than if we believe there is no point in looking, because what we don't know we can never discover. (*Meno* 86b–c)

This is similar to the warning against mistrusting or even hating argument (*misologia* was the term Socrates coined) put forward in the *Phaedo* (89d). We should avoid turning misanthropic when we are let down continuously by so-called friends, and similarly, even if we feel let down by argument after argument failing, we should not turn against the principle of dialectic, but persevere. The very admission of ignorance is an improvement on thinking that one knows when one does not; some advances are made even if one never reaches a definite conclusion, and, in the very self-searching and intellectual endeavour involved, the best human life is lived. In an echo of Xenophanes saying that "by searching we find a better path" (B18), Socrates summed up his position in the famous phrase "an unexamined life is not worth living" (*Apology* 38a).

In much the same way as Pyrrho, the founder of Scepticism, would find a use for "probability" as a criterion when knowledge was an impossible objective, in the *Meno* the suggestion was raised that perhaps "true opinion" would be an adequate substitute for knowledge as a guide in daily life. The example given was of the "road to Larissa", where it was noted that a traveller would arrive at a previously unknown destination after receiving correct directions from someone who had been told the right way as effectively as from someone who had actually been there himself. In such a situation, believing the truth would do just as well as knowing it, but, to tie the opinion down and to stop it shifting under persuasion or duress, one must be able to defend it (97b–c).

In the *Theaetetus*, Plato shows Socrates returning to the earlier format of *elenchos*, with knowledge itself (*epistēmē*) as the term at issue. The first definition identifies it with perception. Here the ghost of Protagoras is summoned to give a vigorous defence of his view that an individual relies on his senses for what he knows (and this claim is tied in with and supported by Heraclitus' theory of flux), but the definition of knowing as perceiving is finally refuted. The second suggestion is that knowledge is true opinion (*orthē doxa*), but, when problems about false opinion arise, it is refined by the addition of *logos*, a rational justification for the opinion held. In the *Meno*, as we have seen, knowledge as true opinion plus *logos* had been accepted, but here in the *Theaetetus*, the definition fails under the closer scrutiny of three different meanings of *logos*. It could be: (i) "an image of thought in speech"; (ii) the understanding of a whole from its unknowable elements or letters (the Greek word *stoicheia* covers both); or (iii) the naming of a unique differentiating feature that would make the object count as "known" (208c). It is, however, agreed that none of these, if added to true opinion, would produce knowledge.

Is it possible to work out Plato's own contribution to the debate, even when he is still using Socrates as his main spokesman? If it is agreed that Socrates himself was a doubter, searching for knowledge by examining himself and others, but eventually being unsuccessful and admitting ignorance, then, in those dialogues where he is portrayed as reaching positive conclusions, the spokesman is likely to be speaking for Plato rather than keeping to the *persona* of the historic Socrates. The most important of these positive conclusions concern what is conventionally called the theory of forms, and this is particularly relevant to the enquiry about knowing, believing and doubting, and their objects.

Plato on knowledge

The Presocratic Parmenides had earlier contrasted knowledge with opinion (*doxa*). Knowledge of what there is was said to be accessible to the goddess, and available to a favoured individual, only after following a long and difficult argument, but men in general, the "dazed uncritical crowds", relying on their perceptions, had only a mistaken opinion about reality. This contrast was taken up by Democritus in opposing *nomos* ("custom", "what is generally accepted") to *physis* (what is true in nature). Both Presocratics were against Heraclitus' view of the world as continually in a state of flux, although controlled by a cosmic *logos*. Plato's compromise was to agree with Heraclitus on the basic instability of the perceived world, and allow it to be accessed only by perception, and discussed in terms of opinion (*doxa*). However, he set apart from the perceived world an intellectual realm, akin to Parmenides' unchanging and eternal reality, unique in itself but, for Plato, populated by a number of "forms", one for every set of particulars with the same name, although the focus was on forms of moral and mathematical terms. Plato describes such forms as perfect in every respect, and acting as ideal standards and models for their imperfect instantiations here. They alone are the objects of knowledge (*epistēmē*) and accessible to reason (*nous*), whereas we cannot *know* the particular phenomena that are around us, but only have beliefs and opinions, based on our shifting perceptions of them.

The key texts come in the central books (V–VII) of Plato's *Republic*. The first book of this long work is a standard Socratic *elenchos*, with three definitions of justice offered, all failing, and *aporia* (the inability to find a way out) the expected result. A fresh start, however, is made in the following two books, which set out to look for justice "writ large" in the state, and this involves building up a state from modest beginnings to a fully fledged *polis*. Then book IV tracks down the meaning of justice in its application in both public and private contexts. The central books are a digression, as Socrates has to elaborate on three provocative issues that were briefly raised, and now require more detailed examination. The first is that women would be equal to men in the state, the second that there would be no individual families but women and children would be "in common" and the third that the smallest change that would bring about the ideal state would be to have philosopher-rulers (473d–e). In the context of this last controversial point, it is clear that a definition of a philosopher is needed before a study of the qualifications required for government can begin. Socrates suggests that a philosopher is a lover of wisdom (as the name implies), and wisdom involves knowing (and loving) what is really there. The clarification of this point and the contrast with belief and ignorance occupy the last part of book V.

The first move (at 476e) is taken from Parmenides' main thesis, reiterating that to know is to know something, and that is to know something that exists, that is there. The opposite state is ignorance, related to what does not exist. Given these two faculties or states of mind (which Plato calls *dynameis*), it is possible to distinguish a third, *doxa* ("belief" or "opinion") between the two, and relate them all to different objects. The object of knowledge (*epistēmē*) is what exists, the object of ignorance (*agnoia*) is what does not exist, and between them then must be the object of *doxa*, what is and is not. This is said to characterize phenomena generally because they are imperfect and unstable. Beautiful sights and sounds, for example, shift according to circumstances, being beautiful at some times and not others, or the expression "double" can sometimes mean its opposite of "half" (as 4 is double 2 and half 8). Plato is saying in effect that we cannot believe and know the same things: we can have beliefs or opinions about the *unknowable*, such as life after death or the origins of the cosmos, but the unchanging objects of mathematics are *knowable*, we can claim knowledge of them, and be assured of their truth. The mathematician works with ideal circles and numbers when making his calculations and reaching true conclusions, and his diagrams drawn in the sand are only particular rough reminders of the real objects. Similarly, it is expected that the true statesman or philosopher would know ideal justice and look to this and apply his knowledge of it when dealing with particular cases of just and unjust actions. In a contrast reminiscent of Heraclitus, most people are said to be like those asleep or dreaming in their state of *doxa* related to the changing world around them, while the few, the true lovers of wisdom, are awake, having knowledge of unchanging forms.

Sun, line and cave

The contrast between, on the one hand, knowledge, which is secure, based on sound reason and concerned with reality, and, on the other hand, shifting opinion, related to perceived particulars, which themselves are constantly changing, was developed further in book VI of the *Republic* and at the beginning of book VII in three famous passages known as: (i) the simile of the sun; (ii) the diagram of the line; and (iii) the allegory of the cave. These are introduced when Socrates says that the highest *mathēma* (object of knowledge) is the form of the good. This he refuses to define directly, but he is ready to give some indication of its nature in analysing the functions of its offspring, the sun. As the sun gives light to this world, and allows the eyes to see both the sun itself and other phenomena, so the form of the good gives truth to forms, and allows the mind to know both itself and other forms. Furthermore, as the sun is also responsible for the birth and nourishment of what is seen, so the form of the good is responsible for the being and reality of the forms that are known. The distinctions are developed further in (ii), the divided Line, which starts:

> Take a line divided into unequal sections (*A, B*) and divide each section again in the same proportion, and you will have the parts related in respect of *clarity* and *obscurity*. In the visible (section *A*) one subsection (*a'*) represents *images*, the other subsection (*b'*) the *objects which the images resemble* – animals, plants and the whole range of manufactured articles.   (*Republic* 509d)

The longer section (*B*) is divided into subsection (*a*), mathematical forms, which are not completely independent of the physical world in that images from it (such as triangles drawn in the sand) are used in theorems about mathematical form (such as triangularity itself), and section (b) which deals only with forms "through them and to them and concludes with them". Each section has its own related state of mind: (*a'*) "guessing" (*eikasia*); (*b'*) "conviction" (*pistis*); (*a*) calculation (*dianoia*); and (*b*) understanding (*nous*). The ratios of the sections (*a'*:*b'* :: *a*:*b* :: *A*:*B*) show, in terms of "clarity" and "obscurity", that true understanding relates to calculation as the conviction coming from seeing an original relates to the previous guessing from a shadow or reflection.

A		B		
visible, belonging with opinion		*intelligible, belonging with knowledge*		
a'	*b'*	*a*	*b*	
guessing	conviction	calculating	understanding	(states of mind)
images	*originals of images*	*mathematical forms using images*	*forms*	(objects)

In (iii), the allegory of the cave (514a–518e), these distinctions between the states of mind of opinion and knowledge and their related objects – perceptible phenomena and cognitive reality – are vividly and dynamically portrayed. The setting is an underground cave, with prisoners tied to their seats, looking straight ahead at a wall on which move shadows cast from a fire, which illuminates moving objects carried along a low barrier behind the prisoners.[5] Suppose one of the prisoners is released and turned round. Having previously seen only shadows, he would now first see the objects that are the originals of the shadows, and then the fire behind them, which provides the illumination for the shadows. If he then staggered up the incline from the dark cave to the bright world above, his eyes would be dazzled, and, to adjust his vision, he would look first at shadows and reflections, then at the trees that cast the shadows, then up at the night sky and finally at the sun itself in broad daylight. The process is painful; the prisoner is unwilling to make the effort and he is dazzled and confused at each stage. Only when he sees the sun (which represents the highest form, that of the good), does he understand everything; he is happy for himself, and feels pity for the others. His journey represents a long and arduous progress in education, from having opinions about appearances during his time in the cave to knowing the true reality of the upper world. The capacity for knowledge, comparable to that of sight, is innate in everyone, but the soul, which has this capacity, must be turned round *as a whole* from the world of change until the mind's eye can bear to look straight at reality.

Knowledge through education, *erōs* and memory

In the *Republic* the way for the soul to make the journey from opinion to knowledge is through a strict and difficult ten-year programme of higher education, consisting of a study of the principles of arithmetic, geometry, stereometry, astronomy and harmonics. These disciplines are an appropriate preliminary to philosophy in that they train the mind to turn from the world of sight to the world of thought: from particulars to the forms. Finally, the student is ready to study dialectic, which makes no use of the senses, but by means of reason goes to the essential reality of each entity and does not stop until it reaches the forms, and ultimately the form of the good. Education here would supplement, perhaps even replace, two other means that had been suggested for bridging the gap between the visible world and that of the forms, namely love (*erōs*) in the *Symposium* and *Phaedrus*, and memory in *Meno* and *Phaedo*.

The journey of love, described in the *Symposium* by the priestess Diotima, moves, like that of education in the *Republic*, from the particular to the universal. The lover first falls in love with a beautiful body, which enhances his appreciation of physical beauty in all its instances. From this appreciation he recognizes that beauty of soul is superior to that of the body as discourses (*logoi*) are generated between the lover and the beloved. But then a superior beauty is recognized in actions and laws, and higher still are the sciences and technical knowledge. Finally the lover faces the "vast sea of beauty", and the desire to know drives him, through reasoning and thinking, to catch sight of a special kind of knowledge, which has as its object the constant and eternal form of beauty (*Symposium* 210a–211b). Later, in the *Phaedrus* myth, there is a development of the relationship described in the *Symposium*, in that the two together, lover and beloved, cooperate in their moral and intellectual partnership, and eventually may "grow their wings" and return to their place in the revolution of the heavens. There they contemplate the true reality with which true knowledge is concerned: "that absolute knowledge which corresponds to what is absolutely real in the fullest sense" (249c).

Alongside the process of education and the power of love, Plato suggests that the third means of reaching the intellectual world from the visible is through memory. This comes first in the *Meno* in the "geometry experiment" (82b–86a). To show a way out of the dilemma that we cannot start on the search for knowledge from a state of complete ignorance (for we would not recognize the truth even if we chanced on it), Socrates draws in the sand a square of side two units with an area of four square units, and questions a slave about it. If the square is doubled to eight square units what then would be the length of the side? The slave's first, obvious, answer is to double the side to four units, but this gives an area of sixteen square units. His second answer therefore is a number higher than two and less than four, so obviously three, but this gives an area of nine square units, when an area of eight is needed. The slave gives up, so Socrates takes him through the geometrical representation of the puzzle until the slave answers correctly that the square of area eight square units is the square on the diagonal of the 2 × 2 square. Socrates draws two conclusions for Meno, who is observing the dialogue. First, the *elenchos*, the examination of the slave, has removed his false knowledge on the length of the side, and has stimulated the search for true knowledge: what *is* the correct answer? Secondly, since he has not learnt geometry in this life, he must have known it before he was born, and he has *remembered* the correct answer. Therefore, "If the truth about reality is always in our soul, then the soul must be immortal, and we must be brave and try to discover – that is to remember – what we do not happen to know (or more correctly remember) at a given moment" (*Meno* 86b).

In the proofs for the immortality of the soul in the *Phaedo* we have seen how Plato, through Socrates, again brought forward the suggestion that knowing is remembering. This argument started from the assumption that we do not meet with any perfect examples of qualities such as "equal", "beautiful" or "just" in this world, but we are able to recognize their imperfections and judge how far they fall short of the ideal. We can only do this because we already *know* about perfect equality, beauty, justice and the like from an existence before birth, and are reminded of them now. The next *Phaedo* argument previewed the contrast of two worlds, the visible and the intelligible, which was to play a central role in the *Republic* in the illustrations of sun, line and cave. Here Socrates compares the simple, unchanging, immortal, invisible, pure and divine forms that are the objects of knowledge with composite, changing, mortal, visible particulars that are the objects of sense-perceptions. The body belongs with the latter, but the soul, although not one of the forms, is like them in being imperceptible and connected with ruling and knowing; it is therefore likely to have the other characteristics of divinity and immortality (78c–80d). These two points from the *Phaedo*, of knowledge as recollection and forms contrasted with particulars, become entangled with the philosophical discussion of the life of the soul as separate from the body. This is resolved in the end by an eschatological myth, the truth of which is guaranteed, not by knowledge, but by persuasive opinion (114d).

The use of forms and their apprehension by reason was crucial to the arguments concerning philosophical activity in *Phaedo* and *Republic*, but, as we have seen, in the later *Theaetetus* the attempt was made to examine the nature of knowledge without bringing them into the discussions. This would suggest, along with the criticisms of forms at the beginning of *Parmenides*, written at about the same time, that Plato was becoming increasingly dissatisfied with a two-level ontology, which restricted knowledge and truth to the eternally unchanging, and opinion to shifting phenomena. This tendency is supported by the dialogue *Sophist*, linked to *Theaetetus*, where only five forms are used – being, same, other, rest and movement – which are compared to "vowels" interweaving among consonants; they make discourse meaningful, without any moral implications.

Knowledge and the structure of the sciences

Aristotle's main reaction to Plato's approaches to the problem of knowledge was to challenge the *separation* of forms from perceptible objects. In the "middle" dialogues, Plato's forms had been set in a world of their own, characterized as the true, consistent subject matter of knowledge accessed by reason, and contrasted with our familiar, constantly changing world, about which there could be no knowledge, but only opinions and beliefs. For Aristotle the two worlds are contiguous, defined by the path of the moon. In his theory the realm above the moon in which the planets move continuously in perfect circles is for ever unchanging, whereas that below is subject to generation, growth and decay. Knowledge of both is possible but, whereas that of the eternal is eternally true, that of the shifting particulars that make up the natural world cannot be invariably true but only "for the most part", a position midway between certain knowledge of timeless and necessary truths and ignorance of the unknowable, which is due to accident or chance.

From another perspective, Aristotle regarded objective knowledge as "theoretical", contrasting it with both "practical" knowledge, which is concerned with day-to-day living, and "productive" knowledge, which aims at some beautiful or useful result, such as a sculptor's statue or a doctor's cure. Then he made a further threefold subdivision of theoretical science into: (i) mathematics; (ii) natural science; and (iii) theology (*Metaphysics* 1026a18). Where Plato had seen the mathematician using diagrams of triangles and squares as visual aids to abstract reasoning about the perfect triangle and the square, Aristotle claims that the mathematician studies actual physical objects but *as* triangles or squares: "the unchanging but material", in his terminology. Natural science is concerned with physical objects, animate and inanimate, changing and material, in the world around us, to be studied as they are; from them we can deduce comprehensive principles that are relevant to generation, movement and decay. Theology, or "first philosophy", on the other hand, is not at all related to the world around us, but deals with the immaterial and unchanging, concerned with the heavenly bodies in their rotations, and including the cause of their rotation: the "unmoved mover" or "pure being", named as *theos*.

All of these divisions of *theoretical* knowledge, according to Aristotle, are pursued for their own sakes, in the disinterested study of what there is, and the related primary principles. *Practical* knowledge, in contrast, has as its subject matter human beings themselves, in their individual interests, characters and decisions (the study called *ethics*), and also in their relationships with each other in institutions and societies (the subject matter of *politics*). Lastly there is *productive* knowledge, which deals with art, poetry and rhetoric. Philosophical *logic*, the development of which is regarded as one of Aristotle's greatest achievements, he viewed as the pervasive *organon* (literally "tool"). It is involved in all the different spheres of knowledge, laying down the general principles, the standards of truth and the methods of argument that govern their study.

This great structure of the patterns of human knowledge had a place for all the branches of learning. Aristotle's colleagues in the Lyceum would be able to slot into this framework a particular subject of investigation and make some advances, keeping to the principles of that subject and interweaving its essential properties. Geometry, for example, starts from geometric data to solve geometric problems through deductive theorems, and arithmetic works with numbers in its own calculations. Each science has its own distinctive nature, although one might help another with *practical* difficulties such as arise with mechanics or harmonics. Only random coincidences or chance occurrences are illogical and inexplicable, and so unknowable. The results for each science can be true (or at least hold "for the most part"), and the body of knowledge can be increased in any given area, provided that the reasoning involved is valid; and it was to this end that Aristotle devised his complex system of logic.

Aristotelian advances in knowing

There are two ways in which new truth may be acquired, according to Aristotle. In the first, one moves from the particular to the general, by the method of *induction* (which, he said, originated with Socrates). By taking a characteristic common to a series of instances we can discover a general rule that would cover cases not yet examined. This is the way in which doctors and lawyers work to produce a set of medical or legal principles. On the other hand there is *deduction* or "demonstration" (*apodeixis*), which moves from the general to the particular. This can be through perception and familiarity, as in the engaging example of toddlers, who at first call all men "daddy" and all women "mummy" until they learn to differentiate the individual from the class (*Physics* 184b12).

In formal deduction the *syllogism* is used, explained as a *logos* (a "type of argument") "in which statements are made, and something other than what is stated follows necessarily from them" (*Prior Analytics* 24b18). Here the starting-point, the initial premise, may be: (i) a self-evident truth (such as the "law of contradiction" – that at the same time and in the same respect "is" and "is not" cannot both be true); (ii) a mathematical axiom (for example "if equals are taken from equals, equals remain"); or (iii) a common conception in ethics that is generally acceptable (such as "self-control and endurance are praiseworthy"). The syllogism then makes a valid deduction from the initial premise through a middle term to a conclusion. The most common are the "always true" type (all B is A, all C is B, therefore all C is A), and those partially or "for the most part" true (all B is A, some C is B, therefore some *C* is *A*). The conclusion could then in turn be the first premise of a further syllogism in a continuing thread of argument.

As he worked through the ways in which schemes of study could be classified and validated Aristotle was concerned above all to find *order* in the advances of human reasoning. This was shown especially in his comprehensive biological works, where he focused on classifications into *genus* and *species*. By such means it would be ultimately possible to reach correct definitions that would pin down what a thing is in its essence. This relates to his famous "four causes" (or, more exactly, "explanations"). Aristotle expected that understanding the fourfold explanation of (i) *agent* (who or what is responsible for *x*?), (ii) *matter* (what is it made of?), (iii) *form* (what is its shape or structure?) and (iv) *purpose* (what is it for?) would secure knowledge of particulars. He recognized that this method of explanation linked him to the Presocratics, who foreshadowed his own position as philosophers concerned with truth, and dealing with principles and causes, although in a more restricted way (*Metaphysics* 983a24–b5). The fact that none of his predecessors dealt with any causes or explanations not covered by his own fourfold scheme encouraged him to see his own as complete. His disagreement with Plato on "formal cause" was not on the principle that explaining the form was the main indication of knowing what a thing is, but that for Aristotle form was not separate and unique (as in Plato's theory), but inherent and multiple, present in the many particulars that shared the one essential nature.

Epicureans and Stoics on knowledge

In many ways the Epicureans and Stoics who came after Plato and Aristotle followed the guidelines laid down by their distinguished predecessors in their theories of knowledge. They too recognized the power of dialectic, which brought with it the assurance of valid argument, a firm foundation for knowledge and the tools to withstand opposition. The notion of a *criterion* of truth was developed, and Lucretius' poem shows that a variety of arguments, evidence and literary devices was used to explain and support the wisdom of Epicurean teaching. The Stoics, in contrast, extended Aristotle's forms of syllogism into propositional logic, reducing complex arguments to their simplest format and then setting out rules for the interaction of the propositions involved (as in the example "if it is day, it is light, but it is day, so it is light" or "but it is not day so it is not light"). They also believed in the innate capacity for reason, arising from primary natural instincts, and maintained that, as children mature, encouraged first by the appropriate environment and then by education, they begin to understand how actions follow instinct and to choose accordingly; when the habit of so choosing is formed, the conditions are ripe for the emergence of wisdom and for action as a moral agent. Subsequent knowledge is built up from first impressions in a series of stages that were illustrated by the founder of Stoicism as follows:

> Zeno would spread out the fingers of one hand and display its open palm, saying "an impression is like this". Next he clenched his fingers a little and said "assent is like this". Then, pressing his fingers close together to make a fist he said that this was cognition, and finally he brought his left hand over his right fist, gripping it tightly, and called this final stage "scientific knowledge" (*epistēmē*, Latin "scientia").   (Cicero, *Academica* 2.145)

Although only the "wise man" would reach complete knowledge, progress towards the ideal was possible for all, and in reaching at least as far as the "clenched fist" position, the Stoics recognized that all human beings, since they are endowed with reason, have the natural faculty to distinguish genuine from misleading impressions, and therefore truth from falsehood.

According to Plato it has been shown that our capacity for reasoning is innate, and should be directed to the goal of recognizing the enduring objects of knowledge and their interaction with each other. Those with the brightest minds have a duty, on maturity, to engage in political leadership, but may return gratefully in retirement to the better life of intellectual studies. Aristotle similarly claimed that the desire to know is instinctive, and found that it could be developed in the pursuit of individual sciences as well as in theoretical contemplation. Epicureans and Stoics followed them in the recognition, central to their epistemology, that the very processes of learning and understanding are advanced human activities, and justify the direct engagement in philosophy.

7. Leadership, law and the origins of political theory

This chapter explores some aspects of ancient political philosophy concerned with the emergence of political communities, leadership, freedom, justice and democracy, natural law, social contracts and constitutional theory.

Political anthropology

Modern theories on the emergence of states tend to focus on their origins in conquest or in social and economic cooperation; the Greeks, however, looked for the origins of states in the willing consent of individuals to submit to law to ensure the freedom, security and territory of the political unit. This thesis was often supported by narratives of founding heroes, national rituals and patron divinities, even as the ideology might be undermined by questioning the validity of the traditions. Human skills in establishing states could be viewed mythically as the gifts of Prometheus, Athena or Hephaestos, or be praised as achievements in their own right: "Humans have taught themselves speech and swift thought, / and how to live in a city and abide by its laws" (Sophocles *Antigone*, 354–60).

The first articulated view of the past was in the "golden age" mythology set out in Hesiod's *Works and Days* (109–201). First there was a "golden race of mortal men" under Kronos; they lived a simple, pastoral life, free of toil and sickness, enjoying the bounty of nature in innocence, peace and mutual friendship. This was followed by a degeneration into a "silver" and then a literal bronze age, of powerful war-loving soldiers with weapons and tools of bronze, who brought about their own destruction. The sequence was interrupted with the race of heroes (to account for the tradition of the Trojan war and the Theban sagas), and now we have the race of iron, where life is hard, as we work, grieve, waste and die. There is also moral degeneration, rife with insolence, perjury, wickedness and godless destruction, and soon "Justice and Honour will leave the blood-soaked earth" (Hesiod, *Works and Days* 196–200).[1] Remnants of the original "golden age" were still thought to exist in remote parts of the world: in the south among the Ethiopians, in the north among the Hyperboreans, and in the centre, hemmed in by mountains, among the Arcadians, the oldest race on earth. This mythology of simple people, remote from civilization and uncorrupted by the wrongs of social and political life, led to the idea of the "noble savage" in historical times. Examples were the Persians, who were taught to "ride, shoot a straight arrow and speak the truth" (Herodotus 1.136), and the Scythians, beyond the Danube. In Rome there was admiration for the Germans and the Parthians, and sometimes for foreign chieftains brought to Rome in triumph, such as Jugurtha from Africa and Caractacus from Britain, whose moral superiority shamed their technically advanced conquerors. The history of civil wars in Rome, and the memory of their origins as simple farmers, also strengthened the Roman sense of degeneration from an earlier age.[2]

Contrary to this nostalgia for the past was an optimism, advanced in myth and argument, of progress from an earlier brutish cave-dwelling existence, and pride in human inventiveness and advanced technology that was continually improving the standard of living. The tragedy *Prometheus Bound*, attributed to Aeschylus, lists, in the gifts of Prometheus, the means of advancing from a primitive existence; they included the discovery of housing, recognizing the changing seasons from the stars, taming animals for physical labour, and the use of numbers, writing, sailing ships, medicine and mining. Protagoras similarly, in Plato's dialogue named after him, tells of human beings, aided by Prometheus, discovering articulate speech, building shelters and acquiring the basic necessities of life. But they were dying out for want of political skill, and so Zeus sent Hermes to impart the virtues of *aidōs* and *dikē* ("self-respect" and "fair dealings with others", which together make up political *aretē*), to the human race: not to just a few (like medical or musical skill) but to everyone (*Protagoras* 322d). Because of the universal nature of these gifts, Protagoras argues that everyone can contribute to the well-being of the state, the *polis*, and democracy is justified. Even so, care, practice, training and instruction from childhood are still needed, to bring the natural talent for *aretē* to fruition in the life of justice, holiness and self-mastery (325a). When their education is complete the citizens are expected to follow the laws that the *polis* has established for the good of all.

In the *Republic*, Plato, through Socrates, gives a version, in a "thought experiment", of the emergence of a *polis* from the mutual needs of individuals who pool their basic resources and their specialist skills. The result is a small, self-sufficient community living a peaceful, healthy life, and enjoying a simple vegetarian diet. Far from being considered an ideal, this community is scorned as "a city of pigs" (*Republic* 372d). Surely some comfort and a few luxuries are required, but their acquisition leads to contact with outsiders, and eventually the need for an army. Then one or more rulers are necessary, to maintain the unity and harmony of the whole. The metals that were used by Hesiod to characterize different races are here applied to classes, in Plato's own "myth of the metals" (415a–c). The citizens must come to understand that they were all born from the earth and so are one family, but the guardian-rulers, the most prestigious, are "golden", with gold in their composition, the military "silver" and the industrial and agricultural classes "bronze" and "iron". Although occasionally the child of a "golden" citizen may be demoted or that of a silver or bronze citizen promoted, in general the class divisions are to be accepted as a permanent feature in the state, necessary for its order and stability.

Aristotle takes a different line in his reconstruction of the formation of the *polis*. He starts from the natural pairing of male and female, which ensures the continuation of the species, and then proceeds with a second natural pairing, that of ruling and ruled, master and slave, the one providing guidance and the other the physical strength to carry out the work required. In this way a household was formed, of man, wife, child and slave, and the combining of several households resulted in the first grouping of a village. A number of scattered villages then cooperated for mutual advantage, and the *polis* emerged, still based on the pattern of the household with a senior member or "king" (*Politics* 1252a24–53b1). The power of speech brings with it the ability to communicate, and this, along with the perception of good and evil, makes the *human* association, which started from the need for self-preservation, the natural environment for living the best kind of life. Human beings are "political animals" in that they reach their full potential in the life of the *polis* maintained by justice and law; only creatures below them and gods above them can survive and flourish in isolation.

The most striking and detailed account of primitive life and its development into the civilized life of the city is found in the fifth book of Lucretius' poem (5.925–1149); this is the official Epicurean view, which goes back to Epicurus and perhaps even further to Democritus himself.[3] It is a direct attack on "golden age" mythology, and is based in the beginning on a version of the "survival of the fittest". Lucretius describes the life of human beings in the Stone Age as nasty, brutish and short. They were physically tough, roamed naked with stones and clubs, living in woods and caves on a raw diet of acorns and berries. What was needed to survive was the ability to feed and reproduce, and then to excel in cunning, strength and speed. In time the men built shelters, were clothed in skins, discovered fire (which was essential for warmth, cooking, protection and the beginning of technology), and, most importantly, developed language and the means of communication.[4] Family units joined up into societies for mutual protection and cities were built, and ruled by kings, who promoted ability, beauty and physical strength.

Eventually gold was discovered and mined, and, with the acquisition of property, wealth became the criterion for success. The kings were overthrown, and there was widespread violence and disorder, with each man struggling for himself. It was at this stage that a "mutual contract of social peace" arose:

> Some showed how to form a constitution, based on fixed rights
> and recognised laws. The human race, worn out by a life of violence
> and weakened by feuds, was the more ready to submit, of their own free will,
> to the bonds of statutes and strict laws.   (5.1143–6)

Leadership in Homer

Before considering the implications of such a "mutual contract" for social peace in the reality of democracies in fifth-century Greece, there is a third tradition concerning prehistory to add to those of degeneration from a better age in the past and progress from a primitive life to one of an advanced society. This derives from ideas about the criteria for authority and leadership, the restraints placed on the leader, and the voluntary cooperation with him, that are found in Homer's *Iliad*.

The commander-in-chief (Agamemnon in the *Iliad*) claims that his authority, which gives him rule over "many islands and all Argos", is a "divine right" from Zeus, legitimized by his sceptre, which had been passed down in hereditary succession to its present owner. In addition to this honour the leader is "better" in that he is physically stronger, rules more men and has superior armed forces, but, if he becomes avaricious and inconsiderate towards his men, this power base cracks, as Achilles reminds Agamemnon: "How can you expect loyal service from the soldiers, / when you send them on a raid or into battle, / if you are always aiming at your own profit?" (*Il* 1.150–51).

Another claim to authority rests on seniority. Because he is older as well as more kingly, Agamemnon demands submission from Achilles, and also argues that Patroclus is less noble and less strong than Achilles, but he is older, and so should restrain him. The aged Nestor above all has this authority, and with it the wisdom of the years and the voice of experience. Yet the younger leaders, too, who are expected to be outstanding in personal courage and fighting skills, must also have *euboulia* (wise counsel), if they are to maintain their control; there is glory to be won in the assembly as well as on the battlefield.[5]

The practice of holding an assembly of the commander-in-chief with the "warrior-lords" acts as a check on the power of the leader and his "divine right" to authority. In formal assembly the warrior-lords could oppose the "king", and he must tread warily since he needs their support. He cannot be too greedy or self-assertive, for, if the honour of the individual lords is not respected, or they do not share in an equitable division of the spoils of war, they may well just leave the fray with their contingent of soldiers, as Achilles threatens to do. The sceptre, as well as legitimizing kingship, also ensures authority in truce-making, law-giving and advising. The sceptre Achilles uses has been held at different times by judges to safeguard their judgements and verdicts (their *themistes*). It is passed round in the assembly to give an individual the right to speak and to command respect while he holds it, even if he speaks against the leader; the leader would do well to listen to any opposition and be ready to carry out the advice offered.

In addition, the privileges of leadership have to be paid for on the battlefield. Odysseus is told that he should be ahead of his troops, since he is first to be invited to table and enjoys the finest meat and wine. And an alternative version to "divine right" as the basis for authority occurs when the best fighters and thinkers may be given privileges *voluntarily* by their people, but in return they are expected to fight in the front line and bear the brunt of battle. Rights bring obligations.[6]

Political communities and the rule of law

In the *Iliad*, the Lycians were willing to submit to authority especially because it was in their own interest; in time of war their survival depended on the heroism of their leaders. But how could such willing cooperation be transferred to civilian life in the *polis*? There is one reference to the solution in Sparta in a fragment of a poem called *Eunomia* (Hesiod's word for "good government") by the Spartan Tyrtaeus:

> The kings (who have their honour from the gods) and the elders
>   should begin;
> then the men of the people should say what is honourable and
>   do what is just,
> and none give crooked counsel to the city;
> then victory and power will belong to the people. (fr. 3, Bergk)

The Homeric trilogy of kings, lords and soldiers is here replicated in the "mixed constitution" of kings, elders and commoners. The combined assembly now includes the third class, who enjoy the ordered rights of speech and are free to give advice. If *their* counsel is wise and honourable, and their actions just, then the city as a whole will prosper.

It was the Athenians who claimed to be the inventors of law and to have established the first constitution. This is brought out in Pericles' famous funeral speech in the second book of Thucydides, and summarized by the orator Lysias:

> The early Athenians conducted the city's affairs by law in the
> spirit of free men, for they thought it the action of wild animals
> to prevail over one another by violence. Human beings should
> make law the touchstone of what is right, and reasoned speech the

means of persuasion, then subject themselves in action to these two powers – law their king and reason their tutor.   (2.18–19)[7]

In sixth-century Athens, the political reformer and poet Solon, who was given a year to bring order to the *polis*, started with the basic principle of respect for ordinary people. "Goodness" (*aretē*) was no longer to be the exclusive prerogative of birth and rank but was open to everyone, and so emerged as a general *moral* quality rather than being focused on excellence in leadership. The worth and rights of the *dēmos* were beginning to be recognized and the people were given a share in government as a way of ending the disorder (*dysnomia*) caused by a combination of their self-destructive anarchy and the avarice of the nobles plundering the city's wealth. Solon's reforms aimed to reconcile the two factions; he defended both sides, as he claimed in his fifth *Elegy*, and "did not allow to either an unjust victory". His theory was that mutual tolerance and respect result in good order (*eunomia*), and the political restraints imposed by the recognition of rights and obligations between the classes enable the state to function. It is in the citizens' interest to maintain its stability and smooth progress through the observance of its own just laws. A passage from Herodotus illustrates the advantage of this willing submission to law in wartime. The exiled Spartan king Demaratus explains to Xerxes how a small contingent of Greeks can dare to oppose the vast Persian army, with no one commanding them:

> The Greeks are free, but not entirely free, for they do have a master and that master is law, whom they fear even more than your subjects fear you. They do whatever this master commands, and his commandment is always the same: not to retreat in battle, against whatever odds, but to stand firm, to conquer or to die.
>
> (7.104)

The *polis* then emerges as a limited, independent, self-governing and self-defending citizen body, regulated by its own constitution, bound into a social and political unit, and fiercely conscious of its own individuality. The underlying principles continued to be put into effect in the spread of *colonies*, sent out by a mother-state. The colonies again are independent units, peopled by citizens who have equal standing, are allotted equal land rights, and are all bound by the constitution of the initial duly appointed "law-giver".

The understanding of the *theory* of political progress and its significance was set out before the citizen body in Athens when they assembled in the theatre. This is illustrated by two examples from the tragedies of Aeschylus. At the end of the *Oresteia* trilogy the tradition of blood-vengeance was finally replaced by due process of law. The Furies, who had implemented the old order, were transformed and incorporated into the new order, and the earlier terror was replaced by that civilized respect for law that would ensure the security and defence of the emerging *polis*. The city's patron goddess Athena, who herself is identified with the reconstituted city, and represents its wise seriousness, summarizes the position:

> Respectful awe (*sebas*) and fear his kinsman, shall keep the people from acting unjustly by day and night … I counsel the people to despise both anarchy and despotism, and not to cast out fear entirely from the city, for what man will be just who has nothing to fear? Respect for law, held in due dread, safeguards the city and defends its territory, such as is found nowhere else.
>
> (*Eumenides* 690–702)

The second example is from the *Suppliants*, and shows the power of the king restrained by the will of the people. The Argive ruler has to choose between refusing asylum to the suppliants, or becoming involved in a war with Egypt. Although he is sole ruler, he cannot act without the people's endorsement, and so gives their decision: "The city's vote, democratically taken, has decreed that the women should not be surrendered. It is fixed permanently, not inscribed on wax or parchment, but clearly spoken by free men" (*Suppliants* 942–5). The single ruler is bound to act according to the collective will of his people.

One further and famous example from drama, however, in Sophocles' *Antigone*, shows a conflict between a ruler and his people, and between constitutional law and a higher, unwritten law. Creon, the king, is attempting to restore stable government to Thebes after civil war. His opening "policy speech" introduces many familiar points, including the city's guarantee of the security of its citizens ("our city is our life"), the "ship of state" analogy when the state is set back on course after the political storms, and a summary of the evils following civil discord. But the opposition of abstract concepts here is not between Solon's *dysnomia* and *eunomia* ("bad law" and "good law"), but between destructive anarchy (literally *an-archia*, "no government") and a more sinister addition to the political vocabulary, *peitharchia* (unremitting obedience to the established government). Creon's thesis is that strong rule at the top, accepted by all the citizens, is in everyone's interest as the way to survive. Antigone's counter-thesis is that transient human laws are themselves subservient to a greater authority:

> Zeus did not declare this to me nor did Justice,
> who lives with the gods below, define such laws for men.
> I did not think that you, a mortal, had the power to override
> the unalterable, unwritten laws of the gods.
> These are not for today or yesterday but live for ever,
> and no one knows from where they come.   (450–57)

And Antigone sacrifices her life in obedience to these higher laws.[8]

Law and justice in individual, state and cosmos

So the rule of one man over many, which Aristotle saw as the natural order based on the unit of the household, came to be abandoned in the Greek states, whether as monarchy or its obverse of tyranny. In war individual heroism shown by the leader in the dash for glory was replaced by ranked hoplite fighting, where cooperation was essential for survival, as each man defended his neighbour on one side and was himself defended on the other. And in peacetime, as we have seen, the state prospered when the citizens freely respected rights and obligations under the rule of law.[9] The political vocabulary of balanced equality became so entrenched that it could be applied by analogy to quite different contexts. Anaximander, right at the beginning of philosophical thinking, in his one surviving fragment, transferred the vocabulary of justice, injustice, reparation and order achieved over time from the *polis* to the *kosmos*. As hot summers follow cold winters, and wet plains balance dry deserts, opposite forces become too powerful and then pay the penalty for their aggression; the behaviour of city-states provides both metaphor and model for cosmic checks and balances.

Alcmaeon made use of a similar pattern of political metaphor and model, applied not to the larger organism of the cosmos, however, but, on a smaller scale and in a medical context, to the individual human being. A variety of opposites (later interpreted as "humours") can, in a sick man, behave like warring factions within a state, and health results when they are evenly balanced. The doctor aims to bring those who are ill back to health by reducing the dominance of one power (*monarchia*) and restoring equilibrium. Far from being the ideal, monarchy is in fact harmful to the organism, and should be checked by a "blending" with its opposite in due measure.[10] This may well connect with Pythagorean political interests in a well-governed city requiring a specific concord among its citizens for the best environment for their moral development. Pythagoras seems to have suggested that a state emerges from the rule of law, which binds the different classes into a *harmonia*, a fitting-together, in a way comparable to the concordant blending of high and low notes producing a melody, and the balance of physical forces resulting in a healthy body and temperament. In addition, the mathematical foundations of the *technai* of music and medicine could be extended to social and commercial relationships, and, in a political theory based on mathematics, the early Pythagoreans applied the vocabulary of ratio, equality and reciprocity to proportionate civil rights.[11]

Heraclitus' *logos* linked human understanding with state law and universal order, but he also used the concept of inter-state strife as a metaphor for opposition on a cosmic scale. On the human battlefield, war reveals those who will achieve heroic status, and among the survivors some men obviously will be slaves and others free, but war (*polemos*) is also given the rank of the Homeric Zeus, and, as the principle of universal opposition, is responsible for and controls all generation.[12] Strife (*eris*) is paired with justice (*dikē*) in that, for Heraclitus, the permanent tension between opposed forces maintains the structure and functioning of both *polis* and *kosmos*. And cosmic justice, backed by cosmic law, is sanctioned by the Furies (the Erinyes, daughters of justice), who were traditionally the avengers of any violation of the natural order. The human perspective may see injustice, but Heraclitus points to an ultimate reconciliation of the apparent inequalities: "To god all things are fair and just, but men suppose some to be just, others unjust" (DK 22B102).

Heraclitus was also ready to connect the one divine law, which binds the universe through all its fluctuations, with human law, which unites the *polis* and maintains its integrity even more than the physical encircling defences:

> Those who speak with sense must put their strength in what is common to all, as a city does in its law, and much more strongly, for all human laws are nourished by the one divine law; for this

165

has as much power as it wishes, and is enough, and more than enough, for all. (B114)

The citizens "must fight for their law as for their city-walls" (B44), for it derives the strength to support the life of the city from an ever-living world-wide law secured by *logos*. This idea was later taken up by Empedocles, who spoke of "a law for all extending through wide-ruling air and measureless sunlight".[13] These Presocratics – Anaximander, Pythagoras, Heraclitus and Empedocles – agreed on independent standards that apply to individuals, the *polis* and the cosmos as a whole. In a tripartite structure the fully human life was seen to be embedded in the *polis*, the *polis* was intermediate between the individual and the cosmos, and the three were linked by harmony and law. The political vocabulary of conflict, justice and restitution, therefore, was related in one direction to parts or opposed forces within the individual and, in the other, to the structure and functioning of the universe. As a median between the two stood the body politic, seen as the individual "writ large", and as a small-scale cosmos.

Plato's analysis of human body and soul in the *Timaeus* was modelled on that of the cosmos and made from the same material, but in a less perfect form. The circuits of human soul strive to imitate the movement of planets and stars and replicate their harmony, and the similar interplay of Same and Different provides the basis for reason about permanent being and the realm of generation and decay. In the *Republic*, however, the emphasis was on the analogy between human soul and the state in the detailed correspondence between political classes and parts of the *psychē*. The task set is to define justice in the individual, and show that one should be just (and moral in a more general sense) for its own sake, whatever the circumstances. Socrates' approach is first to look at justice "writ large" in the *polis*, and then to see "if anything in the conformation of the smaller entity corresponds to what has been found in the larger" (369a). It is assumed that what is right for the state is right for the individual, and this assumption is supported throughout in the details of the analogy derived from the three classes in the state (philosopher/guardians, military/executive and workers/producers) and the three parts of the soul (reason, spirit and appetite). Virtues in state and soul are found to be comparable, as is the parallel degeneration of both, through oligarchy, democracy and finally tyranny in the state and the corresponding individual. Aristotle was in agreement with Plato on two counts here. First, he accepted the three lifestyles in order of merit, ranking as the lowest that which aims at pleasure, the next the one that values honour (gained from the *political* life rather than the military), and the highest that devoted to philosophy; this means that philosophers, who have wisdom and understanding of right and wrong, justice and injustice, would be most suited to government (*Nicomachean Ethics* 1097b17–35).[14] Secondly, since the aim of individuals and the city is the same (to achieve the best life), then the same life is best for each human being individually and for his city, and the same virtues will be relevant for both (*Politics* 1325b30–32).

Making and breaking social contracts

Various forms of cooperation and adaptation were recognized by the Greeks as necessary to enable society to flourish. In the rule of kings in Homer and Hesiod the people would give their kings honour, loyalty and the best of everything, in return for their leadership and heroism in battle; or the authority of the kings might be restrained by the need to maintain the loyalty of the warrior-lords or by the verdict of formal assembly. In peacetime the justice of the king towards the people would bring them prosperity, and, it was expected, blessings from the gods. With the rise of the Greek city-states and the emergence of democracy within them it was realized that efficient government could result from abandoning monarchic rule, and acknowledging instead the rights of all, bringing the citizens together into a complex but healthy organic structure. This brought with it the concept of law, which could have authority over and above the individuals who proposed and ratified the constitutional changes. The citizens *consented* to government in their own interests and for the good of the whole, since respect for their law was likely to bring victory in war, and freedom, security and stability in peace.

When Socrates was in prison awaiting execution, according to Plato, his friend Crito tried to persuade him to escape. Socrates' response was to reject the offer of life in exile, and to suppose that the personified Laws of Athens gave the reason why. The Laws explain that there is a form of "contract" between them and the citizens of Athens. For their part the Laws legitimize marriages and the birth of subsequent children, ensure their education and throughout their lives give them protection and security in a prosperous environment. In return the citizens agree to defend the city when required, and to obey the Laws in courts of justice, in extreme cases even submitting to execution if that is the verdict resulting from the due processes of the court. The citizens agree to the terms, and show their agreement by living permanently in the city; if they disagree, then they are free to leave and live elsewhere, in a lawless or supposedly more lenient state. Socrates had lived all his life in Athens, enjoying the advantages of life there, and now he must keep to his part of the "contract". Socrates insists that he has to do as the Laws of Athens require, and not leave in a dishonourable way, "returning wrong for wrong, breaking agreements and injuring those who should be most honoured – himself, his friends, his country and his country's laws" (*Crito* 54c).

There was, however, another version of the "social contract" put forward by the more unscrupulous sophists: that there was an agreement among the weaker citizens in the *polis* to band together and make up laws to keep the strong in check. This was the tradition according to *nomos*, the voluntary surrender of individual freedom in exchange for the benefits of social order, but by nature, *physis*, the strong could do as they wished, if they had the power, and rewrite the laws to their own advantage.

The first statement of this glorification of the "state of nature" that brings with it the boast that "might is right" comes in Hesiod's fable of the hawk and the nightingale:

The nightingale, gripped in the hawk's talons, begged for mercy, but the hawk replied: "Miserable creature, why are you crying? One far stronger than you holds you fast, and you will go where I take you, for all your lovely singing. I shall eat you if I want to, or set you free. Only a fool tries to fight against the stronger, for he loses the contest, and suffers pain as well as shame".

(*Works and Days* 202–12)

The Athenians as a whole took up this attitude in the famous "Melian debate", as reported by Thucydides. Melos was a small island in the Cretan sea, a colony of Sparta, which stayed neutral in the Peloponnesian War. The Athenians, however, in 416 BCE, insisted that the Melians join the Athenian Empire and pay tribute. An embassy was sent from Melos to present their case before the Athenians, and the historian gives the arguments on both sides in the form of a frank debate (Thucydides 5.17). The Melians asked to remain neutral. They claimed that their cause was just and favoured by the gods, and warned that if the Athenians moved against Melos it would arouse further hostility to the empire from both their allies and the Spartans. The Athenians replied that, as the stronger, they would act in their own interests and not take moral issues into account; they believed that the gods, too, rule where they can, that the Spartans would, as always, follow the safe path of expediency, and that the allies would consider prudence before honour. The Melians refused to submit, and the Athenians immediately used their superior force against them, destroyed their city, killed the men and sold the women and children into slavery.[15]

Protagoras had explained, in the mythical form of the gifts of Hermes, how human beings are by nature self-respecting in their private lives and just in their dealing with others, but he also put forward a relativist view, according to which individuals make up their own minds about right and wrong and act accordingly. Morality, in fifth-century Athens, became a tussle between the creation of shifting codes of conduct to suit the individual, and the assertion of unchanging values. In the political sphere, those who maintained that there are external guidelines for behaviour, based on objective goods and enshrined in laws that have intrinsic force, now had to *argue* against those who would say that justice may well consist in obeying the laws and customs of the city, but the contrary demands of natural desires and expediency struggle against such imposition, and will override them if the opportunity allows. So there was a second source of disagreement concerning the "natural state": whether we are good by nature, and "born for citizenship" in Aristotle's phrase (*Politics* 1252a24), or whether, in the natural condition, men are selfish and rapacious, and it is according to nature, for human beings and animals alike, that the stronger should have more than the weaker. In the latter view "taking what one can" may be called shameful and wrong by the weaker citizens as they try to frighten the stronger into obeying the city's laws, but any laws so devised as a restraint will be broken with impunity by the unscrupulous and powerful, following their natural instincts.

This point of view is set out by the sophist Thrasymachus, as represented by Plato in the first book of the *Republic* (which may well have been written earlier, and independently of the rest of the dialogue). He makes a blistering attack on Socrates' agreement with the previous speaker that the true ruler, on the analogy of the good shepherd, looks to the interest of his subjects, and everything he says and does is for their advantage. Thrasymachus instead retorts that the shepherd tends the sheep and fattens them up not for *their* well-being but for his own gain. Justice, similarly, is for the good of the stronger and the one in command, and harmful to the one who obeys and serves. A person of great power outdoes everyone else; justice and morality[16] are as he defines them, and he acts accordingly. If he robs the citizens in the process and deprives them of their liberty he is admired and congratulated. Injustice, on a large enough scale, is stronger, freer and more masterly than justice; it is given its bad name only by those who are afraid of suffering it (*Republic* 343a–344c). Thrasymachus' argument is revived by Glaucon in the second book, and presented in a more cogent and orderly manner. First, Glaucon gives the common opinion on the nature and origin of justice, which again involves a form of "social contract". Doing wrong, people say, is preferable to being wronged, but the advantages of wrongdoing are outweighed by the consequences of suffering it, and, since people cannot have both, they agree to forego both. So they make up laws and mutual covenants, and what these laws decree they call "right". Justice has a relative value owing to our failure to do wrong with impunity, and those who practise it do so under compulsion, and not because they think it a good in itself. Anyone who had the power to do wrong would never make any such agreement with anyone – he would be mad if he did (*Republic* 358e–359b). The speech of Callicles in the *Gorgias* vividly portrays this "real man" who is strong enough to flout the conventions that condition good behaviour in the citizens:

> If there arises a man sufficiently endowed by nature, he will shake off and break through and escape from all these trammels; he will tread underfoot our texts and spells and incantations and all our unnatural laws, and by an act of revolt reveal himself our master instead of our slave, in the full blaze of the light of natural justice. (*Gorgias* 484a, trans. Emlyn-Jones)

Constitutional theories

What would be the constitution most adept at keeping blatant self-seeking in check, given the choice of government by an individual, a few men or many? One-man rule (*monarchia*) was, as we have seen, the pattern in Homer, both among human beings and in the rule of Zeus over the Olympians. It was taken up as the ideal condition in

Plato's proposed rule of the philosopher-king, and assumed to be the natural state of affairs for Aristotle, in the household, the *polis* and the cosmos itself (*Metaphysics* 1076a).[17] The first *arguments* for and against monarchy, oligarchy and democracy come in the third book of the historian Herodotus (3.80–82). The setting is the Persian court in 521 BCE, when the king had died without an heir and there was the possibility of a change of constitution, but the debate reflects the fierce controversy in fifth-century Athens over the best form of government, and many of the points raised were taken up by Socrates and Plato.

The first speaker, Otanes, suggests replacing monarchy with democracy. The arguments against a king are that he transgresses ancient laws, is subject to no constraints and, as a result of envy and hubris, breaks out into violent behaviour; in his situation even the best of men would be bound to change for the worse. With democracy, on the other hand, we have *isonomia* (equality before the law); the magistrates are selected by lot and are accountable for their time in office, and there is open debate. The second speaker, Megabyzus, disagrees. The people cannot rule themselves, he says, because they are irresponsible and violent; they have no moral awareness of right and wrong and no intellectual qualifications, but rush blindly into politics like a river in flood. He recommends an oligarchy, for "the best men produce the best policy". Darius in his turn objects to oligarchy because competing for the top offices leads to violent personal feuds, then anarchy and finally bloodshed. In a democracy there are problems with corruption in government and with the strong *philiai*, the tightly knit cartels that are always causing trouble. One ruler is preferable, when he has the wisdom to govern and the ability to control the people.[18]

Aristotle's analysis of constitutions had the same three possibilities: rule by one, few or many. He found for each a correct form, in kingship, aristocracy and republic, which work for the good of the whole, and the corresponding incorrect forms in tyranny, oligarchy and democracy. His preference also was for kingship, but, since it was difficult to find a person endowed with the necessary knowledge and virtue to take on the responsibility of kingship, it could easily slip into tyranny. Similarly with aristocracy (which means, literally, the best, the *aristoi*, in power), there would be a tendency for the class to act in its own interests, and, without any restraints, it would become an oligarchy, characterized by the possession and pursuit of wealth. Democracy, on the other hand, would further the interests of the poor, and their sectional cabals. He therefore advocated the checks and balances of a "mixed" constitution as most likely to ensure the good of the individual citizens and of the *polis* as a whole (*Politics* 3.1). Aristotle suggested that where all the citizens rule and are ruled in turn there would be the framework for cooperation among them for the common good. This could be achieved through a system of rotating "offices", which would be the foundation of the constitution and the source of law. The power of those holding office would be guided by the collective law, and limited by the time of tenure. Citizens would be united to each other and to the *polis* through distributive justice, which would treat them all equally in the context of judicial procedures, recognizing rights and obligations, and, if necessary, imposing penalties if they should be infringed. Although the holders of office would be constantly changing, the laws defining and maintaining government would be permanent and stable, and indeed passed on from one generation to another to ensure the continuity of the common good achieved.[19]

Citizenship

In the Greek *polis* the citizens (*politai*) who were actively engaged in the political life of legislation, attendance at assembly and on juries, voting, office-holding, deliberation and decision-making (and military service when necessary) would be adult free-born males, formally registered, at age eighteen, in the local "deme" (ward or village). Children and slaves were excluded, and also women, who, although free-born, played no part in the public life of the city, except in religious ritual and some festivals. The position of women was clearly a subject for discussion in classical Athens. Women had no political rights, were subservient to a male in the household – father, uncle, brother or husband – and were expected to stay at home, bearing and raising children, and engage in spinning, weaving, cooking and other household tasks. In the theatre, however, powerful women were portrayed on the stage, and three of Aristophanes' comedies show a dominant female character: in *Lysistrata* organizing other women to withhold sex from men as an anti-war protest; in *Thesmophoriazusae* in an attack on Euripides for his depiction of female characters in his plays; and in *Women in Assembly* taking over the legal and executive powers of the city from the men. Plato saw no reason why women should not be as qualified as men to become philosophers and rulers of the state. They may be physically weaker but that is irrelevant when it is a question of intellectual capacity and training. In the constitution described in the *Republic*, given the universal childcare arrangements available to parents in the guardian class, and their freedom from financial worries, male and female are equally eligible for practical politics and intellectual dialectic. Later in the dialogue, in the summary of the qualifications needed for success in philosophy and politics (*Republic* 540c), there is a further reminder that the discussion applies as much to women who have the appropriate talents as to men.

Slaves, who made up a considerable proportion of the population, also had no political rights, or any free activity, but they were considered the property of their master as a result of purchase or conquest. Slaves might work in the house or on the farm along with the family, be hired out to industries, or hold positions in the bureaucracy of the state, as secretaries or even bankers. Only in extreme situations would they be enlisted into military service (because of the internal risks posed by armed slaves), and then they would be freed first. Freed slaves would have the status of "metics", that is, resident aliens; exceptionally, those who had fought with the Athenians in the battle of Arginusae were immediately given full citizenship. Aristotle was inclined to say that some human beings are slaves by nature, in that they are not capable of rational thought; these, like oxen, benefit the citizens with the use of their physical strength, and in return have food, shelter and protection as working members of the household. The Stoics argued against this in claiming that slavery and freedom are states of mind rather than natural conditions. "Slavery is all the nervousness of a spirit weakened, degraded and broken", and humiliation results from being unable to follow one's own will when in the power of such "masters" as lust, fear, avarice and ambition. On the other hand, only those whose will and judgement ensure their independence in whatever circumstances are doing what they really want; true freedom comes with virtue and the right use of reason.[20]

Utopias

An ideal type of political arrangement, such as is found in Plato's *Republic*, his *Laws* and, to some extent, in Aristotle's *Politics*, has come to be known as "utopia".[21] There were various examples of non-political utopias in Greek literature, starting with the accounts of Homer's Phaeacians in the *Odyssey*, and Hesiod's "golden race of men", who lived in the distant past. An innocent and simple pastoral lifestyle similar to that described by Hesiod was attributed to remote areas such as Arcadia, and shared some features with after-death places of reward for a good life, in Elysium and the Isles of the Blessed. Plato's myth of Atlantis, in the early stages when its people were close to their divine origin and before the city degenerated, could also be described as utopian. Somewhat similar is the idealization of two leaders and their associated rule: that of the Persian prince Cyrus by Xenophon, and in Plutarch of the Spartan legislator Lycurgus, a semi-mythical figure who was credited with establishing the long-lasting Spartan social order (*eunomia*) of an elite, highly successful military force, educated as equals under two kings, with a number of unusual features, including the famous austerity and endurance. Aristophanes produced a satire on the genre in the *Birds* in which a new "bird-city" is established in the air, with laws passed for the common good of the bird-citizens, and to the detriment of gods above and human beings below them.

The theoretical *polis* generated by Socrates in Plato's *Republic* was, however, the most influential utopia from the ancient world. In it the citizens were divided into three classes – philosopher-rulers, military/executive and workers/producers – each showing the virtue characteristic of their group, and participating in the justice of the whole. Among the ruling class an extreme form of communism would be practised, with the abolition of the family, a sharing of husbands and wives, and children brought up to regard all adults as mother or father. Initially it seemed as if utopia could be brought into existence quite easily: if politicians studied philosophy or philosophers went into politics. Later a more drastic first move was thought necessary, to "wipe the slate clean" by exiling everyone over the age of ten, but eventually the *polis* described was recognized as an impossible ideal, "laid up in heaven". In Plato's last and longest work, *Laws*, the blueprint of a (fictitious) city to be founded in Crete was set out in great detail, in accordance with the general custom of a legislator advising on the constitution for the settlement of a new city or colony, or the revival of a former community. The content of the *Laws* is more practical than idealistic, and some features have been found repugnant, as Plato grappled with the problems involved in the excessive details of a body of legislation to be adopted as a stable and permanent working model. Aristotle had a similar aim in his *Politics*. He would have preferred a monarchy based on virtue and wisdom, but he admitted that the ideal was not realizable, given the frailty of human nature. So in the last sections of the treatise he explored the possible constitutional amendments that would aid a city's progress towards its natural end of providing for the welfare and general good of its citizens.

The Stoics had a utopian ideal of the "city of the wise", described by their founder Zeno as "a dream or image of a philosopher's well-regulated society" (Plutarch, *Moralia* 329a–b). He was in favour of abolishing social and political institutions, including temples, law courts, gymnasia and even the family unit, managing without a currency, and in general adopting an austere way of life as advocated by the Cynics and well known in Sparta. Individual legal systems would disappear, and the "city of the wise" would be regulated by universal law "like a herd grazing together, and nourished by a common pasture".[22] From another aspect compliance with this law was interpreted as "following god" by consistent living and willing cooperation with the workings of nature. In addition, it was thought that, when the wise man brings his own reason in accord with cosmic intelligence (*pronoia*), his actions would always be virtuous, and he would be at one with the world and his fellow "world citizens".

But in politics, as in other areas, the rigour and idealism of Zeno's Stoicism was made more accessible by his successors, and, especially when the philosophy came to Rome, the "middle" Stoicism of Panaetius and Posidonius was in many respects in sympathy with Roman *mores*. Rather than replacing individual civic institutions with one world-city restricted to the wise, these Stoics envisaged an *extension* of affiliation from the *polis* to the *cosmopolis*, to which all human beings belong. According to their theory, the initial instinct for self-preservation leads to assimilation with parents, family and tribe as "one's own", and then, in maturity, to the state. So there was a duty to participate in government, protecting the weak and promoting laws to further the well-being of the citizens.[23] In the final move, the mutual affection that started in the home and spread outwards to kin, friends, fellow citizens and allies, ends in the embrace of all humanity (*totius complexus gentis humanae*; Cicero *De finibus* 5.65).[24]

8. Ethics, goodness and happiness

Plato's dialogue *Meno* opens with the following question: "Can you tell me, Socrates, whether virtue (*aretē*) can be taught, or, if it is not teachable, is it the result of practice, or does it come to people, not by practice or through teaching, but from their nature, or is there some other explanation?". Socrates refuses to answer until a definition of virtue itself is established, but the question sets out several criteria for marking out the good from the bad. Some people perhaps have it *in their nature* to be kinder or braver and generally more good than their neighbours, others *may have been taught* courage and self-discipline, and others again *may work continually* at controlling their tempers or being more prudent. On the other hand, what is responsible for a child's unruly behaviour? Is it *bad parenting* exacerbated by *weak teaching*, is it a question of getting into *bad habits* or keeping *bad company*, or *does it just happen* that there are black sheep in the most respectable families? Meno has put his finger on problems that were as perplexing for the Greeks as they are for modern educationists.

The goodness of the Homeric hero

For Homer, being good (*agathos*) was mainly a question of class. The adjective is applied to those of noble birth who are leaders in the assemblies and outstanding warriors; its opposite is *kakos*, which refers especially to one who is cowardly, weak or of low birth. *Aretē* ("goodness", usually translated "virtue", the noun associated with *agathos*) is also related to class and wealth, and characterizes those who are first and bravest on the battlefield, and rich enough to afford chariots and fine armour. In return for their splendid and courageous leadership, these heroes prosper, enjoy a fine reputation and have certain privileges, such as the choicest dishes at table. Competence in other areas can also be linked with *aretē* in the Homeric poems; the Phaeacians, for example, are not war-like, but have skills in sailing, and a woman's virtue is in her beauty and her chastity. Such attributes provide the material for song, and win for the individuals a long-remembered fame on earth, to compensate for a grey existence in the world of the dead.

Any *moral* aspect to *aretē* in this sense, however, is undermined by being linked to the favour or interference of the gods. To safeguard those under their protection, gods can take away the opportunity for a display of *aretē* by making an opponent invisible, or removing a hero from danger, whereas if men incur divine anger, however unwittingly, then their prosperity is doomed. The kindly Phaeacians were destroyed by Poseidon, and Hector, despite his bravery and determination to defend his city, could not win against Achilles, who enjoyed the patronage of the goddess Athena, and the unfair advantages she secured for him. In situations like these the poet frequently presents the vulnerability of the heroes in their mortality in a more favourable light than the careless arrogance of the immortals. There are two passages, however, that show the heroes acting independently, according to their own principles of death and glory, and in defiance of divine warning and protection. In the first, Achilles is given a choice between two fates – an early death at Troy with honour and undying fame in song, or a long life in his homeland in obscurity (*Il* 9.410–16) – and he takes the former. In the second example it is Hector who is urged to stay within the city and not face Achilles, for this is the prudent way, advised by his aged parents and supported by omens from the gods, but Hector recognizes only one omen, the call to battle, and replies: "For me it would be better by far / to meet Achilles face to face, to slay him and return home, / or to die gloriously at his hands in sight of the city" (22.108–10).

Habits and dispositions in Heraclitus and Empedocles

The word "ethics" comes from the Greek *ēthos*, translated as custom or habit. It first appears in Heraclitus in the enigmatic three-word sentence *ēthos anthropōi daimōn* (DK 22B119), which means, literally, "habit [is] human destiny". Heraclitus was the first to consider moral action as a problem requiring philosophical analysis, and he linked it to a combination of physical structure and continued endeavour, where the personality resulting from the habit of certain kinds of thoughts and actions affects the physical composition of the soul. The individual soul for him is made of the same constituents as the cosmos: fiery *logos* and its "turnings" of water and earth. Given these constituents, he believed that we are able to improve or diminish the powers of soul. In particular, we may extend its range of knowledge through searching and enquiring, for the more we know, the more there is yet to know in the unfathomable depths of the soul's *logos*. In an almost literal way, such learning makes for a "drier" soul, and "dry soul is wisest and best" (B118). On the other hand, although resistance is hard, the gains of indulgence are at the expense of soul, and giving in to desire decreases our psychic powers. Evidence for this can be found in the behaviour of the drunkard, who has literally dampened his soul; this reduces his ability to control his body (so that he stumbles) and to express his thoughts in clear speech (for the words are slurred). But Heraclitus was still Homeric enough to recognize that the best choose undying glory above all else, and that the greatest honour is due to the young who die in battle, the "Ares-slain" (B29, 24).

Empedocles followed Heraclitus in seeing character as dependent on physical structure and habitual behaviour. He claimed that people, like animals and plants and the cosmos itself, are made of the four elements of earth, air, fire and water in varying proportions. Their thinking and choosing depend on the mixture of these elements in the blood around the heart, where the quality of thought is related to the approximation to the ideal ratio (one to one) of the ingredients. Individuals can improve their thinking and their character through their own efforts, although this may prove difficult, as he advises his student Pausanias:

> If you push [my words] firmly under your crowded thoughts, and contemplate them favourably with unsullied and constant attention, assuredly all these will be with you through life, and you will gain much else from them, for of themselves they will grow into the character (*ēthos*) of each, according to its nature. But if you yourself should reach out for things of a different kind, for the countless trivialities that come among men and dull their meditations, straightaway these will leave you.　　(31B110)

The knowledge conveyed by Empedocles' thoughts and words, after being received and contemplated, becomes embedded in the heart area; it thus brings Pausanias closer to the condition of being wise and acting appropriately by causing the number of right thoughts to grow, and by making him more the receptive to such thoughts. Underlying the arcane language is a recognition that the thinking mechanism is determined by the body's elements, but that the consequent predispositions can be countered by teaching and motivation. (The problem tackled here surfaces in modern theories of gene-determined behaviour and methods of countering it.) In addition, Empedocles is with Heraclitus in establishing a connection between the individual and the workings of the cosmos, in Heraclitus' case in the common *logos* and, for Empedocles, not only in the comparable elemental composition, but also in the forces of attraction and repulsion. Siding with Strife brings disaster, but aligning oneself with the power of universal Love contributes to personal and universal well-being. Those who act in this way achieve the best kinds of human life, that of prophets, poets, physicians and statesmen.[1]

Ethics in an atomic theory

Along with quotations and reports on the atomic theory of Leucippus and Democritus there are over 160 "ethical" fragments attributed to Democritus, which are found in the collection of Stobaeus. These are now generally accepted as genuine, and, if so, place Democritus in the tradition of Heraclitus and Empedocles in claiming a physical structure for body and soul. According to the atomists' theory the outcome for an individual's psychological state depends on the movements of the aggregation of "soul" atoms (i.e. those that are small and round and move swiftly) both within the body and in response to external stimuli. The ethical fragments attributed to Democritus are short statements of a bland and non-controversial nature,[2] but there is a general tendency to encourage cheerfulness, moderation and serenity. *Euthumia*, the word translated as "cheerfulness", is more literally connected with a feeling of well-being in the heart area, and, according to Empedocles' theory and the later atomism found in Lucretius, the feeling depends on the physical state and is a consequence of it. For Democritus this would relate to atomic movements in the heart area being smooth and harmonious, whereas the contrary feelings of anxiety or pain are

179

the result of such movements being disturbed, either by a blow from an external object or by inner psychic turbulence. The advice given would be relevant to reducing the turbulence and achieving tranquillity. At the least, it is seen as part of the philosopher's remit to recommend in some detail guidelines for leading one's life in the best way, which would be in accord with the physical principles involved. And Democritus does take a stand on the "Meno" question given above, on whether goodness results from teaching, practice or nature, when he says that "More people become good by practice than by nature" (68B106).[3]

Teaching virtue

At about the same time as Democritus came to Athens, the sophists were converging on the city, and their livelihood depended on *aretē* being teachable. But, in the new context of the democratic city-state, *aretē* had shifted its meaning from the main Homeric sense of success in battle. Prosperity and "being best" now depended on political power, the respect of one's fellow citizens and the ability to persuade others, especially in the assemblies and law courts, to adopt one's point of view. New skills were required that conventional education was unable to provide, and so the sophists moved in to teach such skills (for a considerable fee). Political theory, law, history, literary criticism, linguistics and above all the art of speaking were subjects in their curriculum. The tradition made famous by Hesiod of a golden age in the past from which the human race had degenerated was replaced in the new science of anthropology by a theory of the human race *making progress* from an earlier cave-like existence through their inventions and intellectual efforts. Bright young men in fifth-century Athens were dazzled by such optimism and the new opportunities the sophists offered, while also listening to challenges to traditional moral values.

In Plato's dialogue *Gorgias*, the first of three conversations the character Socrates is engaged in is with the respected orator, teacher and sophist, Gorgias himself. When pressed by Socrates, Gorgias maintains that his field of activity is in the area of right and wrong, and he sets out to persuade the citizens in the law courts and assemblies to adopt his views on moral issues, and teaches others to do the same. His type of persuasion is not, however, based on an understanding of the issues involved, but is concerned merely to obtain conviction without comprehension (455a). The teacher passes on his expertise for his pupils to use when it is appropriate to do so, namely in defence and not aggressively. The teacher is no more to blame for a student's subsequent bad behaviour than a boxer is if his pupil uses his new-found skill to beat up his parents. But in fact Gorgias claims to teach morality if the student does not already know it; a rhetorician is incapable of putting his skill to immoral use and deliberately doing wrong, and his students would follow his lead (460e).

The subject of right and wrong, subsumed under the term *aretē*, is linked in this context with success in politics, and is seen as a necessary means to this end. Another sophist who was concerned with the teaching of such political *aretē* is Protagoras, and, in the dialogue named after him, he is shown as ready to defend his point of view with both a myth and an argument. In the myth Zeus sends Hermes to impart to the human race the virtues of *aidōs* (self-respect) and *dikē* (fair dealings with others), which together make up political *aretē*: not just to a few (like medical or musical skill) but to everyone (323d). Even so, care, practice, training and instruction from childhood are still needed to bring the natural talent for *aretē* to fruition in justice, self-mastery and holiness of life (325a). The *argument* Protagoras puts forward for being a teacher of virtue is by analogy with musicianship. If the state encouraged everyone to be a flute-player children might not be as talented as their parents, but even the weakest would have some skill that could be improved by teaching: "So it is with virtue. If there is anyone who is just a little better at setting us on the road to virtue, he should be welcomed. I think I am one of these, better than others at making a man fine and good, and worthy of the fee I charge" (328a–b).[4] In this way Protagoras can answer Meno's question on all three counts. Everyone has a natural talent for political *aretē*, and this can be enhanced by practice, in the environment of family upbringing and regular schooling, and then by the higher education provided by the sophists.

Later in the *Meno*, however, the problem arises of finding suitable teachers. The hypothesis is put forward that being good involves knowledge of some kind, and in that case it will be teachable and there will be teachers of it. But then it is difficult to find such teachers. Respectable citizens and even distinguished statesmen have hired teachers in riding, music, athletics and the like for their sons, but not experts in goodness, presumably because they could not find any, or did not think the subject teachable, especially when it was seen that the sons of good fathers have sometimes gone to the bad. And if the sophists, along with parents and poets, are rejected as qualified instructors, then doubt is thrown on goodness being teachable, or, indeed, linked to any special kind of knowledge or skill (96c). Here we need to explore Socrates' own position.

Defining virtue and the Socratic paradoxes

If we are going to live rightly, then we must know what we are talking about, and Socrates is represented in Plato's early dialogues as searching for definitions of different virtues. He is not after a list of instances, of courageous actions or pious deeds, but he wants to know what the virtue actually is – how to define the key ingredient that stays constant and holds true in all circumstances. Once we know this then we shall act accordingly. In the cases recorded, however, in the search for definitions of courage, piety, self-control, beauty, friendship and virtue itself, the results are always negative. Socrates' respondents end up uncertain, bewildered, numbed and often angry, and Socrates himself turns away disappointed, for the so-called experts have not been able to help him. There have, however, been some gains, in that the definitions offered, although eventually failing, improve through the dialogues, both in having wider applications and in their eventual link with knowing something. The painful process of the *elenchos* removed errors, and brought the respondent to an admission of ignorance, but it also provided the stimulus to think more deeply about some moral issues that had previously been taken for granted. Socrates was like the sophists in questioning traditional assumptions, but where they tended to scepticism and relativism his purpose was always for the good of all concerned. The most promising of the company would stay with him and continue the search for solutions to the problems raised, and it was in this very searching and self-examining that we are best employed: "the unexamined life for any human is not worth living" (*Apology* 38a).[5]

The study of individual virtues and their eventual link with knowing something, although finally rejected, was the basis of two "paradoxes" attributed to Socrates, namely that "virtue is knowledge" and "no one does wrong willingly". In the interpretation of these statements we find that Socrates was looking for an art or skill in living comparable to the skills displayed by professionals and craftsmen. A doctor builds up expertise from treating a number of patients, derives some principles from the results, and is better equipped to effect a cure with the next patient who comes to him. A potter becomes skilled in making pots from understanding the clay he works with and the heat required in the kiln, and with practice turns out a work of art each time. In life too, as a whole, is it possible similarly to have a set of theoretical principles and apply them in such a way that right action results? The study of different virtues tended to the conclusion that in different situations *an understanding of good and evil* is appropriately applied. Courage, therefore, turns out to be an awareness of what is truly frightening, justice involves recognition of the rights of other, and self-control ("temperance") is based on self-knowledge; these virtues all depend on, or are aspects of, an overarching wisdom. People can be called courageous, for example, only if they are fully conscious of the dangers to be faced and still act bravely; otherwise they are simply being reckless. To be just they need to know what is right and wrong in social situations.

If being good is a question of knowing something, then being bad would result from ignorance, and a consequence of this is that the remedy rests with education, not punishment. This is the point Socrates makes in his own trial: if he has acted against the law, the act, he claims, was involuntary; he did not *intend* anything illegal; and the court should therefore be correcting his ignorance, not putting him on trial for his life. Punishment should not be blind vengeance, but reformative, and the most effective means of reform is through education, for "no one does wrong willingly".[6] It is recognized that this is by no means a common view, for surely one can know what is right, but deliberately do wrong for various reasons? Socrates, however, is able to persuade even Protagoras to agree with him when he puts the following question:

> Most people think that often it is not the knowledge that a man has which he follows but something else – at one time anger, at another pleasure or pain, sometimes love and frequently fear; they regard knowledge as a slave, pushed around by these other emotions. Do you agree, or would you rather say that knowledge is a fine thing, and master of a man, and, if he can distinguish good from evil, *nothing* would force him to act contrary to knowledge, since practical wisdom (*phronēsis*) is all that he needs?
>
> (*Protagoras* 352b–c)

The point is that if we truly understand what is best for us in our long-term interests then we follow the path of virtue. Being afraid to do the right thing, for example, or supposing the wrong is more pleasant, results from a basic misunderstanding of the nature of good and evil.

Doing wrong and suffering wrong

Such a stand further involves another surprising opinion attributed to Socrates: that it is always better to suffer than do wrong. This was a most difficult point of view to persuade others to support, since it struck at the heart of traditional Greek opinion. In a variety of different situations, for Homeric warriors, tragic heroes and heroines, political leaders and writers of history, it was taken as normal and expected behaviour that one would defend the family, help friends and inflict maximum harm on enemies, especially in retaliation for wrong done. Socrates' stand is shown in Plato's *Crito*,[7] where he is in prison awaiting execution and Crito tries to persuade Socrates to escape. He has forceful arguments on his side, but Socrates abides by what he has always believed – that the really important thing is not to live, but to live well (*Crito* 48b),[8] and this means that one must never commit injustice, whatever the provocation:

> The truth is what we have always said. Whatever the popular view is, and whether the consequence is pleasanter than this or even tougher, the fact remains that to commit injustice is in every case bad and dishonourable for the person who does it. In no circumstances must one do wrong, not even in retaliation for being wronged unjustly … I have believed this for a long time and still hold to it. (49b–d)

The reason for this belief for Socrates is that any injury that is done to one affects only material possessions or physical health, whereas doing wrong to another affects the *soul* of the wrong-doer. Care for the soul is of overriding importance, and any kind of decent life requires it to be given precedence over the body. Socrates' own austerity was well known. He had no interest in personal comfort, wearing the same tunic summer and winter, and living in poverty, impervious to heat and cold and physical danger. Nor did he worry about what people might think of him, but instead showed his own concern for others in constantly encouraging them to reassess the values they lived by. He wanted them to make their own integrity the most important consideration, and resist any move to damage it in the interests of improving their material well-being.[9] As he said to the Athenians in the speech at his trial, "I spend all my time going about trying to persuade you, young and old, to make your first and main concern not for your bodies or your possessions but for your soul, that it might be in the best possible state" (*Apology* 30a).

That Socrates was willing to adhere to these principles in his own "care for the soul" is shown on two occasions. In the first, at his trial, he supposes naturally enough that the Athenians were mainly interested in repressing his philosophical activity. Criticism of their lifestyle, their politics and their politicians was tolerated when the Athenians' democracy was strong, but, after the war with Sparta, the imposition of the rule of the Thirty Tyrants and the eventual return of the democrats, the political situation became fragile. The former tolerance was no longer advisable, and it seemed more prudent either to compel Socrates to abandon his provocative confrontations or to send him into exile. Socrates then sees himself faced with the same kind of choice as Achilles: of keeping to his heroic principles with an early death, or sacrificing them for a long and quiet life in obscurity. Like Achilles, he chooses death rather than disgrace, and says: "Where a man has once taken up his stand, either because it seems best to him or because that was the position assigned to him, there I believe it is his duty to stay and face the danger, taking no account of death or anything else before dishonour" (*Apology* 28d).

The second occasion concerns another chance Socrates had to avoid execution, when, as we have seen, his friend Crito offered to arrange his escape from prison. Socrates' reasons for remaining are again concerned with staying true to the principles he has always lived by. Even if he has been unjustly condemned, he reiterates his preference to suffer wrong rather than to do wrong, and harm his city by disobeying its laws.[10]

Why should we be good?

At the beginning of the second book of the *Republic*, Glaucon and Adeimantus raise the question, in the strongest possible terms, of *why* we should be good. The discussion is formally about "justice" and "injustice", but the Greek terms *dikē* and *dikaiosynē* are much broader than that, covering morality as a whole as well as the specific virtue. Glaucon speaks first, saying that in general people think that it is best to do injustice without paying a penalty, and worst to suffer it without being able to take revenge. Justice is between the two, valued not for itself but because the weak cannot act unjustly with impunity, and need to develop measures to prevent the stronger wronging them. The desire to outdo others and get from them as much as possible is pursued as a natural good, but this is countered by state laws and conventions, which require us to treat others with respect. But suppose one came upon a "ring of invisibility", like Gyges in the Lydian story? When Gyges found that no one could see him when he turned the ring round on his finger, he at once killed the king, married the queen and did whatever he wanted with no risk of retaliation. Glaucon claims that any one else, just or unjust, would do the same in that situation, and Socrates is challenged to show why one should not take advantage of such an opportunity. The case could be made more extreme by giving the unjust man the reputation and rewards that accompany a good name, and taking away from the just man *his* good name, exchanging it for the reputation for injustice and all the sufferings and punishments that go with that. In such circumstances why should we be good for its own sake if we can get away with misusing our position and doing whatever we like? Adeimantus chimes in with further support for Glaucon's challenge. It is generally the case, he says, that doing wrong is more profitable than doing right; those with wealth and power, however acquired, are thought fortunate, and the weak and poor are despised, even though they have higher standards of behaviour. Can we expect punishment in the next life for our injustice, if not in this? Perhaps, Adeimantus suggests, there are no gods, or they are not concerned with what we do, and, even if they are, we have been told that they can be influenced and persuaded by prayers and offerings. A young person might well suppose that it is best to create a facade of illusory goodness to deceive those around him, but keep behind it "the greedy and crafty fox" of the fable (*Republic* 358c–367e). How then will Socrates defend right action for its own sake in all circumstances? The subject is crucial and its importance is recognized, for "our argument concerns no ordinary topic, but how we ought to live" (532d).[11]

In the long reply, a more affirmative Socrates takes over from the doubting *persona* of the first book, who had finished on the usual note of an admission of ignorance, not knowing what justice is, whether it is a virtue or not, and whether a person who has it is happy or unhappy. Now, when faced with these strong challenges, Socrates sees two tasks ahead of him: to show that we should do the right thing for its own sake, with no regard to reputation, rewards or punishments; and to counter relativist views with the affirmation of external guidelines for behaviour based on objective standards of good and bad that remain true whether or not individuals decide to make up their own minds about how they are going to behave.

The first task he tackles with the search for justice in the political model of three classes in a state – rulers, soldiers and workers – which are found to correspond to three parts of the soul – reason, spirit and desire.[12] The virtue of wisdom is connected to the rulers in the state and reason in the soul, and courage belongs with the army, and with spirit in the individual. Moderation (*sōphrosynē*; also called "self-control" or "temperance") is the friendly relations between the parts, and justice turns out to be "having and doing one's own thing", as is appropriate to the divisions in city and soul. This somewhat strange conclusion links different aspects of virtue with the three key functions in the state and the three parts of the soul, in the interests of social and individual prospering. The aim of the whole discussion was to find out what justice is and why, in the broader perspective of moral action, it is to be followed. When reason rules, the right choices are made in the light of its wisdom, spirit aids reason in providing the motivation for acting and pride in the achievements, moderation submits to the arrangement in the interests of the whole, and the resulting harmony secures a well-integrated, properly functioning "just" individual.

The converse of this is shown in detail in later books, when failing regimes are related to individual degenerate psychic states. The first move in the decline comes when spirit overcomes reason, and the demands of "honour" prevail. This is followed by reason and spirit being made subservient to the overriding desire for wealth and possessions in the "oligarchic" regime of the moneyed classes and in the corresponding profit-driven individual. In a democracy, the next stage, the people do as they wish with no restraints from a ruling or military class, and the democratic man gives in to his desires at random. The final degradation is in tyranny (akin to dictatorship), where the best citizens are soon imprisoned or murdered, the tyrant's cronies put in their place, the treasury ransacked and the people impoverished and downtrodden. The corresponding "tyrannical" soul is the contrary of the just one, for here the voice of reason is silenced, and all the man's energies work to satisfy his rampant desires. The differ-ence is shown especially at night time. Through the day the good man shows wisdom in his intellectual activities and choices, deals with his desires in moderation, perhaps calms his spirit after an angry outburst and then sleeps peacefully at night. His direct opposite, the "tyran-nical" man, who is described here as "envious, untrustworthy, friend-less, host and nurse to every kind of vice", lives in fear and self-loathing by day, and at night has violent dreams. While his reason is asleep the wild part of his soul, bloated with food and drink and out of control, goes on the rampage, and, maddened by the attempts to satisfy itself, brings on nightmares of incest, murder and every kind of wickedness. By means of some dubious mathematics, it is concluded that the phil-osopher-king is 729 times happier than the tyrant, and the tyrant the same number of times more wretched (*Republic* 587d). Although the "tyrannical" man is deliberately portrayed as an extreme case, we are told that "it is clear from our dreams that there is a dangerous, wild and lawless form of desire in us all, even in those who seem to be moder-ately inclined" (571d–572b).[13] The detailed psychological analysis of the previous discussion had provided the tools and the incentives for keeping such lawless desires in check in the interests of the best type of individual life in the best managed constitution.

Objective values and the form of the good

So far, then, it would seem that the first challenge had been met, and the case made for acting rightly for its own sake. It had been shown to be best to have a balanced personality, using discernment to make sensible decisions, and harnessing our energies to achieve an organized and harmonious life. Our natural desires to quench our thirst, eat well, enjoy sexual relationships and have an adequate standard of living are to be respected but not allowed to dominate or get out of hand. But there is still the further question of whether *objective* standards of morality do exist, or whether we are to define our own values in a random way, as each thinks fit. Plato takes it for granted that we all pursue "the good", that we want something that really is good, and are ready to do every-thing for its sake, but we do not know exactly what it is (505a–d). The subject is given its most detailed treatment in the context of the role of the philosopher-rulers in books 6 and 7 of the *Republic*, in what is tech-nically a digression from the first challenge. Socrates is now dealing with an elite few, or perhaps only one person in the state, but even so he refuses to discuss "the good" in the same way as he had treated the individual virtues, "and even to arrive at my own view is too big a topic for the discussion we are now started on" (506d). Instead he offers as guidelines the simile of the sun and the allegory of the cave.[14]

The theory of forms is introduced for the first time in the *Republic* in this digression. It is agreed that there does exist "justice itself", which acts as a standard for individual just acts and gives them its value; similarly for other entities that have a common name there is a paradigm case, imperceptible but accessible to reason. Above all there is the form of the good, (also called "good itself" or "essence of goodness"), which is found to have a special status. Its offspring is the sun, and, as the sun allows eyes to see and objects, including itself, to be seen, so the good allows mind to know, and forms, including itself, to be known. In the allegory of the cave the sun is like the fire that illuminates the carved figures and allows their shadows to be seen on the facing screen, but, in the world above, the good itself takes the place of the sun, illuminating the objects of knowledge in the intelligible realm. The prisoner who is dragged up from the cave to see the sun eventually understands how it explains everything in the cave as well as in the upper world, and this throws light on how the philosopher-king or -queen,[15] after a gruelling higher education, can achieve knowledge of the good. This involves an understanding of how objective values depend on the good, of the place of the cosmos in the sum of things, and of the correct assessment of human action in relation to what is perceived and known. Philosophers would then be required to return to the cave, to the sphere of human associations, to "labour in politics", applying their greater understanding to practical matters of state and society, before being allowed to retire, and spend their lives as they would wish, in the contemplation of eternal moral truths.

It could also be conceded that such a life brings the greatest pleasure. In the final discussion of the three types of lives in the *Republic* it was agreed that that of the philosopher was most pleasant. Each of the three would have its champion. The money-maker or the gourmet is content with his or her life and would have little interest or experience in the pleasures of sports or of learning. The athlete, similarly, might not be an intellectual, but would have been excited at the thrill of winning a prize in the games,[16] and claim the superiority of that achievement over making a profit. Only philosophers have the experience of intellectual enquiry, and so are in a position to assess the three lives; in their judgement, the life of the philosopher would be most pleasant.

This position, however, is somewhat modified in the discussion of the *Philebus*, a later dialogue devoted almost exclusively to the subject of pleasure. The "middle" life discussed in the *Republic*, and represented by the athlete and warrior, is dropped, and the discussion focuses here on the claims of pleasure in contrast to intelligence as the main ingredient in the good life. A straight antithesis between the two is rejected, however, in the context of the *totality* of the good life for human beings. Intellectual activity on its own is said to belong to the divine, whereas pleasure without consciousness or understanding of it characterizes only the simplest forms of animal species. The satisfactory life for human beings, and the one to be commended, requires both ingredients combined in moderation. Reason brings intelligence with it, together with order, truth, moderation and beauty[17] in the pattern of right living, involving not only theorizing and dialectic (which produce "pure" pleasures) but also the *application* of knowledge in sciences and crafts. These activities, along with those concerned with health, result in the "mixture" of advantages that would be available to everyone. Plato's mature conclusion here makes the "best life" more accessible to people generally than the Socratic view that the life of the philosopher is the only one worth living. It is also closer to the recommended choice of Odysseus in the Myth of Er: to take up, from all the possibilities offered, the undistinguished life of an ordinary man.

Aristotelian ethics

Aristotle treated the question of how we are to live our lives as a scientific exercise, spelled out in the *Eudemian Ethics* and the more significant *Nicomachean Ethics* (which has some overlap with the *Eudemian*).[18] He starts with given data, which in this case are common opinions, and the consensus is that everyone wants to be happy. It is our aim in life, and why we act as we do. Sometimes there are "intermediate" goods, where one thing leads to another (as money to buy a house, education to enhance a career), and there might be further intermediate goods (as the house being needed for a family, the career for greater prestige), but these intermediates have to end at some point in an ultimate good, and this is agreed to be happiness. It is curiously pointless to ask: why do you want to be happy? Happy people have fulfilled their desires and achieved their aim, but the problem comes with defining the *content* of their happiness, and this is what Aristotle sets out to do.[19]

He opens with an attack on the most distinguished candidate for the best good of all, namely Plato's form of the good. The first failing is that this is too abstract and transcendental to be relevant to daily life. Secondly, Plato did not take account of the various uses of the word "good", whereas Aristotle analyses the different applications of the adjective and the relationship between them, and finds a primary meaning around which other senses cluster.[20] In phrases such as "a good knife", "a good flute-player" and "a good drink", the primary meaning relates to successful functioning, as, for these examples, in cutting effectively, playing well or quenching thirst. What is good, therefore, for human beings would relate to their practical functioning as human beings, and the outstanding characteristic of human life, which distinguishes it from that of plants and animals, is the ability to think. Aristotle concludes that happiness is to be found in the active life of reason, "in the perfect realization of the true self", which, in non-Aristotelian language, means something like "in working to the best of our abilities".[21] But we cannot live by reason alone, and Aristotle is ready to admit that basic needs should be met, and a length of time allowed for their enjoyment, "for one swallow does not make a summer, nor one day a happy life" (*Nicomachean Ethics* 1088a18). He summarizes as follows:

> The happy man is one who is able to achieve excellence in his activities and who is adequately provided with external goods, not just for a time but throughout his life; and we should perhaps add that his death will be in accord with the pattern of his life.
>
> (1101a14–20)

We see here that the successful and happy life should satisfy the whole person, since it combines the exercise of reason in contemplation with considered action and the enjoyment of leisure and moderate comfort. The virtuous activity that belongs with reason is *sophia* (theoretical wisdom), which is concerned with scientific study and the intellectual life of philosophy, and this takes the highest place, being close to the divine. But human beings are *political* animals, as Aristotle famously said, and they function best in a well-regulated society. It is in this context of political activity that the moral virtues of justice, courage, generosity and the like flourish; *phronēsis* (practical wisdom) then comes into play in regulating desires, impulses and ambitions, and making appropriate choices in the best interests of the individual and society as a whole. Aristotle would also want to say that patterns of moral behaviour can be built up, through education and under the guidance of *phronēsis*; it is then easier to continue to make the right choices and live a moral life. As we can only become competent flautists by continually playing the flute, so "by doing just acts we become just" (1103b1).

Moderation of feelings and impulses is also a key feature of *phronēsis*, and ensures that in a spectrum of related activity a *mean* between extremes is chosen. Indulging his tendency for classification, Aristotle tabulates individual virtues as "means" between a vice of defect and one of excess. In dangerous circumstances, for example, *phronēsis* understands the situation, and controls the defective instinct of cowardice (which is to run away) and the excess of rashness (namely charging in without thinking), and promotes the mean between the two, the virtue of courage. Again the virtue of generosity occupies a place between the defect of meanness and the excess of prodigality, and sincerity between false modesty and boastfulness. Righteous anger also has a place in Aristotelian morality. The Stoics later would see all emotion as a failure of reason, but Aristotle found a role for anger as a stimulus to positive and justified reaction in situations where *phronēsis* recognizes an attack on one's honour or that of family or friends.

In this context Aristotle thought that the problem of "weakness of will" is to be explained as a failure of *phronēsis* to restrain desire. When we know right from wrong, Socrates had said we would always do what is right; not to do so would be a failure in knowledge, for then we have not really understood where our true good lies. Aristotle claims, rather, that in a particular instance where *phronēsis* recommends right action but we do the opposite, the *akrasia* (weakness of will) is a *psychological* failure on our part. Because appropriate patterns of behaviour have not become sufficiently ingrained, an occasional lapse allows an irrational appetite to overturn a rational decision.

Aristotle's general view of happiness and the good life has enjoyed a revival in recent discussions of moral philosophy in the concept of "virtue ethics".[22] There has been a move away from considering external criteria, such as duty or utilitarianism, to a focus on moral *agents* and their choices and conduct that is in agreement with Aristotelian theory. Aristotle is also seen as a champion of "virtue ethics" in providing an ultimate explanation for moral actions that is bound in with human rationality. And finally the problems concerned with defining and classifying individual virtues can find a resolution in the unity of apparently different virtues when they are explained as aspects of wisdom in action in the functioning of *phronēsis*.

Stoic virtue

The linking of virtue with reason and understanding had started with Socrates. It was further developed by Plato in his concept of the ultimate reality of goodness itself, and adapted to a more realistic lifestyle by Aristotle. The Stoics, however, reverted to the Socratic line and took it to extremes. The fundamental connection between knowing right and doing right meant that, for them, the slightest deviation was a failure of intellect. Since they also adopted the suggestion that individual virtues were interrelated as particular applications of a general theory of conduct known as the "art of living", they concluded that either a person was completely virtuous, knowing the principles of right action in every situation, or, being ignorant of them, was both foolish and vicious. They thought of the soul as literally highly strung and, comparing it to an instrument that is either in tune or out of tune, they claimed that the state of the soul is either in harmony with itself and producing right actions according to nature, or is in discord, with wrong actions resulting.

This theory started from a study of primary natural instincts.[23] Against the Epicurean theory of pleasure as primary, the Stoics claimed that the initial stimulus was for self-preservation. It is instinctive and natural behaviour for animals and young children to make for what protects and nourishes them and to turn away from whatever might endanger their well-being, as they struggle to gain a foothold in life and overcome their initial weakness. As children grow, however, while still retaining this natural and appropriate behaviour, which is shared with animals, they begin to show their specific humanity in an awareness of rational processes. They start to act from choice rather than instinct, and maturing reason encourages them to choose consistently what is appropriate and in accord with nature as a whole. When such a pattern of behaviour has been established the true good finally comes to be understood. This is none other than virtue (*aretē*), which alone has intrinsic merit and is to be desired for its own sake. As adults they now understand that virtue is the one true good and its opposite, vice, the one evil, and that only in practising virtue under the guidance of reason will they realize their humanity to the full and so be truly happy.[24]

Those who reach the highest good are few and, in the daily lives of most of us, moral issues are not always pressing or dominant; advice is needed, therefore, on how to make decisions on a non-moral level. Provided it is always recognized that virtue is the only good and vice the only evil, the Stoics were ready to divide everything else into what is to be preferred, what rejected and what is of no consequence at all. What is preferable is natural, and so obviously includes life itself[25] as well as health, a moderate amount of wealth for one's comfort and the enjoyment of the respect of others. The continual selection by reason of the preferable according to our natural requirements, and the rejection of the opposite, are "appropriate actions" that are open to all. *Progress* towards the goal came to be emphasized rather than the difficulty (or near impossibility) of reaching it, so that education in the family and encouragement in the community were important in building up the habit of choices that are consistent with our human nature.[26]

It was central to Stoic ethics that the merit of an action has to be judged by the psychological state of the agent, which means that the inner motive is more important than the outward result. Where there is psychic harmony[27] then the actions performed will be rational and right, but, where there is discord within, then vicious action will follow. This means that there will be no improvement if the wrongdoer is physically punished, but attention should be given to treating the individual's psychological state and the underlying *pathos*: the sickness or disorder that caused the eruption into violence. An encouraging aspect, however, was the assertion that human beings are programmed by nature to be good. It is in accord with our humanity that reason develops from sound foundations, and the life of virtue to which it will lead us is consistently in harmony with that humanity, and indispensable to happiness. If we do not reach the goal the fault may be due to many causes, for example weak parenting, ill-health, unsympathetic environment, bad company or misguided education, all of which would work against progress towards the best life. More positively, the application of virtue to our natural affinities meant that the Stoics emphasized duty to parents and relatives, service to the community and responsible government in the wider sphere of politics.

The happy life of the Epicureans

Epicurus required philosophy to be practical, relevant and therapeutic. It needed to give a recipe for a happy life, but the recipe had to find its ingredients within the limits of human life on earth. Epicurus rejected divine government of the world or interference by divine powers in its working either now or in the future. Death, on his theory, is the dissolution of the atomic matter that makes up both body and soul, so that we should be as unconcerned with the time after death as with that before birth. There will consequently be no rewards or punishments at the end of life in return for how that life was lived, and it should not be governed by the expectation of either.[28] Reincarnation, with the prospect of another life, better or worse than this according to our present behaviour, was likewise ruled out.[29] It is the assurance given by the study of natural science that frees us from the consideration of divine retribution either now or later; there is only this life, to be lived on its own terms, and within its defined boundaries. Furthermore, since body and soul come into existence together, and mature and finish together, they should be regarded as partners rather than antagonists.[30] The happy life, therefore, will be more readily attainable if each is given its due, and the partnership fostered rather than ignored or suppressed. And it is open to everyone. Greek philosophy tended to be contemptuous of ordinary people, and to offer its choicest fruits to a mature and intellectual male elite; the Garden of Epicurus was unique in opening its gates also to women, the poor and the ignorant.

Stoic ethics, as we have seen, started from primary natural instinct, which they said was for self-preservation. The Epicureans on the contrary claimed that this instinct was for pleasure:

> We maintain that pleasure is the beginning and the end of the happy life; for we recognise it as the primary good inborn in us, we make it the starting point of our every choice and aversion, and the standard to which we return in judging all that is good.
>
> (DL 10.129)

Epicurus is with Aristotle in supposing that living things tend towards and want to obtain the good appropriate to their own kind. To discover what it is for human beings, he looks at them in their most primitive and uncorrupted condition, that is as newborn babies, and finds there that the instinct is towards what is pleasant and away from what is painful. This instinct, rooted in human nature, would be for what is of benefit, so Epicurus claims justification for his first move, that pleasure is good and pain bad. This goodness of pleasure is an immediate subjective experience, a direct perception, no more requiring argument than that fire is hot and honey sweet; and as such it is not liable to error. Consequently it just is the case that, in a natural condition, or at leisure, "when our power of choice has free range and nothing prevents us from doing what we like best, every pleasure is welcome and every pain avoided" (Torquatus, at Cicero, *De finibus* 1.33). Since this is so, Epicurus gives advice on how to achieve this aim most efficiently and effectively, and bases a practical rule of life on the universal experience of pleasure being natural, desirable and beneficial.

Sometimes, however, pain can be viewed as good if it will result in an increase of pleasure (as when nasty medicine brings relief), and pleasure evil if the consequence is greater pain (one more drink producing tomorrow's headache). At other times we may seize on an immediate pleasure and be caught by it "as by a bait", without looking ahead. An art of measurement is needed, an estimate of advantages and disadvantages, and a broad view of the whole of life, to keep us from making the wrong choices.[31] But what is to be measured? The primary natural and necessary desire is for food and drink, and Epicurus candidly maintains that someone who is hungry is unlikely to be happy; hunger is an obsession that has to be satisfied before attention is turned elsewhere. But it is not difficult to satisfy this most pressing need, and the pleasure of the satisfaction is independent of the simplicity of the means: "Plain food brings enjoyment equal to that of a lavish banquet when the pain of want is removed; and a starving man reaches the peak of pleasure in a meal of bread and water" (DL 10.130). The case is similar with other natural and necessary desires, which are best satisfied by simple means, to provide the foundation for a happy life. Luxurious clothing and housing, for example, can vary the pleasure involved but not increase its density, and the pursuit of ever more luxury panders to unnecessary desires and can be harmful in the long run. If we understand the limits of living and realize that it is easy to remove the pain caused by want, then life can be complete, and there is no need to struggle. Excess of any kind is liable to endanger the state of well-being:

> Not uninterrupted drinking and parties and love-making and
> exotic meals bring about the pleasant life, but sober reasoning,

> which examines the motive for every choice and rejection, and
> drives away those beliefs which cause the greatest tumult in the
> mind. (DL 10.132)

The resulting stable condition produces a strong and positive feeling of pleasure, along with a continuous sensitive awareness of abiding joy.

Happiness, therefore, depends on us and our attitude to external circumstances, rather than on the external circumstances themselves. Epicurus thought that we could, for example, be distracted from present pain by memories of pleasures in the past or anticipation of those to come. The study of science and cosmology, as has been shown, removes fears about divine displeasure and *post mortem* suffering, but the thinking involved has a pleasure of its own, which accompanies the effort. Furthermore, while pursuing its own pleasure of learning, the mind is securing the happiness of the whole, in giving support to the understanding of the limits of physical fulfilment, enjoying tranquillity in the present and being free of fear for the future. As with Aristotle, *phronēsis* (practical wisdom combined with sound judgement) has an important part to play in evaluating and balancing pleasures and pains, and making decisions towards achieving the aim of the happy life. In the long run, Epicurus concludes, *phronēsis* recommends virtuous activity as the most necessary and overriding means to happiness, since this is indispensable for the pleasant life. Because of the close interconnection it is impossible either to live pleasantly without practising the virtues, or to practise the virtues and not live pleasantly. Self-restraint (the virtue of "temperance"), controls vain desires and chooses moderation; courage enables us to meet pain and death with tranquillity, and justice promotes harmonious relationships with family and friends, and consequent peace of mind. Where the Stoics suppressed emotions as intellectual failures, Epicurus realized that they are natural to us. In the animal world, deer are always afraid and run away, cows are placid and lions roar because of the preponderance of different types of atomic molecules in their constitution, whether tending to be of the "windy" kind, or producing an excess of cold or heat. Some people, similarly, are more inclined to be afraid, or are too placid or too ready to lose their temper as a result of their physical make-up, but where animals stay true to type, human beings can exercise some control:

> Although education can produce a similar veneer, it leaves
> untouched original traces of each character, so that one person

too quickly loses his temper, another gives in to fear too soon, a third meekly accepts an insult. In many other respects there are different human characteristics, and different habits following from them, but one thing is sure – the traces of natural faults that reason cannot over-ride are so insignificant that nothing prevents us from leading god-like lives.   (Lucretius 3.307–22)

Friendship

Friendship was a topic that interested all the main philosophers. Plato wrote a dialogue called *Lysis* that attempted to analyse friendship (*philia*), starting from the assumption that a friend is the most precious of all possessions, and moving on to the question of how a friend is acquired. Are my friends the people I like or those who like me? But perhaps friendship unrequited is not true friendship, and there has to be mutual attraction. This then raises the topic of whether "likes" or "unlikes" are attracted to each other. Does my best friend have a background, character and habits similar to mine, or are we opposites, laughter-loving balanced by seriousness, for example, or impulsiveness by calm? In either case, where the friendship is reciprocated, the true friend becomes "my own".

Plato's *Symposium* and *Phaedrus* deal with erotic friendships. *Erōs* is the subject of the different speeches of the guests at the symposium, and the culmination is the speech of the priestess Diotima as reported by Socrates. In this, the "ladder of love" is explained. A person is first attracted by the handsome appearance of another, then realizes that beauty of soul and character is more commendable than a pretty face. But then the move is made away from the individual to understanding fine laws and institutions and the beauty in mathematical theories, and finally beauty itself is reached in all its splendour. The journey, however, seems to be a selfish one, as the beloved is abandoned for a higher object of desire, but in the *Phaedrus* myth this position is modified. Lover and beloved together help each other to "grow their wings" and ascend to the contemplation of forms.

Aristotle devoted two books of his *Nicomachean Ethics* to the subject of friendship. Like Plato, he would regard a friend as "one's own", in fact a "second self", and so value his or her welfare with the same consideration as his own. The company of business colleagues may be useful, and that of acquaintances often pleasant, but that of good people is independent of other considerations. Such "virtue-friendship" involves loving others for themselves, with no thought of gain or convenience for oneself. It will happen *incidentally* and as a bonus that one's own life is enhanced and its happiness increased by the other's company: joys are doubled and troubles halved in the sharing. It is in our nature to be sociable, and, in contrast to Plato's ideal of solitary contemplation, Aristotle is closer to Socrates in suggesting that philosophy advances further and is more enjoyable if two people argue through a topic together.

The Epicureans went further than their predecessors, and gave friendship top priority for long-term happiness: "Of all that wisdom provides for blessedness throughout life, by far the most important is the possession of friends" (*KD* 27). It is more important even than the fulfilment of the most basic needs. Before eating, for example, they encourage us to look for a friend to share the meal, for otherwise we are living like lions or wolves (Seneca, *Letters*, 19.10). The connection with fellow citizens in the societies in which we live is an enforced one, and justice can do little more than establish conditions for restraining them from harming and being harmed; in general Epicurus recommended avoiding any overt political activity as guaranteed to disturb one's peace of mind. But friendship freely entered on, and based on individual character and inclination, is another matter. If we are always asking for help from our friends, this is not true friendship but "petty trading", although the *confidence* that they will be there in times of need brings a pleasant feeling of security. If the confidence is reciprocated and we love our friends as ourselves, then, in the promotion of the happiness of the other, the source of greater happiness for both lies: "Great men are concerned above all with wisdom and friendship; the first of these is a mortal good, the second immortal" (*Vatican Sayings* 78).[32]

Compared with the Epicureans, the Stoics had a problem with friendship. In stressing the indifference of philosophers to external circumstances, and their own freedom and independence of spirit, the Stoics were led to the conclusion that there is no need for friends. A friend, according to their theory, is not of intrinsic value or necessary for happiness, but merely allows *scope* for the practice of virtue in generosity and benevolence. Furthermore, if only the wise are capable of true friendship, then it is out of reach for most people. From another point of view, however, the Stoic theory of friendship was more encouraging. From the development of the primary natural instinct for self-preservation, it is clear that children extend awareness and affection to parents and family; then, as they grow to maturity, they reach out to the community and the state. As a result, in contrast to the Epicureans, the Stoics fostered the sense of duty towards one's fellow citizens, and expected active participation in the political life of the city: "The human race has been given by nature such a need for virtue and such a love of defending the common welfare that its force defeats the charms of leisure and the pleasant life" (Cicero, *Republic* 1.1).[33] The theory extended the sense of belonging even further, from family to state (*polis*), and from state to the world-state (*cosmopolis*), for "we are born for the company of others, and the social fellowship of the whole human race" (*De finibus* 4.4). According to the Stoics, the interconnection of justice, law, reason and nature is therefore in the interests of citizens and world citizens alike. Altruism and utility ultimately coincide in both civic justice and philanthropy, for acting justly strengthens civic ties to the advantage of all citizens, and acting kindly towards a fellow human being enhances all human life.

Epilogue

This introduction to Greek philosophy, which began with the Milesians in Asia Minor, finishes with Lucretius and Cicero in the last century of the Roman Republic. After this period philosophy in the Roman Empire tended to focus on ethics (rather than logic or natural science) in the search for guidelines for living the best life, under whatever circumstances. Stoic ethical theory was most favoured,[1] but the rigidity of the early formal Stoicism was adapted to deal with contemporary problems, and its practitioners were ready to find support and encouragement in other philosophies, even accepting aspects of Epicureanism. Three well-known figures popularized this trend from different standpoints: Seneca, at one time adviser to Nero, Epictetus, the former Greek slave, and the emperor Marcus Aurelius. Within a general Stoic framework the letters of Seneca, the teachings of Epictetus in the "Handbook" (*Encheiridion*), and the *Meditations* of Aurelius had an immediate appeal, and they are still read today for their direct approach, sound advice and good sense.

Epicureanism was handed down from its founder as a complete system, which meant that there was little development in the philosophy. Although it was officially out of favour in Rome for rejecting the state gods, speaking against participation in politics and generally advocating an easygoing lifestyle, it had many adherents. These included Cicero's friend Atticus, Cassius the conspirator against Caesar, the poet Horace (who called himself "a pig from the sty of Epicurus"), and Plotina, the wife of the emperor Trajan. The philosophy continued to thrive for centuries in communities throughout the empire, and to arouse controversy. Galen and Plutarch wrote extensively condemning its principles, whereas Diogenes of Oenoanda set up his massive public inscription to win over Greeks and foreigners alike to Epicurean wisdom.

Theophrastus and then Strato and Lyco succeeded Aristotle at the Lyceum (which became known as the "Peripatetic School") and continued many of his projects. From then on the main interest of the school was in studying and interpreting the works of the founder, starting with Andronicus of Rhodes, who published commentaries on Aristotle's physics, ethics and the surprisingly popular *Categories*. A whole industry of writing commentaries on Aristotle flourished in Athens, Rhodes and, after the Macedonian conquests, in the great library at Alexandria. Among the most influential were those by Alexander of Aphrodisias, and, in the sixth century CE, by the Christian Philoponus and the Neoplatonist Simplicius. The interest in Aristotle passed into Islamic culture from Alexandria, with translations and commentaries of major works in Arabic, the most important of which were by Avicenna (Ibn Sīnā) in the East, and later by Averroes (Ibn Rushd) in Spain.[2]

Significant original work in philosophy is to be found in the development of Platonic thought in the Academy and beyond. After Plato's death in 347 BCE, the leadership of the Academy passed to his nephew Speusippus, who revised the relationship of forms to mathematics, and then Xenocrates, who also introduced the principles of the One and the Indefinite Dyad, which may have originated in "unwritten doctrines" of Plato. Some decades later there was a breakaway movement under Arcesilaus, which became known as the "New" Academy. This movement, developed further by the brilliant Carneades, favoured scepticism, connecting the dialectical tradition of Plato to a general suspension of belief. Philo of Larissa was head of the school from 110 to 88 BCE and then moved to Rome; he was interested in reconciling the different trends in his focus on moral education. Antiochus, who had studied under Philo, disagreed with his approach, and re-established the Old Academy. This initiated a period recognized as "Middle Platonism", in which Stoic and Pythagorean influences pervaded Platonic metaphysics and ethics. There was some dispute about the assimilation or rejection of Aristotelian material, but little direct evidence for this period survives. We know of Eudorus, famous for recommending "becoming like god" as the human ideal, and Philo of Alexandria, the interpreter of Hebrew scriptures along Platonic lines. A century later, Numenius of Apamea in Syria, an influential philosopher and an important predecessor of Plotinus, attributed much of Plato's philosophy to Pythagorean influence. Also in Syria, Albinus, Galen's teacher, had a particular interest in Plato's *Timaeus*, and in his writing explored ways of synthesizing it with some aspects of Aristotelianism. The "Platonic Underworld" of the *Corpus Hermeticum*, Gnosticism and the *Chaldean Oracles* are also to be found in this period.

Plotinus arrived in Rome from Alexandria in the third century CE, and this move marked the end of Middle Platonism, and the establishment of the first phase of Neoplatonism in the third century CE. Plotinus started a school in Rome, where his work was continued to the end of the century by his pupils Amelius Gentilianus and the more famous Porphyry, who had come to join him in Rome from Athens. Plotinus' philosophy, along with his biography, was set out in a series of essays collected and edited by Porphyry, in six sets of nine, and so called the *Enneads*. The chief features focus on a reworking of Plato's form of the good into a principle superior to both intelligence and being, called simply "the One". From this Plotinus derived Intellect and then Soul in a series of eternal "outflowings". The One, the "First Hypostasis", is the primary causal principle of all existence. The Intellect, the "Second Hypostasis", possessing perfect self-knowledge and eternal life, is derived from the One, and Soul, the Third Hypostasis, is in its turn a by-product of Intellect.[3] Soul produces, animates and controls the visible world in the generation of time as it projects its light onto the negative force of matter. As well as publishing this work by Plotinus, Porphyry wrote an introduction, *Isagōgē*, to Aristotle's *Categories*, which was translated into Latin by Boethius, and so directly influenced medieval discussions of the "problem of universals". Porphyry's own philosophy was concerned with the metaphysics of the divine nature and the One, and ways in which individual souls could be detached from passions and enter a higher reality.

The second phase of Neoplatonism centred on the Syrian Iamblichus, who had studied under Porphyry in Athens, and had then set up his own school near Antioch. Iamblichus wrote extensively, introducing into Neoplatonism a particular interest in Pythagoreanism, now known as "Neopythagoreanism", as well as a more elaborate form of Porphyry's metaphysics. Neopythagoreanism had started in the first century CE, and went on to combine the three hypostases from Plotinus with features from Plato's *Timaeus* and *Parmenides*. In the next century, Nicomachus of Gerasa in Syria had brought Pythagorean "number mysticism" into the system with his *Theological Arithmetic*, and so influenced both Iamblichus and Proclus.

Around 325 CE, the year of Iamblichus' death, the emperor Constantine confirmed Christianity as the religion of the Roman Empire. Thirty years later Julian "the Apostate" attempted to reverse his decree and return to the earlier cults. He used Iamblichus' work, which had been brought to him by Maximus of Ephesus, as the basis for a Hellenic theology to rival Christianity, but he failed in his attempt to turn the tide. Aristotelian studies, along with mathematics and astronomy, continued in Alexandria, but suffered a setback when the philosopher and mathematician Hypatia, one of the most famous teachers there, was brutally murdered at the instigation of the archbishop Cyril in a wave of protest against pagan teaching.

In the third phase of Neoplatonism, the school returned to Athens, where Plutarch of Athens re-established Plato's Academy. He was succeeded by Syrianus, who had come to Athens from Syria, and then by Proclus, a major figure in the fifth century CE, whose writing on *Elements of Theology* was extremely influential. Proclus' own commentaries were mainly on Plato, complementing to some extent the major studies on Aristotle's works. In 529 CE the Academy was officially closed by the emperor Justinian; Damascius was its last director. Simplicius, who came originally from Cilicia in Asia Minor, had first studied in Alexandria and then been a pupil of Damascius in Athens. As a result of Justinian's action he was forced to leave with Damascius and five other philosophers. From 531 CE they were welcomed at the court of Khosrau I of Persia, and Simplicius continued to work there undisturbed on his monumental commentaries on Aristotle from his own Neoplatonic standpoint.

Augustine of Hippo in North Africa, and contemporary with Hypatia, admitted that his conversion to Christianity was stimulated by reading "certain books of the Platonists". They would have included the *Timaeus* (the only one of Plato's works available in Latin translation, by Cicero, and which had a commentary by Chalcidius) and parts of Plotinus and Porphyry, probably in Latin translation, although Augustine did have a little Greek. In much of his own work he "Christianized" this reading; he suggested, for example, that Plato's eternal and unchanging forms were the thoughts of God, existing in his mind, and adapted Plotinus' cosmology and psychology to the new religion. In the century after Augustine, Boethius was a further link between Greek philosophy and the Christian theology of the Middle Ages. Having a comprehensive knowledge of Greek he worked with original texts, probably in Alexandria, and his translations of Aristotle into Latin and his related commentaries on them meant that it was Aristotle rather than Plato who dominated medieval philosophy. Boethius himself attempted to reconcile the two in following Plato in his own metaphysics and theology, and Aristotle in logic and natural science. His famous *Consolation of Philosophy*, written in prison, was an exploration of many of the themes running through Greek philosophy. The *Summa Theologiae* of Thomas Aquinas marked the culmination of the merging of Aristotle and Neoplatonism with Christian theology.

Throughout the Middle Ages, Aristotle had continued to be the dominant figure from Greek philosophy studied in the Church and the universities. It was in the early years of the Renaissance that a much wider range of texts from Greek philosophy became accessible in what is known as "Renaissance Platonism". A Platonic school had been established at Mistra in the Peloponnese by Pletho, who was sent as a delegate to the Council of Florence to negotiate the reunion of the Western and Eastern Christian Churches. Pletho inspired Cosimo de' Medici to found the Platonic Academy of Florence and, as a result, Italian scholars from there began to travel extensively in Greece. They returned with manuscripts that, under Pletho's influence, they settled down to translate. Included among them was Diogenes Laertius' *Lives of Eminent Philosophers*, which covered biographies of all the main philosophers with quotations and summaries of their views, and was translated into Latin in 1433, the year of the birth of Marsilio Ficino. Ficino joined the Platonic Academy of Florence as an adult, where he translated the whole of Plato and Plotinus into Latin, and, with the advent of printing, saw these key texts immediately circulating throughout Europe.

From 1470 onwards, when the first philosophical texts were printed, thousands of editions of Greek philosophers were made public. Presocratics, Stoics and Sceptics were also joining ranks with Plato, Plotinus and Aristotle, and there were various attempts at reconciling all these different teachings. Giovanni Pico della Mirandola, for example, a younger contemporary of Ficino, wrote 900 theses (all condemned by the Church) as well as starting on a *Concord of Plato and Aristotle*. Giordano Bruno, in the next generation, travelled and taught widely in Europe, but was eventually executed in Venice

Figure 2. Raphael, *School of Athens,*, in the Apostolic Palace, Vatican City.

as a heretic. He favoured Neoplatonism, but, as he was dissatisfied with Aristotle's related cosmology and metaphysics, he went back to the Presocratics, and found antecedents for the One of Plotinus in the pantheism of Xenophanes and Heraclitus, Parmenides' unity of being and Anaxagoras' principle of "everything in everything". On the Epicurean side, the poem of Lucretius barely survived the hostility to its teaching. The poem is found in only two manuscripts (now in Leiden), but, with the publication of the poem, Epicureanism also became part of the philosophical scene of the Renaissance.

The great reconciliation of the different Greek philosophies with each other and with Christianity came with Pope Julius II in 1510, when he commissioned Raphael, then just twenty-seven years old, to paint a quartet of frescoes in a room in the Vatican Palace (Stanze della Segnatura) which would be his private library. They were to represent philosophy, theology, poetry and law, with *"causarum cognitio"* (knowledge of causes) as the motto above philosophy. The related fresco became known as the *Scuola di Ateni* (School of Athens), although it incorporated figures from East and West as well as Athenians, in a setting where the architecture is Roman. The long-lasting rivalry between the supporters of Plato and Aristotle is settled by the two philosophers standing as equals in the central position, Plato holding the *Timaeus* and pointing upwards, Aristotle the *Nicomachean Ethics*, and embracing with a sweeping gesture the surrounding physical world. Some other figures in the fresco are generally identified: Socrates in discussion with Antisthenes; a group of Presocratics including Pythagoras, Parmenides and Heraclitus; Epicurus, Plotinus and Hypatia; Diogenes the Cynic sprawling on the steps; Euclid with students; and Ptolemy as a bystander. The figures cover a range of ancient philosophers, shown in action engaged in mathematics or talking in groups (with contemporary Italians joining in) or lost in thought; the whole is a magnificent celebration of Greek philosophy in the heart of Christian Rome. From then on the influence of the Greek philosophers spread to the countries of western Europe, to Descartes and Malebranche in France, Erasmus and Spinoza in the Netherlands, Leibniz and Hegel in Germany, to Bacon, Hobbes, Locke and Berkeley in England, Hutcheson and Hume in the Scottish Enlightenment and Richard Price in Wales.

APPENDIX
Sources for Greek philosophy

Twenty-six original works of Plato and an extensive range of Aristotle's writings survive; there is also a hymn by the Stoic Cleanthes, and three letters and some maxims from Epicurus, reinforced by the Latin poem of Lucretius. Thales, Pythagoras, Socrates and Pyrrho wrote nothing. For these and the other Greek philosophers in the period BCE we have to rely on quotations and reports from later authors, who refer to their predecessors in different contexts and for widely differing purposes, and vary considerably in accuracy and general reliability. In the case of the Presocratics there is also a network of doxography, that is, comments, summaries and paraphrases of views attributed to the Presocratics on a range of topics. Most of this material is descended, directly or indirectly, from *Opinions of the Physicists*, a history of early philosophy written by Theophrastus, the student and successor of Aristotle at the Lyceum. In this secondary literature, even with straight quotations it is often difficult to tell where the original words begin and end, and how much of his own terminology and bias the reporting author has introduced. In some cases the quotations are from memory, or reported at second or third hand, where the original work is not available. The problem is further compounded by different and sometimes conflicting manuscript readings.

In addition to the original texts, the following are the main sources available for Greek philosophy, with a note on the authors and their interests.

Aetius (1st–2nd century CE): This is the name given to a second-hand summary of Theophrastus' *Opinions of the Physicists*. The source was reconstructed by Diels from parts common to Stobaeus and the pseudo-Plutarch *Placita*, and published in his *Doxographi Graeci*.

Aristophanes (*c*.445–385 BCE): Aristophanes' comedy *The Clouds* presents Socrates as a character in the context of the new learning introduced by the sophists. Socrates is shown doing cosmology, running a school, and teaching the young to argue against their elders. Although the Platonic Socrates denied these claims, Aristophanes gives a contemporary view of him as hardly distinguishable from the more unscrupulous sophists.

Aristotle (384–322 BCE): Aristotle often takes his predecessors' opinions as a starting-point for his own discussions. He is inclined to use his own terminology, and to see others as tackling a problem from his point of view. He can be brusque and sometimes, especially in the case of the Eleatics, unsympathetic or unfair, but he is pre-eminent as a source for the Presocratics (including Pythagoras and the Pythagoreans), and for valuable comments on Socrates. Apart from direct quotations, his main contribution to the history of philosophy is his summary of Presocratic explanations of the world in the first book of his *Metaphysics*, when he looks to his predecessors for confirmation of his own theory of causation. In his *Physics* we also have the first presentation and criticism of Zeno's famous four puzzles on motion.

Alexander of Aphrodisias (2nd–3rd century CE): Alexander is one of the most important of the earlier commentators on Aristotle's work. His commentaries on *Metaphysics*, *Meteorologica* and *De anima* expand Aristotle's comments on the Presocratics involved, and his work *On Fate* is important for contrasting Stoic ideas on fate and determinism with those of Aristotle.

Arius Didymus (1st century BCE): This philosopher was a friend and adviser to the emperor Augustus. He wrote works entitled *On Sects* and *Epitome*, both of which contain summaries of previous philosophies, including an important survey of Stoic physics and ethics; some of this material is preserved in Eusebius and Stobaeus.

Cicero (106–43 BCE): Towards the end of his life, in enforced retirement from politics, the famous Roman orator and statesman devoted himself to philosophic writing. He presented, in Latin prose, the views of the post-Aristotelian Hellenistic schools, with his own friends and teachers acting as spokesmen for the different positions. His *Academica* summarized Carneades' scepticism, and the more dogmatic response to it from the later followers of Plato. *On the Nature of the Gods* first gives an unsympathetic summary of the Epicurean stand against conventional religion, which is answered by Balbus as spokesman for Stoic theology, the third book contains a compromise between the two. More important are the five books *On Supreme Good and Evil* (*De finibus bonorum et malorum*), which give a derogatory account of Epicurean ethics, but, in the person of Cicero's friend the younger Cato, the most complete summary of Stoic ethics available as a continuous text.

Clement of Alexandria (1st–2nd century CE): One of the most erudite of the early Church Fathers, Clement was a convert to Christianity who continued to be interested in Greek literature and philosophy. The *Stromateis*, a miscellaneous collection

209

in eight books of comparisons between paganism and Christianity, is a treasure house of quotations from Greek philosophers, especially from the Presocratics and Stoics. There are also some fragments of Heraclitus in his *Protrepticus* (an "exhortation" to convert to Christianity) as well as a brief account of the Stoic "good".

Diogenes Laertius (3rd century CE): This name (sometimes given as Laertes Diogenes, and here abbreviated to DL) is attached to a compendium with the title *Lives and Opinions of Famous Philosophers*. The ten books of biography, anecdote, summary and report cover the spectrum from Thales to Epicurus. However unreliable and uncritical he was as a historian, Diogenes frequently names his primary and secondary sources, and quotes extensively. The material is important for all the major philosophies, but book VII is especially valuable as a Stoic source, detailing the lives and works of Zeno of Citium, Cleanthes and Chrysippus.

Diogenes of Oenoanda (2nd centrury CE): This Diogenes is famous for the long wall he erected in Lycia in central Turkey, around 200 CE. The wall is over forty metres long and four blocks high, and is inscribed with columns of Greek text relating to Epicureanism. It is a main source for Epicurus, including summaries and direct quotations, which Diogenes publicized with the declared aim of encouraging his fellow citizens to follow the Epicurean way of life.

Hippolytus (2nd–3rd century CE): In his main work, *Refutation of all Heresies*, Hippolytus, Bishop of Rome, set out to combat different heresies by showing their kinship with particular pagan philosophies. He is a main source for Heraclitus, whose theories he assimilates to the heresy of Mardonius, and for quotations from Empedocles.

Iamblichus (*c.*245–325 CE): Iamblichus is an important Neoplatonist who wrote commentaries on Plato and Aristotle, as well as the essay "On the Pythagorean Way of Life". As with his contemporary Porphyry (who wrote a *Life of Pythagoras*) much of the material relates to later practices and tenets of the Pythagoreans, and is unreliable as a guide to Pythagoras himself and his immediate followers.

Lucretius (*c.*90–50 BCE): Little is known about Lucretius' life. He is famous as the author of one hexameter poem in six books known as *De rerum natura* ("On the nature of things", or "How things are"; abbreviated as *DRN*). This is an extensive exposition in Latin of Epicurus' physical theory and is a main source for it, covering the nature and movement of atoms, the structure and mortality of the soul, the early history of the human race and various natural phenomena.

Philodemus (*c.*110–40 BCE): The "Fragments of Philodemus" were discovered in Herculaneum in southern Italy. These are numerous charred scraps of papyrus from the library of the Epicurean Philodemus, which was buried in the eruption of Vesuvius in 79 CE. They were excavated in the mid-eighteenth century and are still being deciphered. They are especially valuable as a defence of Epicurean teaching against attacks from Stoics and others, and an adaptation of it to contemporary issues.

Plutarch (50–*c*.120 CE): As well as his *Lives* of Greek and Roman statesmen, Plutarch wrote numerous essays on ethical themes, known collectively as *Moralia*. These essays are packed with quotations from most of the philosophers, but often inadequately remembered, and interspersed with Plutarch's own comments. His most valuable quotations from the Presocratics are from Xenophanes, Heraclitus and Empedocles. Two essays have a considerable amount of Epicurean material, "Against Colotes" and "Against Epicurean Happiness", but presented from a hostile point of view, and he is similarly unsympathetic to the Stoics in his essay on Stoic self-contradiction.

Sextus Empiricus (2nd–3rd century CE): Sextus is the main source for ancient scepticism, in three books on *Outlines of Pyrrhonism* and eleven *Against the Mathematicians*. *Outlines* is a summary of the work of the early Pyrrhonists, especially that of Aenesidemus, and compares scepticism with other Hellenistic schools. *Against the Mathematicians* similarly involves quotations and reports from a variety of philosophers, especially Epicureans and Stoics, but also includes some Presocratics such as Xenophanes, Heraclitus, Pythagoras and Democritus, who were seen as forerunners of the sceptics in raising doubts about the possibility of human knowledge.

Simplicius (6th century CE): Simplicius' commentaries on Aristotle's *Physics* and *De caelo* are monumental works of erudition. When Aristotle refers to a Presocratic, Simplicius usually gives the relevant quotation, sometimes at greater length than necessary where the original was hard to find and worth preserving (as was especially the case with Parmenides' poem). In the commentaries there are also many references to Stoic and Epicurean theories, but Simplicius has a Neoplatonic bias, and tends to interpret all philosophies in terms of the contrast between the worlds of reason and perception.

Stobaeus (5th century CE): John Stobaeus compiled an anthology of quotations from Greek writers as a course of instruction for his son in various topics. The collection is in four books: the first two are abridged, and known as *Selections* (*Eclogae*) and the third and fourth make up an *Anthology* (*Florilegium*). The collection relies on earlier extracts and summaries from the first centuries CE, and contains a large number of valuable quotations from Presocratic and Stoic philosophers.

Xenophon (*c*.430–350 BCE): A successful Athenian general, Xenophon wrote several works on his contemporary Socrates: like Plato an *Apology* and *Symposium*; a dialogue on managing an estate (*Oeconomicus*); and *Memorabilia*, a valuable source for the philosophical activity of Socrates. Although it is commonly said that he was unable to understand or follow Socrates' deeper meanings, Xenophon's evidence is still useful to set beside that of Aristophanes and Plato in the search for an accurate reconstruction of the historical Socrates.

Some further sources

The philosophers of the Roman Empire, Seneca, Epictetus and Marcus Aurelius, favoured Stoicism, but they often reported or quoted from other philosophies where they found passages to be relevant and useful. In addition there are some summaries and quotations from all the philosophers in the ancient dictionaries of Hesychius and the *Etymologicum Magnum*, and also in "scholia", anonymous notes in the margins of the manuscripts of related works.

Diels-Kranz (DK)

The standard collection of fragments of the Presocratics and Sophists is H. Diels & W. Kranz, *Die Fragmente der Vorsokratiker*, 6th edn (Berlin: Weidmann, 1951). It is in three volumes (the third is a comprehensive index) and, in a section for each philosopher, gives the sources for the passages under "A", and then direct quotations with author, context and textual apparatus under "B". DK 22B93, for example, would be the reference for fragment 93 of Heraclitus, the subject of section 22. Even if translators or commentators use their own order for the fragments, there would always be a reference or concordance to the DK numbering.

Glossary of Greek philosophical terms

agathos good, brave, virtuous
    aristos best, most good (superlative of *agathos*)
    auto to agathon the good itself, form of the good
    aretē virtue, excellence (abstract noun for *agathos*)
    eu well, in a good way (adverb for *agathos*)
aithēr bright blue sky (above misty *aēr*); as "ether", Aristotle's fifth element
akrasia loss of control, weakness of will
alētheia truth
apodeixis demonstration, deduction
apeiros without boundaries, limitless
    to apeiron: the limitless
aporia perplexity (literally "no way out")
aitia explanation, cause (*aitios*: responsible)
archē beginning, rule, first principle, hence
    anarchia without government, anarchy
    monarchia rule by one man
ataraxia freedom from disturbance, tranquillity
atomon uncuttable, atom (from *temnō*, "I cut")
dikē justice, morality
    adikia injustice, wrong-doing
doxa opinion, belief
elenchos examination, refutation
eidos form (plural *eidē*); *idea* was also used; (both words connect with "see",
    idein, and "know", *eidenai*)
ekpyrōsis conflagration
epistēmē knowledge

eudaimonia happiness, prosperity, flourishing (literally "having a good
    daimōn/spirit")

harmonia fitting together, attunement, harmony

hēdonē pleasure

historia enquiry, research

hylē matter (as opposed to form)
    prōtē hylē prime matter

kakos bad, cowardly, wicked (opposite of *agathos*)

kalos beautiful, fine, right, moral (linked to *agathos*)
    to kalon beauty, what is fine and right

kinēsis movement, change, alteration

kosmos order, the world order, cosmos

kenos empty
    to kenon void

logos spoken word, reason, account, formula, ratio

nomos law, custom, convention, tradition
    eunomia good order, with good laws (also, well-managed pasture)
    isonomia equal distribution, equality of rights

noēma thought
    to noēton the intelligible world (contrasted with *to oraton*, the visible world)

nous mind, intelligence

oikeiōsis self-regard, affinity (from *oikia*, "home")

on being (neuter participle of *eimi*, "I am")
    to on what is; *to mē on*: what is not
    ta onta what there is; *esti*: is, *ouk esti*: is not
    ousia being, essence

pathos suffering, passiveness (plural *pathē*, "passions", "emotions")

phronēsis practical wisdom

physis natural structure, nature (often contrasted with *nomos*)

pneuma breath, warm breath

polis independent city-state
    politēs citizen
    politeia "state" in the abstract, constitution, republic
    ta politika what concerns the city-state, politics

psychē soul, principle of life

stoicheion element (also for a letter of the alphabet)

sōphrosynē self-control, modesty, temperance

technē skill, craft

telos end, aim, goal

Notes

1. Mapping the territory

1. "Presocratic" is the collective term traditionally assigned to the first philosophers, in the sixth and fifth centuries BCE, who came before Socrates and the Sophists. The last of them is Democritus, who is included in the "Presocratic" group, although he is contemporary with Socrates, because his atomic theory marked the culmination of the earlier ways of thinking.

2. The *cosmological* background to the poems was of a simple structure of earth as a central circular disk, around which flowed the freshwater river Ocean, with sky above and Tartarus below.

3. "Hellas" and "Hellenes" are the original words (still used) for the land and its people; "Greece" and "Greeks" are from the Latin *Graecia* and *Graeci*.

4. The letter B before a numeral refers to the numbering of the fragments of the Presocratics according to H. Diels & W. Kranz, *Die Fragmente der Vorsokratiker*, 6th edn (Berlin: Weidmann, 1951); see Appendix, p. 212.

5. Given a right-angled triangle with the two sides about the right angle of length 2, the length of the hypotenuse is $\sqrt{8}$, which cannot be represented by a whole number; the hypotenuse length was therefore called an "irrational" number (*alogos arithmos*). Hippasus, an early Pythagorean, was said to have been drowned at sea for revealing this uncomfortable fact.

6. This is a direct adaptation to time of Anaximander's spatial argument that there is no "sufficient reason" for the earth to move in one direction rather than another, and so it stays in the same position; see p. 66.

7. Recorded by Plato at *Phaedrus* 270a, where discussions of cosmology, being literally "high talking" (*meteōrologica*), helped to improve Pericles' own public speaking.

8. The citizens of Lampsacus erected an altar in memory of Anaxagoras, and,

215

at his own request, the date of his death was an annual school holiday; cf. Aristotle, *Rhetoric* 1398b10 on honours given to the wise.

9. His crucial question was: "how could hair have come from what is not hair, and flesh from what is not flesh?" (DK 59B10).

10. The main dialogues may be classified as follows: (i) Socratic defence and literary criticism – *Apology, Crito, Ion, Hippias Minor*; (ii) Socratic *elenchos* – *Laches, Charmides, Euthyphro, Hippias Major, Lysis, Euthydemus*; (iii) mainly Socratic – *Gorgias, Meno, Protagoras, Cratylus, Symposium*; (iv) Socratic/ Platonic – *Phaedo, Republic, Phaedrus, Timaeus*; (v) also Socratic/Platonic – *Theaetetus, Parmenides, Sophist, Politicus, Philebus*; and (vi) dogmatic/anti-Socratic – *Laws*.

11. This is the first word the modern traveller to Greece sees on arrival, as it is used for searching and examination by customs officials.

12. In Diogenes Laertius, *Life of Plato* 3.37, and Aristoxenus, *Harmonics* 30–31, it is reported that only Aristotle stayed to the end of the *Phaedo* reading, and that the audience gradually deserted the lecture when it became clear that the content was seriously mathematical.

13. The works in the Platonic corpus of doubtful authenticity are: *Alcibiades I* and *II, Cleitiphon, Epinomis, Erastae, Hipparchus, Menexenus, Minos* and *Theages*. The main authentic dialogues are listed above in note 10.

14. Two of the *Phaedo* proofs involve the assumption of "forms" as perfect and unique paradigms of the many imperfect particulars found in this world; this is the first appearance of the so-called "theory of forms"; see pp. 118–19.

15. The exact text is: "The safest general characterization of the European philo-sophical tradition is that it consists of a series of footnotes to Plato. I do not mean the systematic scheme of thought which scholars have doubtfully extracted from his writings. I allude to the wealth of general ideas scattered through them" (*Process and Reality: An Essay in Cosmology* [Cambridge: Cambridge University Press, 1929], 39).

16. The following is a summary of Aristotle's main works: (i) on logic – *Categories, On Interpretation, Analytics (Prior and Posterior), Topics* and *Sophistic Refuta-tions*; (ii) on natural science – *Physics, On the Heavens, Generation and Decay, Meteorology, On the Soul* (and some related short essays); (iii) on zoology – *Animal Studies, Parts of Animals, Animal Movements, Progression of Animals, Generation of Animals*; (iv) on first philosophy/theology – *Metaphysics* (this title means simply "[written] after (*meta*) *physics*"; "metaphysics" acquired its later meaning from the subjects discussed by Aristotle in the work); (v) on practical and productive sciences – *Nicomachean Ethics, Eudemian Ethics*; (vi) and *Politics, Rhetoric* and *Poetics*.

17. Translated into Latin as *quinta essentia*, from which the word "quintessence" is derived.

18. Plato had realized that the organ of thought was located in the head, but Aristotle's biological studies are weakened to some extent by his reverting to earlier theories, placing the centre of thought and perception in the heart

area, which obviously seems to house the life force of the body at its centre. Epicureans and Stoics followed Aristotle in this view.

19. *Hamartia* has often been translated as "sin" or "tragic flaw", which has caused critics to look for a "flaw" in famous characters in tragedy, but the meaning is simply "mistake", which the protagonist may try to avoid but which eventually causes the reversal of fortune.

20. The Cynics were literally the "dog-philosophers" (the Greek word for dogs is *kynes*), so called because of their bark-like scolding and shameless street behaviour.

21. Diogenes reduced his needs to a minimum, starting the philosopher's "uniform" of staff, cloak and food-bag; when he saw children drinking from their cupped hands, he threw away his own cup as unnecessary (DL 6.57). The famous "tub" he is said to have lived in was more probably a large storage jar.

22. None of Xenocrates' works survive, even in fragments. He was famous for saying that philosophy "heals life's disturbances" (Clement, *Stromateis* 2.22).

23. The most famous Megarian paradox was the liar paradox, which in Cicero's version is: "if you say that you are a liar and this is true, you are lying" (*Academica* 2.95).

2. Language, logic and literary form

1. Thales' sayings are from Aristotle: "All things are full of gods" from *De anima* 411a8 amd the magnetic stone moving iron from *De anima* 405a21. Aristotle gives the arguments for water as first principle at *Metaphysics* 983b20–26. The comment on the style of Anaximander is from Simplicius *in Phys.* 24.16, and on Anaximenes from DL 2.3. The Hecataeus quotation is from the first sentence (fr. 1) of his *Genealogia*. Anaximander uses legal language in DK 12B1, and Anaximenes a mathematical ratio in his fragment 13B2.

2. Of the *logos*, which is as I describe it, people always prove to be uncomprehending both before they have heard it and once they have heard it, for, although all things happen according to the *logos*, people are like those of no experience, even when they do experience such words and deeds as I explain when I distinguish each thing according to its nature and declare how it is, but others fail to notice what they do after they wake up just as they forget what they do when asleep. (22B1)

3. See Cicero, *Stoic Paradoxes* 1, 3 and 5, and *Pro Murena* 61, discussed in my *On Stoic Good and Evil* (Warminster: Aris & Phillips, 1991), 197–201.

4. An elegiac couplet is a six foot hexameter line, followed by a pentameter, of two and a half feet repeated. For the Pythagoras fragment see above, p. 113. Solon used elegiacs for his political manifesto; see p. 162.

5. Empedocles is said to have taken the opportunity to recite part of his philosophy in the poetry competitions at the Olympic games.

6. On chariot symbolism see Homer, *Odyssey* 9.295; Parmenides B6.6; Empedocles B17.21, 139.2. On far-wandering people see Homer, *Odyssey* 20.195; Parmenides B16.4; Empedocles B20.5. On philosophical cosmology see Homer, *Iliad* 15.190–93; Hesiod, *Theogony* 108–10; Parmenides B10.1–4; Empedocles B38.1–4.

7. The moon is called *allotrios phōs* by Parmenides, but the meaning here is "light from another place".

8. For example, a literal translation of the "stadium", as quoted by Aristotle, reads: "First that about not moving, because the runner must first reach the half before the end". His version of the "arrow" reads: "if everything is always at rest in its length, and what is moving is always in the now, unmoved is the moving arrow" (*Physics* 239b9–30).

9. Towards the end of the exchange between Callicles and Socrates, Callicles refuses to answer further. In an unusual passage (*Gorgias* 506c–507c), which is both monologue and dialogue, Socrates asks the questions as himself and gives the answers to his own questions, speaking as Callicles.

10. As well as his puzzles, Zeno of Elea is said to have been the first to write dialogues; see DL 3.37, 48, and Plato's discussion at *Republic* 392.

11. The audience was disenchanted and only Aristotle stayed to the end, see above, Chapter 1, note 12.

12. Even the opening words are important. It was well known, for example, that Plato tried out several variants on the first line of *Republic*, and *Timaeus*, one of the most complex mathematical works in antiquity, has a deceptively simple opening: "One, two three – but where, dear Timaeus, is our fourth guest?".

13. *Symposium* is especially difficult syntactically, as it is an account of the evening's conversation by Aristodemus, one of the guests, as told to Phoenix, and then reported by him to Apollodorus, who is retelling it to an unnamed companion.

14. One of the signs that the Atlantis myth is not to be taken as true is the exaggeration of the god Poseidon fathering *five* pairs of twins, who build an exotic city on a faraway island, and set up *ten* dynasties of rulers, whose descendants set out from there to conquer the known world. Plato's *eschatological* myths are discussed further below from the viewpoint of "after-death experiences", pp. 120–23.

15. Plato's myths are relevant in a number of the topics in the following chapters: *Timaeus* for cosmology (Ch. 3), *Gorgias*, *Phaedo*, *Republic* and *Phaedrus* for soul and selves (Ch. 5) and *Politicus* and *Atlantis* for politics (Ch. 7).

16. Further evidence is gradually coming to light from research on Philodemus from the charred papyri from the Villa of the Pisones at Herculaneum, which were buried in the eruption of Vesuvius in 79 CE, and on the wall excavated at Oenoanda in southern Turkey on which Diogenes carved a summary of Epicurus' philosophy.

17. Lucretius' argumentative style is especially telling in his use of the device known as *reductio*, which finishes off a series of arguments with a flourish of an absurd conclusion from the opponent's premises. For example, against

the theory that the sense organs do not have sensation themselves but are the means through which the soul perceives, he says that if sight is to be explained as an immortal soul looking through unshuttered windows, why is it we can *feel* the eyes functioning (as when we screw them up if the light is too bright), and follows this with the *reductio* that, if the eye is a window for the soul, the soul would see better if the eyes were taken out, "frames" and all (3.362–9)!

3. Cosmologies

1. The Greek *to a-peiron* is a neuter singular noun made from the adjective *apeiros* (unlimited) with the definite article; the initial alpha negates the sense in *peiron* (from *peras*) of "limit". In the grammar of the word, Anaximander deprives his principle of gender, character and boundary. *To gonimon* (that which is capable of generating [hot and cold]), which comes out of the *apeiron*, is another neuter noun, similarly invented to depersonalize the primary principle.

2. *Archē* (from *archō*; "I begin" and "I rule") was Aristotle's term, but it may well go back to Anaximander. Its dual sense is as with the English "first": first in time and first in importance.

3. The sources for Anaximander's cosmology go back to Theophrastus, Aristotle's successor; cf. DK 12A9–11 and A14.

4. According to Aristotle, Xenophanes used to look up at the night sky and was the first to "one-ify", making up a verb, *henizo* ("I consider as one"; "I have a unified theory of everything"), from *hen*, meaning "one" (*Metaphysics* 986b24).

5. The phrase in this form is first found in Plato's comment on Heraclitus at *Cratylus* 402a, and connected with DK 22B91 and B12: "you cannot step into the same river twice".

6. The analogy between cosmos as animal, and animal as cosmos, was also used in medical theory. As well as the general connection between cosmic elements and opposites with "humours" in the individual, the Hippocratic text *On Sevens* (ch. 6) relates the seven levels of the cosmic concentric spheres in detail to parts of the body; ch. 11 links geographical sites with bodily parts, and *Airs, Waters, Places* is concerned with the theory that climatic conditions resulted in specific personality traits in the local inhabitants.

7. The verb is *gegonen* (*Timaeus* 28a), the perfect tense of *gignomai*, but the perfect tense in Greek has reference to a *present* state.

8. Cf. "the eight orbits, two of which have the same speed, make distinct notes numbering seven (a crucial number in almost everything), separated by intervals; clever men have imitated this music with strings and in song" (Cicero *Dream of Scipio*, at *Republic* 6.18:). Some Pythagoreans removed the earth from its central position, and replaced it with a central fire.

9. Aristotle typically dismissed this imaginative theory on the pragmatic grounds that, since the force of thunderclaps can shatter stones, the much greater sound of stars in their movement would cause much greater havoc,

which is clearly not the case. "It is fair to say that we do not hear it and that bodies are not observed to suffer any violent effect because of the fact that no noise is produced" (*De Caelo* 290b).

10. This is an expansion of a passage by Epicurus in his "Letter to Herodotus" (DL 10.41).

11. The quotation, which is likely to go straight back to Chrysippus, is from Nemesius, *On the Nature of Man* 38.111 (Long & Sedley 52C). See the edition of Nemesius by R. W. Sharples & P. J. van der Eijk (Liverpool: Liverpool University Press, 2008).

4. Pagan monotheism

1. Here Cicero is reporting the Stoic view. Similarly, for Seneca: "We generally attach great importance to an opinion held by the whole human race, and accept it as convincing argument. We infer that there are gods from everyone's instinctive belief, and no nation has yet been found, so far beyond the reach of law and civilization, as to deny their existence" (*Letters* 117). This argument for the existence of god was known as "*consensus gentium*".

2. The saying is quoted by Aristotle, *De anima* 411a8, and discussed by Plato, *Laws* 899b.

3. The principle had already been used by Anaximander in a spatial sense to explain the stability of the earth; see p. 66 and ch. 1, n. 6, p. 215.

4. *Apology* 23a–b, 28e, 29d, 39a. The language of obedience to god is similar in *Phaedo*, in the injunction against suicide: "it is not unreasonable to say that we must not put an end to ourselves until god sends some necessary circumstance, like the one facing us now" (62c).

5. *Republic* 377b–383c; and Xenophanes B26, Parmenides B8.26–31, Empedocles B28, 29.

6. Envy (*phthonos*) is a typical attribute of the gods of epic and tragedy, which incites them to bring ruin on hubristic mortals who threaten their status.

7. The counterpart to this – not saying that the god is to be interpreted as sky, but that the clouds in the sky are gods – is one of the so-called Socratic beliefs that, along with the denial of the divinity of Zeus, was lampooned by Aristophanes in his comedy *Clouds*.

8. Scepticism goes back to the sophists and especially Protagoras, as in the opening of his work *On the Gods*: "I am unable to discover whether the gods exist or not, or what they are like; there are so many obstacles – the obscurity of the topic and the shortness of human life" (DK 80B4).

9. See the diagram, p. 79, which shows the paths of the rotation of the spheres of the planets and the circle of the fixed stars; the rotation is maintained continuously by their perpetual desire for the prime mover.

5. Souls and selves

1. The verb used here, *syn-kratei*, translated as "maintains", also covers the senses "strengthens" and "holds together". The authenticity of the word in the fragment has been queried, but, even if the compound verb is not the

original Ionian, the sense of strength and power in the *kratos* stem would be genuine.

2. The end of Anaxagoras B12 – "each individual object most obviously is and was what that object has most of" – is similar to the wording of the last line of Parmenides' fragment here.

3. "Simmias is human" is a constant, saying what he is essentially; "Simmias is tall" is an "accidental attribute", since its truth may depend on who is standing next to him or his age at any particular time.

4. In his speech in defence of Murena, Cicero mocked the prosecutor Cato for believing, as a staunch Stoic, that there were no grades of wrongdoing. He also brought out some of the perplexities of this "all or nothing" position in his six essays on "Stoic Paradoxes". But Roman Stoics generally attempted to mitigate the harshness of this conclusion with a theory of *progress* from folly to wisdom.

6. Believing, doubting and knowing

1. Cf. also "indeed we know nothing, for truth is in unfathomable depths" (Democritus B117; echoing Heraclitus DK 22B45).

2. This example was a precursor of the more famous "liar paradox" by Eubulides, the Megarian logician in the fourth century BCE; see Chapter 1, n. 23.

3. The analogy surfaces again in Diotima's instruction to Socrates in the *Symposium*. She speaks of a loved one who, with the encouragement of his lover, gives birth to the kinds of reasoning that advance moral progress, and joins with him in raising the subsequent offspring (*Symposium* 209b, 211c).

4. For virtue, knowledge and the "art of living", see pp. 182–3.

5. The situation could be compared to an audience imprisoned in a cinema, looking at the same film endlessly repeated.

7. Leadership, law and the origins of political theory

1. Homer's *Iliad* tended to show nostalgia for the past, as when heroes are said to be weaker now, and Nestor, characteristically of the old, continually speaks of better times when he was young, but Sthenelos, with the optimism of youth, counters this: "we are better men than our fathers, we took Thebes and we respect the gods, whereas our fathers were destroyed by pride" (*Il* 4.405).

2. Cf. Catullus 64.384–408 and Horace: "The age is fertile in evil … Time corrupts all; what has it not diminished? Our grandfathers sired inferior children, and we in turn shall bring forth a more degenerate generation" (*Odes* 3.6). But there was also a tendency to see the ages of metals as involved in cyclic time, so that the iron age would eventually end and the golden age return. In a political context this could be turned into a compliment to the emperor Augustus, in restoring the "*aurea saecula*". Shelley, in his poem "Hellas", saw the return in the new land of America: "The world's great age begins anew, the golden years return".

3. The account is still of interest to contemporary anthropologists. Democritus is

usually taken as the source for the abridged version given in Diodorus Siculus 1.8.

4. The significance of animal cries and the primitive language of infants was recognized in the development of communication, in opposition to Plato's "name-giver" (*nomothetēs*; the role of Adam in *Genesis*), who named animals and objects, and also to Heraclitus' interest in a name connecting with the *nature* of the object referred to, discussed throughout Plato's *Cratylus*.

5. In the *Odyssey* (6.103ff.) the primitive Cyclopes are noted as exceptional in having no leaders, communal life and assemblies for debate or public laws (*themistēs*), "but they live in mountain caves, and each imposes his private *themistēs* on his own wife and children, and ignores the others".

6. See for example *Iliad* 1.490–91; 2.205–6; 4.341–4; 9.96–102, 438–43; 12.310–21.

7. Cf. Aristotle's summary: "Law is a mutual guarantee of rights" (*Politics* 3.9).

8. Political comment in drama was not confined to tragedy. Most of Aristophanes' comedies have themes relating to the contemporary political scene. It is said that when Dionysius of Syracuse asked for an analysis of the Athenians' constitution, Plato sent him a collection of Aristophanes' plays.

9. Cf. Hesiod's genealogy, which linked justice (*dikē*), good government (*eunomia*) and peace (*eirēnē*) as sisters, born of Zeus and Themis (*Theogony* 901–6). In non-mythical terms, the imposition of divine authority on a primitive form of natural order produced in human society the rule of law, which enables justice to flourish and brings the benefits of peace.

10. The theory comes from Alcmaeon: "What preserves health is *isonomia* between the powers – wet and dry, cold and hot, bitter and sweet and the rest, and *monarchia* among them is the cause of sickness, for *monarchia* of one or the other is destruction; health is a blending in due measure" (DK 24B4).

11. Cf. an early form of communism: "According to Timaeus Pythagoras was the first to say 'friends share everything'" (quoted by Plato at the end of the *Phaedrus*) and "friendship is equality" (Iamblichus, *Life of Pythagoras* 175–6). And: "When Xenophilus the Pythagorean was asked by someone how he could best educate his son, he replied 'by making him the citizen of a well-governed state'. Throughout Italy Pythagoras made many men honourable and true (*kaloi kai agathoi*, literally *beautiful and good*, the standard Greek phrase for the best kind of people)" (Aristoxenus at DL 8.16–17). The hostility roused by the Italian Pythagoreans, which resulted in one incident of a number of them being trapped and burnt to death, seems to have been motivated by their attempts to put their political theories into practice.

12. Cf. "War is father of all and king of all; some it shows as gods and others men, some it makes slaves and others free" (DK 22B53), and "You must understand that war is common and strife justice, and everything happens as a result of strife and necessity" (B80).

13. DK 31B135, quoted by Aristotle in support of the general prohibition against murder, according to "universal law and natural justice". Aristotle himself suggested a cosmos : family analogy in that god manages the cosmos as the

head of a family does his household or as a general manages his army, where the good is shown both in the individual parts and the whole (*Metaphysics* 1074a13–22).

14. A three-part state is in the pattern of kings–nobles–soldiers in the *Iliad*, and in the illustration attributed to Pythagoras of the three sets of people who go to the Olympic games, namely spectators, athletes and money-makers. Cf. also the bribes the three goddesses offer Paris for the prize of the golden apple: Hera brings power, Athena wisdom and Aphrodite sexual pleasure.

15. In the long run, however, the Athenians lost. Their cruelty was long remembered, allies were alienated and the Spartan general Lysander expelled the Athenian power base from Melos and eventually imposed on Athens itself the rule of the Thirty Tyrants.

16. The Greek word for justice (*dikē*) is broader than its English translation, and can cover morality in general. The *Republic* as a whole sets out to tackle the question of the superiority of the morally good life, whatever the circumstances. On the "contract", see also Cicero: "Where there is widespread fear, man afraid of man, class of class, then, because no one is confident of his own strength, a sort of bargain (*quasi pactio*) is made between them … so not nature or desire but weakness is the mother of justice" (*Republic* 3.22).

17. Aristotle quotes Homer with approval here: "one ruler let there be" (*Il* 11.204).

18. Darius won the argument, and was himself appointed king after cheating in what was meant to be open competition for the office (Herodotus 3.85–7).

19. Aristotle's interest in constitutions resulted in his setting up a research project in the Lyceum, which collected and reported on 158 different types found in the Greek world; only the *Constitution of Athens* survives.

20. See Cicero: "only the wise are free" (*Stoic Paradoxes* V), that is, the wise man is (really) free even if in (apparent) slavery. These "paradoxes" are essays by Cicero on Stoic aphorisms that run counter to accepted opinion (*doxa*). The sayings are typical of the provocative rhetoric found in both Cynics and Stoics.

21. The name was coined by Thomas More in 1516, ambiguous in its Greek derivation between *eu-topos* (good place) and *ou-topos* (no place).

22. There is a play on the double meaning of *nomos* here as both "law" and "pasture"; the citizens would be "nourished" by the law like cattle grazing together from the same pasture.

23. Cf. Cicero: "It is consistent with natural instinct that the wise man should be ready to take part in politics and government" (*De finibus* 3.68). The advice given in the *Dream of Scipio* summarizes the application of virtue to the natural affinities: "practise justice and affectionate duty (*iustitia et pietas*) to parents, relatives and then above all to your country" (*Republic* 6.16), and adds that well-run cities (*coetus hominum iure sociati*) are pleasing to god. Stoic theory here contrasted sharply with the Epicurean aversion to participation in politics as a threat to personal tranquillity (*KD* 37).

24. This comprehensive cosmopolitanism perhaps started with Socrates even before the Cynics. It is said that when asked which city he was from, Socrates

replied, *kosmopolitēs eimi* (I am a world citizen). On the virtue of philanthropy following from this theory, see Chapter 8, p. 200.

8. Ethics, goodness and happiness

1. The word is *promoi* in Empedocles (B146.2), used not in the Homeric sense of generals who are first in battle, but according to the later use for leaders in peacetime.

2. Four examples suffice: "good and bad fortune relate to the soul" (DK 68B24); "it is best to live our lives as cheerfully as possible, and with the least distress, this would happen if our pleasure was in the long-lasting" (B53); "if you exceed the measure, the most delightful becomes the most unpleasant" (B97); and "sleeping during the day indicates physical or mental distress or laziness or lack of education" (B76).

3. In the choice of nature, teaching or practice, however, he takes a different stand at B28: "Nature and teaching are similar, for teaching reshapes the man, and in re-shaping sets his nature".

4. The Greek for "fine and good", *kalos kai agathos*, was a standard phrase for the prestigious man of virtue.

5. Cf. a rare positive statement attributed to Socrates in the *Meno* on the value of ongoing enquiry: "One thing I am ready to fight for as long as I can, in word and deed, that we shall be better, braver and more active if we believe it right to look for what we do not know than if we believe there is no point in looking, because it can never be discovered" (86b–c).

6. The main text of the "paradox" is from *Protagoras* 345d, where Plato has Socrates say: "It's more or less my opinion that no wise man thinks a person does wrong willingly, but they are well aware that those who commit shameful and evil acts do so unwillingly".

7. *Crito* is a short dialogue, with only Socrates and Crito present, and is generally taken to be an early work of Plato, and one that comes close to a portrait of the historical Socrates. Socrates is presented not, as at his public trial, often bantering and provocative, but, in the privacy of the prison, seriously engaged in a most important conversation as he attempts to win over his friend to his point of view.

8. The word "well" here (*eu*) is the adverb from *agathos* (good), and "to live well", like "living the good life", is ambiguous between living a *morally* good and a *materially* good life. Socrates takes it in the moral sense, but, as in the English adverb, there is always the hint of "well-being" and "doing well".

9. The "soul" that is to be cared for is the person in the truest sense, cf. "the human being within the human being" (*Republic* 589a).

10. See *Crito* 54c; the passage, with its "social contract" theory is discussed above, pp. 167–8.

11. Cf.: "There can be no finer subject to talk about than what sort of person a man should be, what his work should be and how he should follow it, both in youth and old age ... this topic is one about which we should all be seriously concerned; it is nothing less than how we should live" (*Gorgias* 488a).

12. For more details on state justice, see above, Chapter 7, pp. 126–7.

13. There is a vivid reinforcement of the required restraint in the myth of the "black horse" in the three-part soul, which the charioteer, with the help of the white horse, tries to tame; cf. above on *Phaedrus*, pp. 164–7.

14. For the details of the simile and the allegory see above, Chapter 6, pp. 147–9.

15. For women as philosophers, cf. Chapter 7, pp. 172–3.

16. There were no money prizes in the official games. The prize was just an olive-wreath, but the fame the winner achieved made the effort worthwhile.

17. At *Philebus* 64e, "*to kalon*" combines the senses of being beautiful, fine and appropriate for human living.

18. There is another work on ethics under Aristotle's name, with the title *Magna Moralia*; this is generally accepted to be later, and probably written by one of Aristotle's students.

19. *Eudaimonia* is the word generally translated as "happiness". It involves general "flourishing", success, prosperity and literally "good fortune" (the presence of a good *daimōn*).

20. The term "focal meaning" was coined by G. E. L. Owen and has become the classic term; see his *Logic, Science and Dialectic* (London: Duckworth, 1986), ch. 10.

21. Aristotle's view here, of happiness arising when we are true to ourselves and do the best we can, surfaces again in Cicero: "We should all assess our own character and regulate that one, and not try to see how another's might suit; for the character that each person has suits that person best" (*De officiis* 1.113).

22. Roger Crisp defines virtue ethics as a theory "which makes essential reference to the morality of virtue itself, with a focus on agents and their lives, rather than discrete actions". For Rosalind Hursthouse, "The virtuous person has particular virtues that can be understood as traits humans develop in order to live well. Such motives arise in a natural fashion without someone's having an eye on moral rules and laws". And John McDowell claims that "Rules of any form of rationality can be grounded only in human practice". All quoted in R. Crisp & M. Slote (eds), *Virtue Ethics* (Oxford: Oxford University Press, 1997).

23. The main text here is Cato's exposition of Stoic ethics in the third of five books of Cicero's *De finibus*.

24. This is the "art of living" (*ars vivendi*). The idea started with Socrates, who was searching for a *technē* of living well, combining theory and practice, comparable to that exercised by doctors and artisans. But the Stoics saw the "art" as more like that of dancing, where the movements are not random, but have a pattern. Furthermore, this art does not aim at an external product, but the skill is shown in the actual performance (Cicero, *De finibus* 3.24).

25. If life "for the most part" is according to nature then life is preferable, but if it is "for the most part" contrary to nature then suicide, the "rational departure", is justified (Cicero, *De finibus* 3.60). This could be in serving one's country, to save a friend or to avoid wrong action ("death before dishonour") and

incipient insanity, which threatens the life of reason ("reason or the rope" as Diogenes put it); see the discussion in J. M. Rist, *Human Value* (Leiden: Brill, 1982), 62. To show indifference to life was the ultimate expression of moral freedom, an occasion for a display of "fortitude and philosophic calm" (the more familiar sense of "Stoic"). It accounted for a spate of Stoic suicides under Roman emperors, following the example of Cato, who preferred death to submission to Caesar.

26. The moral of Cicero's *Dream of Scipio*, the Roman Stoic version of Plato's Myth of Er, was to cultivate the virtues of *iustitia* and *pietas*, which together covered respect for family, state and gods.

27. This is shown by the physical aspect of the soul, defined as warm breath (*pneuma*), being in the correct tension (*tonos*).

28. Cf.: "death, the most awesome of evils, is nothing to us, for while we exist death is not present, and when death is present we no longer exist" (*KD* 2). Traditional after-death punishments were seen as *allegories* for the mental torments we bring on ourselves now; see Chapter 4, p. 100.

29. "We have been born once, but it is impossible to be born twice; in eternity, necessarily, there is no future life for us" (*Vatican Sayings* 14).

30. As, for example, in Plato's *Phaedo*: "as long as we have the body with us, and our soul is kneaded into this evil thing, we shall never have unqualified possession of the object of our desire" (66b); "we must have no association with the body beyond what is absolutely necessary, nor allow ourselves to be affected by its nature" (82e).

31. This is known as the "hedonistic calculus", as explained in Plato's *Protagoras*:

> Like a skilful trader, put into the scales the pleasures and pains, and their nearness and distance, and weigh them, and then say which outweighs the other. If you weigh pleasures against pleasures, you should of course always take the more and the greater, or if you weigh pains against pains you take the fewer and the less; or, if pleasures against pains, then, if the pains are exceeded by the pleasures – whether the nearer by the distant or the distant by the nearer – you would choose the course of action in which the pleasures are to be found, and avoid the one in which the painful exceeds the pleasant.
>
> (356b–c)

The similar Epicurean version is given at DL 10.129–30.

32. Cf. "Friendship goes dancing round the world, telling us all to wake up and give thanks for the happy life" (*Vatican Sayings* 70).

33. The political life allows one to show "greatness of spirit" (*De officiis* 1.72), and it is given as a condition for the soul returning to the stars after death in the *Dream of Scipio* (Cicero, *Republic* 6.16, 26).

Epilogue

1. Interest in Stoic logic revived later, and its underlying principles had a considerable influence on medieval methods of argument.

2. In the twelfth century, Arabic philosophers, such as Suhrawardī of Aleppo,

focused more on Plato and Neoplatonism, adapting various theories of the One, the Intellect and Soul.

3. Intellect here combines aspects of Aristotle's "self-thinking god" and Plato's theory of forms.

Further reading

General

Annas, J. 2000. *Ancient Philosophy: A Very Short Introduction*. Oxford: Oxford University Press.

Cohen, S., P. Curd & C. D. C. Reeve 2000. *Readings in Ancient Greek Philosophy*, 2nd edn. Indianapolis, IN: Hackett.

Furley, D. (ed.) 1999. *From Aristotle to Augustine*, Routledge History of Philosophy 2. London: Routledge.

Guthrie, W. K. C. 1962–81. *A History of Greek Philosophy*, 6 vols. Cambridge: Cambridge University Press.

Hamlyn, D. W. 1989. *The Penguin History of Western Philosophy*. Harmondsworth: Penguin.

Irwin, T. 1999. *Classical Thought*. Oxford: Oxford University Press.

Kenny, A. 2004. *A New History of Western Philosophy. Vol. 1: Ancient Philosophy*. Oxford: Clarendon Press.

Taylor, C. C. W. (ed.) 1997. *From the Beginning to Plato*, Routledge History of Philosophy 1. London: Routledge.

Sedley, D. (ed.) 2003. *The Cambridge Companion to Greek and Roman Philosophy*. Cambridge: Cambridge University Press.

Zeyt, D. J. 1997. *Encyclopedia of Classical Philosophy*. Chicago, IL: Fitzroy Dearborn.

Translations of the Homeric poems and Hesiod are in Penguin Classics and widely available elsewhere. All classical texts (with facing translation) are published in the Loeb Classical Library (Cambridge, MA: Harvard University Press). This is the best place to find Diogenes Laertius, *Lives of Eminent Philosophers*, 2 vols, R. D. Hicks (ed.) (Cambridge, MA: Harvard University Press, 1925).

Presocratics and sophists
Barnes, J. [1987] 2002. *Early Greek Philosophy*. Harmondsworth: Penguin.
Barnes, J. 1982. *The Presocratic Philosophers*, rev. edn. London: Routledge.
Curd, P. & D. D. Graham (eds) 2008. *The Oxford Handbook of Presocratic Philosophy*. Oxford: Oxford University Press.
De Romilly, J. 1992. *The Great Sophists in Periclean Athens*. Oxford: Oxford University Press.
Hussey, E. 1972. *The Presocratics*. London: Duckworth.
Kirk, G. S., J. E. Raven & M. Schofield (eds) 1987. *The Presocratic Philosophers*, 2nd edn. Cambridge: Cambridge University Press.
Long, A. A. (ed.) 1999. *The Cambridge Companion to Early Greek Philosophy*. Cambridge: Cambridge University Press.
McKirahan, R. D. 1994. *Philosophy before Socrates*. Indianapolis, IN: Hackett.
Rankin, H. D. 1983. *Sophists, Socratics and Cynics*. London: Croom Helm.
Sprague, R. K. 1972. *The Older Sophists*. Columbia, SC: University of South Carolina Press.
Warren, J. 2007. *Presocratics*. Stocksfield: Acumen.
Waterfield, R. 2000. *The First Philosophers: The Presocratics and the Sophists*. Oxford: Oxford University Press.

Individual studies
Coxon, A. H. 1986. *The Fragments of Parmenides*. Assen: Van Gorcum.
Curd, P. 1998. *The Legacy of Parmenides*. Princeton, NJ: Princeton University Press.
Curd, P. 2007. *Anaxagoras of Clazomenae*. Toronto: University of Toronto Press.
Kahn, C. H. 1979. *The Art and Thought of Heraclitus*. Cambridge: Cambridge University Press.
Kahn, C. H. 2001. *Pythagoras and the Pythagoreans*. Indianapolis, IN: Hackett.
Huffman, K. A. 1993. *Philolaus of Croton*. Cambridge: Cambridge University Press.
Inwood, B. 2001. *The Poem of Empedocles*, 2nd edn. Toronto: University of Toronto Press.
Lesher, J. 1992. *Xenophanes of Colophon*. Toronto: University of Toronto Press.
Schofield, M. 1980. *An Essay on Anaxagoras*. Cambridge, Cambridge University Press.
Stamatellos, G. 2007. *Plotinus and the Presocratics*. Albany, NY: SUNY Press.
Taylor, C. C. W. 1999. *The Atomists: Leucippus and Democritus*. Toronto: University of Toronto Press.
Wright, M. R. 1981. *Empedocles: The Extant Fragments*. New Haven, CT: Yale University Press. Reprinted (Bristol: Bristol Classical Press, 1986).

Socrates
Allen, R. E. 1980. *Socrates and Legal Obligation*. Minneapolis, MN: Minnesota University Press.
Gulley, N. 1968. *The Philosophy of Socrates*. London: Macmillan

Kraut, R. 1984. *Socrates and the State*. Princeton, NJ: Princeton University Press.

Santas, G. X. 1979. *Socrates*. London: Routledge.

Stone, I. F. 1988. *The Trial of Socrates*. Boston, MA: Little Brown.

Taylor, C. C. W. 1998. *Socrates: A Very Short Introduction*. Oxford: Oxford University Press.

Vlastos, G. 1991. *Socrates, Ironist and Moral Philosopher*. Cambridge: Cambridge University Press.

Plato

Cooper, J. M. & D. S. Hutchinson (eds) 1997. *Plato: Complete Works*. Indianapolis, IN: Hackett.

Kraut, R. (ed.) 1992. *The Cambridge Companion to Plato*. Cambridge: Cambridge University Press.

Most of Plato's major dialogues are translated with introduction and notes in Penguin Classics, Oxford World Classics and the Clarendon Plato series.

Individual studies

Annas, J. 1981. *An Introduction to Plato's Republic*. Oxford: Oxford University Press.

Grube, G. M. A. 1980. *Plato's Thought*, 2nd edn. Indianapolis, IN: Hackett.

Robinson, T. M. 1970. *Plato's Psychology*. Toronto: Toronto University Press.

Ross, D. 1951. *Plato's Theory of Ideas*. Oxford: Clarendon Press.

Rowe, C. J. 1984. *Plato*. Brighton: Harvester.

Schofield, M. 2006. *Plato: Political Philosophy*. Oxford: Oxford University Press.

Vlastos, G. 1975. *Plato's Universe*. Oxford: Clarendon Press.

Vlastos, G. 1981. *Platonic Studies*, 2nd edn. Princeton, NJ: Princeton University Press.

White, N. 1976. *Plato on Knowledge and Reality*. Indianapolis, IN: Hackett.

White, N. 1979. *A Companion to Plato's Republic*. Indianapolis, IN: Hackett.

Aristotle

Barnes, J. (ed.) 1984. *Aristotle: Complete Works*. Princeton, NJ: Princeton University Press.

Barnes, J. (ed.) 1995. *The Cambridge Companion to Aristotle*. Cambridge: Cambridge University Press.

Some of Aristotle's works are available in the Clarendon Aristotle series, Penguin Classics and Oxford World Classics. They can all be consulted in the Loeb editions.

Individual studies

Ackrill, J. L. 1981. *Aristotle the Philosopher*. Oxford: Oxford University Press.

Cooper, J. 1975. *Reason and Human Good in Aristotle*. Cambridge, MA: Harvard University Press.

Kenny, A. 1978. *The Aristotelian Ethics*. Oxford: Clarendon Press.

Kenny, A. 1992. *Aristotle on the Perfect Life*. Oxford: Clarendon Press.

Kraut, R. 2002. *Aristotle: Political Philosophy*. Oxford: Oxford University Press.

Lear, J. 1980. *Aristotle and Logical Theory*. Cambridge: Cambridge University Press.

Lear, J. 1988. *Aristotle: The Desire to Understand*. Cambridge: Cambridge University Press.

Lloyd, G. E. R. 1968. *Aristotle: The Growth and Structure of his Thought*. Cambridge: Cambridge University Press.

Mulgan, R. G. 1977. *Aristotle's Political Theory*. Oxford: Clarendon Press.

Solmsen, F. 1960. *Aristotle's System of the Physical World*. Ithaca, NY: Cornell University Press.

Hellenistic philosophy

Algra, K., J. Barnes, J. Mansfeld & M. Schofield (eds) 1999. *The Cambridge History of Hellenistic Philosophy*. Cambridge: Cambridge University Press.

Inwood, B. & L. P. Gerson 1997. *Hellenistic Philosophy*. Indianapolis, IN: Hackett.

Long, A. A. & D. N. Sedley 1987. *The Hellenistic Philosophers*. Cambridge: Cambridge University Press.

Long, A. A. 1986. *Hellenistic Philosophy*, 2nd edn. Berkeley, CA: University of California Press.

Individual studies

Annas, J. E. 1992. *Hellenistic Philosophy of Mind*. Berkeley, CA: University of California Press.

Annas, J. E. & J. Barnes. 1985. *The Modes of Scepticism*. Cambridge: Cambridge University Press.

Asmis, E. 1984. *Epicurus' Scientific Method*. Ithaca, NY: Cornell University Press.

Clay, D. 1983. *Lucretius and Epicurus*. Ithaca, NY: Cornell University Press.

DeWitt, N. W. 1954. *Epicurus and his Philosophy*. Minneapolis, MN: University of Minnesota Press.

Hahm, D. E. 1977. *The Origins of Stoic Cosmology*. Columbus, OH: Ohio State University Press.

Powell, J. G. F. (ed.) 1995. *Cicero the Philosopher*. Oxford: Clarendon Press.

Reesor, M. E. 1989. *The Nature of Man in Early Stoic Philosophy*. London: Duckworth.

Rist, J. M. 1969. *Stoic Philosophy*. Cambridge: Cambridge University Press.

Rist, J. M. 1972. *Epicurus: an Introduction*. Cambridge: Cambridge University Press.

Sellars, J. 2006. *Stoicism*. Stocksfield: Acumen.

Sharples, R. W. 1994. *Stoics, Epicureans and Sceptics*. London: Routledge.

Sedley, D. N. 1998. *Lucretius and the Transformation of Greek Wisdom*. Cambridge: Cambridge University Press.

Smith, M. F 1993. *Diogenes of Oenoanda: The Epicurean Inscription*. Naples: Bibliopolis.

Smith, M. F. 2001. *Lucretius, On the Nature of Things*, 2nd edn. Indianapolis, IN: Hackett.

Wright, M. R. 1991. *Cicero: On Stoic Good and Evil*. Warminster: Aris & Phillips.

Themes

Adkins, A. H. A. 1972. *Moral Values and Political Behaviour in Ancient Greece.* London: Chatto & Windus.

Cooper, J. M. 1999. *Reason and Emotion: Essays in Ancient Moral Psychology and Ethical Theory.* Princeton, NJ: Princeton University Press.

Copenhaver B. P. & C. B. Schmitt 1992. *Renaissance Philosophy.* Oxford: Oxford University Press.

Ferguson, J. 1958. *Moral Values in the Ancient World.* London: Methuen.

Gerson, L. P. 1990. *God and Greek Philosophy.* London: Routledge.

Gosling, J. C. B. & C. C. W. Taylor (eds) 1982. *The Greeks on Pleasure.* Oxford: Clarendon Press.

Gould, T. 1990. *The Ancient Quarrel between Poetry and Philosophy.* Princeton, NJ: Princeton University Press.

Graham, D. 2006. *Exploring the Cosmos: The Ionian Tradition of Scientific Philosophy.* Princeton, NJ: Princeton University Press.

Hankinson, R. J. 1998. *Cause and Explanation in Ancient Greek Thought.* Oxford: Clarendon Press.

Herman A. 2004. *To Think Like God: Pythagoras, Parmenides and the Origins of Philosophy.* Chicago, IL: Parmenides.

Huby, P. 1967. *Greek Ethics.* London: Macmillan.

Kahn, C. H. [1960] 1994. *Anaximander and the Origins of Greek Cosmology.* Indianapolis, IN: Hackett.

Kahn, C. H. 1996. *Plato and the Socratic Dialogue: The Philosophical Use of a Literary Form.* Cambridge: Cambridge University Press.

Lloyd, G. E. R. 1973. *Early Greek Science.* New York: Norton.

Luscombe, D. 1997. *Medieval Thought.* Oxford: Oxford University Press.

Nussbaum, M. C. 1986. *The Fragility of Goodness.* Cambridge: Cambridge University Press.

Price, A. 1989. *Love and Friendship in Plato and Aristotle.* Oxford: Clarendon Press.

Sambursky, S. 1956. *The Physical World of the Greeks.* London: Routledge.

Seeskin, K. 1987. *Dialogue and Discovery: A Study in Socratic method.* Albany, NY: SUNY Press.

Sorabji, R. 1980. *Necessity, Cause and Blame.* London: Duckworth.

Sorabji, R. 1983. *Time, Creation and the Continuum.* London: Duckworth.

Sorabji, R. 1988. *Matter Place and Motion.* London: Duckworth.

Wright, M. R. 1995. *Cosmology in Antiquity.* London: Routledge.

There is an online tutorial in ancient Greek language (with a philosophical bias) at www.wrightclassics.com/mathos (accessed June 2009).

Index of passages

Index

For ancient authors see also Index of Passages.

239